6/98

Web

psychos

stalkers and

pranksters

Web psychos stalkers and pranksters

Michael A. Banks

 **CORIOLIS GROUP BOOKS**

an International Thomson Publishing company I(T)P®

Albany, NY ▪ Belmont, CA ▪ Bonn ▪ Boston ▪ Cincinnati ▪ Detroit ▪ Johannesburg ▪ London ▪ Madrid
Melbourne ▪ Mexico City ▪ New York ▪ Paris ▪ Singapore ▪ Tokyo ▪ Toronto ▪ Washington

PUBLISHER	KEITH WEISKAMP
PROJECT EDITOR	DENISE CONSTANTINE
COPYEDITOR	SUSAN HOLLY
COVER ARTIST	GARY SMITH/PERFORMANCE DESIGN
COVER DESIGN	ANTHONY STOCK
INTERIOR DESIGN	NICOLE COLON
LAYOUT PRODUCTION	PROIMAGE
PROOFREADER	STEPHANIE HOON
INDEXER	CAROLINE PARKS

Web Psychos, Stalkers, and Pranksters: How to Protect Yourself Online
Copyright © 1997 by The Coriolis Group, Inc.

Limits of Liability and Disclaimer of Warranty

Trademarks

The Coriolis Group, Inc.
An International Thomson Publishing Company
14455 N. Hayden Road, Suite 220
Scottsdale, Arizona 85260
602/483-0192
FAX 602/483-0193
http://www.coriolis.com

Printed in the United States of America
ISBN: 1-57610-137-1
10 9 8 7 6 5 4 3 2 1

*This book is dedicated to the memory of Martin Caidin—
pilot, explorer, adventurer, writer, and friend.*

Acknowledgments

Thanks to Lt. Jack Banks of the Boone County (Kentucky) Police Department, Beth Frenkel, Becky Lasater, Paul Milligan, Peter B. Olson of DELPHI, Detective Sergeant Jim Bellah of the Portland Police Bureau, and Vince Zema for their contributions to this book.

For their general enthusiasm, and editorial and promotional input, special thanks to: Denise Constantine, Jeff Duntemann, Donna Ford, David Friedel, Lynn Guy, Susan Holly, Sandra Lassiter, Josh Mills, Anne Tull, Keith Weiskamp, and the production staff at The Coriolis Group.

Contents

Contents

Threats
And Other
Promises
In
Cyberspace

Introduction

In one sense, this book started late one night in 1982. It was then, long before the current incarnation of the Internet, that I first realized being online could have unhappy—and perhaps dangerous—consequences.

I had dialed up a new BBS in my home town. As was common practice with BBSes in those days, new callers had to leave their home telephone number and other information with the board's sysop before they would be granted full access. This was so the sysop could verify that a caller was "real," and not a prankster.

This particular board had a new feature; it automated collecting your name, phone number, and other info with a primitive online form. I blithely filled out the form that night, logged off, and went to bed. Sometime after midnight, I started getting strange phone calls. Someone was dialing, not saying anything, then hanging up. After four such calls, I turned off the phone.

By the late next afternoon, I had a verification call from the sysop. I logged on and checked out the system, and logged off along about supper time. The hang-up calls began almost immediately.

This went on for several days and nights before I stumbled onto the reason for the calls. As it turned out, the new BBS had another feature that allowed you to see a list of the day's callers. Unknown to the sysop, the information for that list came from the verification database. So, everyone's telephone number was displayed, along with their name and other information.

I was astonished. Obviously, other modem users looking for BBSes had checked out that list. In their anxiety to find new boards, they assumed any phone numbers they saw online were BBS numbers. Worse, the board's command structure was such that it was easy to select the caller list, when what you wanted was a list of local BBS numbers.

The scores of modem calls I got were the result of some honest mistakes. That didn't make them any easier to take. (I'm sure anyone who has endured harassing telephone calls or had a reason to keep their telephone number private can empathize.) In any event, I had my telephone number changed, and I advised the sysop, who corrected the problem.

In all, the episode wasn't too costly. Aside from a week's aggravation, I was out fifteen dollars to change my phone number. But it made me think: What if *everyone's* phone number was this easy to find online? Ditto their home addresses, employment history, or other personal information.

Okay, okay—such information was (and is) stored in a variety of databases maintained by credit reporting agencies, healthcare providers, various government entities, and so forth. But not just anyone can access such databases. So, take it a step farther: What if a lot of that information was available to *anyone* with a computer and modem—and was available for free?

It's a little scary, isn't it?

It's true.

This Is Your Life—Online And Off

To show you just how true that is, consider how much I was able to learn about an editor to whom I showed this book. I spent 35 minutes looking him up with three Internet search tools, and one service on CompuServe. The whole thing was an exercise designed to underscore the importance of this book.

I knew nothing about him but his first and last names, and his email address at work. I was able to learn the following about him:

- Home address

- Home telephone number

- Middle initial

- Father's name

- Wife's name

- Current address and time there

- Previous address

- Previous employer, and email address there

This is a guy who doesn't surf the Web, and uses email solely for business and interoffice correspondence. He doesn't hang around on online services, either—he's never even seen a Prodigy or AOL screen. Given how little involvement he has in things online, that was quite a bit for half an hour's surfing, and a total expense of 75 cents. (Maybe it was too much; he decided not to work with me on this book!) It's definitely more personal information than most of us would like to have generally available.

The odds are good that similar information is available about you—particularly if you have or have had a listed phone number, and use the Internet or an online service for anything more than private email. You can find out just how much info is available using the search techniques discussed later in this book.

Me? My information? Well, if you follow those same techniques, you won't learn my home address and phone number. But you will learn quite a bit about me, simply because I have quite a bit of history online. You'll see what I mean later in the book, when I demonstrate how easy it is to build a profile on someone who has been active in various online venues.

I'll also show you how easy it is to gather information about your *activities* online. If, for example, you are in any of several areas on popular online services, it's very easy for a determined watcher to learn whether you're at home or on the road, which public messages you've read, which files you may have downloaded, and more. It's a simple matter of following you around, virtually speaking. I will show you how to deal with this sort of situation, as well.

Hey—That's Personal!

Before you blow off the importance of such information being out there for anyone to grab, think again. Would you like anyone you pass on the street to be able to get your home address, phone number, employer, and other personal information just by looking at you? All without having to go through the tedium of checking courthouse and motor vehicle registration information—and all without you knowing it? Of course not! Your first reaction would probably be that your privacy has been invaded.

However, this is exactly what happens online when there's information about you available through search engines and other means. All it takes is for someone else to be aware of your presence, to get your user ID. From that quick, virtual "look," it is possible to get all sorts of info about you. And getting your user ID is easy— it's available to all when you enter a chat room, visit a Web site, post in a Usenet newsgroup, get on a "listserv"-type mailing, sign a Web site guest book, or partici- pate in any number of other online activities.

Still don't feel vulnerable? Even with complete strangers scooping up informa- tion about you? Again, if you're very active online, it is possible to generate quite a profile about you—perhaps including things that you wouldn't want to be generally known. And, have you thought what someone might do if they had enough information to impersonate you, online or off?

In light of all that, consider this irony: Much of the information available about you online was probably given freely, even placed in publicly available venues, by you.

Fortunately, you can do something about that information—you can get it out of circulation, whether or not you provided it. That's one of the purposes of this book—to help you gain and keep control of your personal information.

Go Away, Kid—You Bother Me

Even if you have nothing to hide, and harbor no fears about people having information about you, other threats lurk in the online world. Some of them involve interactions with others. Anger or upset the wrong sort of person, and your life online can be made very, very uncomfortable, indeed. And maybe your life *offline*, as well.

Before you shrug that off, thinking you can just ignore online harassment, you need to be aware of just *how* and how much someone can get at you. It can be much more than a little annoying—and the more dangerous online types do not go away if you ignore them.

At that, even minor pests can become major headaches if they plague you long enough.

Too, *there are no police on the Internet.* Until the real world gets a better handle on what the Internet is all about, law-enforcement is not going to maintain a viable presence online.

This book can help you avoid most problem situations. If you do find yourself the object of someone's ire, you will learn how to deal with it effectively and put an end to the problem.

Now, Here's My Plan...(What You Will Find In This Book)

There are many more threats online—con artists, frauds, outright stalkers, criminal solicitations, and on and on. This book will describe—and provide examples of—just about every sort of threat or danger that lies waiting on the Internet. Before we get into the specifics, though, we'll take a look at how the Internet got where it is today—with some emphasis on its social and not-so-social aspects—in Chapter 1.

As for the specifics, Chapter 2 presents an overview. You will see how some online threats are merely annoying, while others are dangerous, indeed. We will examine the full range of what's at risk, what you need to protect, and why. Chapter 3 extends the theme of self-protection with the basics of online security.

In Chapter 4, you will get to look at things from the other side. You'll see exactly how your personal information gets out to the world. Armed with this knowledge, you'll be better able protect your information from the idle—and active—curious.

Chapter 5 deals with some of the most common sources of trouble online: Dealing with other people. We'll look at both interaction with others, and at online fakes and frauds. Of particular interest here are the dangers posed by public venues, including chat rooms and newsgroups. We'll examine online etiquette in-depth, for it is the lack of etiquette (also known by the sobriquet "netiquette") that can get you in the most trouble online. The emphasis is on self-protection.

In Chapter 6, we switch gears for a look at more "silent" threats. Specifically, the dangers of downloading and doing business with (or even browsing) Web pages. This chapter includes information on viruses, how to avoid giving away information about yourself when you visit a Web page, safe alternatives to credit-card buying on the Internet, and more.

Then, it's on to *spam*, the plague of the Internet, in Chapter 7. Here, I will show you how to work with ISPs to reduce the amount of spam you receive. You will also learn how to keep your ID from getting on those mailing lists that spammers trade and sell to other spammers. For those who are new to the Web, I will explain exactly what spam is, why it exists, and why only the people selling the mailing lists and mailing services make any money.

Chapter 8 gives you all the details on how to track down information about people online. This will bolster your knowledge of how the "other side" gets information about you, and give you an extremely effective tool for tracking down and eliminating sources of online harassment.

Chapter 9 explores Web sites that support safe surfing. Many of these are hosted by organizations that offer tips, advice, and alerts on Internet safety. Some provide a means of reporting threatening incidents and Web sites. In Chapter 10, we'll examine software that enhances Internet safety and security.

Chapter 11 is the wrap-up. It features a compendium of tips and guidance to staying safe online—anywhere, at any time.

Appendices listing all the URLs mentioned in the book (sorted by category), and additional references and resources give you pointers to specialized knowledge, and to updating the information in this book.

Getting The Most Out Of This Book

To get the most out of this book, remember this: I am not writing about some fictional future when everyone is hardwired and "jacked-in" to the Net. Nor is this book about national and international corporations trading information about your finances, health, and other, more personal aspects of your life.

This is about what's happening right now, to people just like you—and how to prevent it.

As you read this book, try things out. Go to the search engines and other online information sources, and experiment with them. Search out your own personal information, to see just how much of your life is already online. Where I show you it's possible, delete that information—or have it removed. Spend a little time looking up others, too—your friends or family, for starters. They, too, may need to know what's online about them, and where.

Keep this book on hand as a reference—and create your own references. Your Web browser's bookmark or a simple text file can be a useful repository for those sites I discuss herein. You should keep all this information handy, and as accessible as possible; you may need it at any time....

Chapter 1

Where We Are And How We Got Here

Chapter 1

Where We Are And How We Got Here

Chapter 1

"A New York woman extorts thousands of dollars' worth of services from major corporations annually.... A Midwestern man complains once too often about junk mail flooding his email box and logs on to find hundreds of angry and threatening letters from complete strangers.... A man misrepresents himself to a person, who blithely agrees to an in-person meeting, unaware of the stranger's malicious intent.... Con artists take dozens of computer users for hundreds of thousands of dollars in an online investment scam...."

These might look like tabloid headlines, but they are not. They're synopses of actual events—the sorts of questionable and sometimes illegal activities that can and do happen in the loose, unpoliced, and often threatening world of online services and the Internet.

Whether you're online as a hobby or for business, hazards await you. Do the wrong thing, get involved with the wrong people, or just be in the right place at the wrong time, and it can cost you—time, money, peace of mind, your online access, or more.

In a word, being online can be dangerous.

The Good Old Days

It wasn't always that way. In its infancy—during the late 1970s and very early 1980s—the online world was a ragged assortment of small and largely isolated communities. All told, fewer than a million people were online, worldwide. Of these, the majority relied on local computer bulletin board systems (BBSes) for messaging and downloads. The major online services—CompuServe and The Source—had fewer than 150,000 users between them.

None of these systems—BBSes, CompuServe, or The Source—were interconnected. Oh, a few "mail relay" networks existed, ferrying email and messages from one BBS to another by direct telephone contact. But these systems—FIDONet and RelayMail among them—often took days to move a message halfway across the country. Furthermore, not every system was tied into these networks, which meant that there was no way to reach everyone then online.

The bottom line was this: Whatever system you used *was* the online world.

Intersystem communication was so rare that even seeing the menus and other screens from a BBS in another state or country was an experience sought after by many. When a member of one BBS or online service community dialed up and "visited" a board in another state or country, he or she logged the session and uploaded it to his or her home system for all to share. It was not realtime, and not really communication—just a few stored-and-forwarded minutes of frozen time. But sharing such glimpses of a "foreign" system was an enlightening and expanding experience—and presaged the eventual trend toward total interconnection of all online systems.

Yes, *some* interconnections existed, but they were more exclusionary than inclusive. Usenet was out there, but that Unix-based experiment was limited to a few hundred college and business sites and held no allure for the average home computer user. Obviously, the Internet as we know it did not exist. In fact, it could hardly have existed with so few people online and no system interlinks. (The Internet *per se* was pretty much an exclusive club back then. One of the admission requirements was a mainframe computer.)

Realtime chatting? Outside of CompuServe and The Source—both of which charged as much as 40 cents per minute—realtime conversation was rare. You could sometimes involve BBS sysops in conversation, if they were near their machines and in the mood. But there was nothing like the multichannel (or "room") systems you find on today's online services. And the ubiquitous Internet Relay Chat (IRC) systems just didn't exist.

Communication, And Why People Are Online

Realtime conversation—in chat rooms, on virtual CB channels, or whatever the venue—was a large source of revenue for online services in the early days. It is, as you have read and perhaps experienced, an addictive activity. Back in the mid-1980s, it was not uncommon for chat-room mavens to have online service bills of $400 or more per month.

In 1990, just before the World Wide Web rolled out, the managers of several online services gave me a breakdown as to exactly what online activities provided how much of their revenues. Downloading—shareware files mainly—was at the top of the list, meaning users as a group spent more time getting programs and support files than doing anything else online. Realtime conferencing, sometimes lumped in with the other forms of two-way communication—email and message boards—came in a close second. Playing realtime games (normally multiplayer) was third. Everything else followed.

I strongly suspect that if we were able to measure what people are doing online today, communications would win out. If you doubt that, take a look at the hundreds of AOL chat rooms occupied on a given evening and see how many IRC groups are available. (A quick search with AltaVista turns up more than 100,000 references to IRC alone.) Then there are those tens of thousands of USENET Newsgroups, with daily traffic in the millions of messages. And, of course, there's email.

I'm not 100-percent certain that chatting would be the number-one online activity with today's Internet users, but you can count on it being high on the list. And I do believe that more time is spent on communication than on any other online activity. I include email and message boards along with realtime conversation, of course.

All of this says something about why people who are online, are online. It has to do with our shared need to communicate. I'll have more to say about this in a later chapter, but I want you to think about this: Communication is a part of literally all online activities—even downloading files. Think it through, and you'll see it.

With the online population confined to so many small, isolated pockets, getting into much trouble was difficult, because everyone pretty much followed the rules (sometimes whether they wanted to or not). Sysops held absolute power over users' access, which served as quite a deterrent to online mischief. Unwritten rules about online conduct in messaging areas, email, and chat rooms held equal power. The small size of the online communities, in which everyone knew almost everyone else, made public censure an effective tool for use against any would-be malefactors.

Modern Times

Those days are gone. Today, if an Internet Service Provider (ISP) or online service cancels your account for breaking the rules, you can demand a "second chance" and abuse it, too. You can often do this several times before you're canceled. When you finally are canceled, you can get another account in minutes—sometimes with the same service provider. Thus, you can harass the Web with impunity.

If you're making a bloody nuisance of yourself in a USENET Newsgroup or another public message base, fouling up threads and insulting everyone and their dog, no problem. Just ignore the requests to stop and the in-kind abuse, and raise hell all you want. It doesn't matter, because nobody knows who you are or where you live, right?

Or so it would seem to people disposed to annoying others for fun and profit. Not to mention those who are more goal-oriented in their online malfeasance— stalkers, con artists, and other sorts of criminals.

But they're wrong.

So, How *Did* We Get Here?

You may well wonder, how has it come about that this marvelous communications medium known as "the Internet" also serves as a venue for others to annoy, abuse, rob, defraud, stalk, and generally harass others? Aside from the technology, what's the difference between being online in the "good old days" and today?

Actually, the technology has quite a bit to do with it. The state of computer and telecommunications technology has always had a direct effect on the demographics of the online world. In the early days, for instance, technology kept those who weren't technically oriented firmly offline. You had to know quite a bit about computer and telecommunications equipment to get online. Too, personal computers were *expensive.*

For our purposes and those of history, the "online world" consisted and now consists of publicly accessible systems. This means computer-based bulletin board systems, commercial online services, and, nowadays, Internet Service Providers and the Internet/Web at large. It also means that the genesis of the online world can be traced to 1978, as you will see.

So it was in the early 1980s. The online world was populated by an elite group of "techies," who shared a limited range of mutual interests having to do with computing. They also shared a mutual respect for one another's technical knowledge

Figure 1.1   The good old days.

and equipment. If they weren't well-heeled, they were sacrificing types who scraped and did without to be able to afford their computer equipment—a fact that underscored how seriously they took their online activities.

They also shared a respect for what they were doing. Whether they were online as a hobby, an experiment, or simply for the experience itself, the prevailing attitude was that being online was Something Important. Nobody knew why, but we were all certain that one day, everyone would be online. Something as fascinating as computer telecommunications in your home had to be useful for something, and until someone figured out some uses, the faithful would—and did—keep it alive.

A little more than a decade later, everything about being online had changed. Using a computer, modem, and associated software to get on the Internet was easy—often simpler than programming a VCR. The techno-elite were a sudden minority; computer *users* had taken over, because you didn't have to be a techie to get online. Rather than regarding the Internet as a hobby, an experience in itself, or an experiment, the new majority considered the Internet just another extension of their computer, to be used as they saw fit.

And respect? The denizens of the new online world asked for or gave no more respect than an interstate highway system commands.

A BRAVE NEW WORLD?

The new Internet population had no really binding mutual interests, and no mutual respect. Why should they? Surfing the Net was not unlike driving a car; all that was required was the desire, the proper equipment, and minimal training. This put the so-called "information superhighway" on the same level as any other superhighway.

Well, almost. With the Internet, you don't need a license, there's no age requirement, and no cops.

What had been predicted for years had finally come to pass: The online world was accessible and accessed by people from all walks of life. But it was far from the glorious new world so often forecast throughout the '80s by pundits and online service advertising.

Rather, it was—and is—about as close to total anarchy as any social gathering short of a riot can be.

MARKET-DRIVEN EVOLUTION

To be fair, online services and the Internet would still cost dearly to use, and wouldn't offer half of what they provide now, without the millions of users now clogging access lines worldwide. As with every other aspect of personal computing, demand drove hardware and software development; prices dropped as features, functionality, and ease of use rose.

At the same time, online services and the Internet were themselves undergoing market-driven changes. Online services, and most of the Internet's offerings, are shaped by demand. That which gets used stays around and is enhanced; that which isn't used goes away. This is true of specific products and services as well as general service categories. (If nothing else, *this* medium provides a truly honest gauging of what people like—and dislike.)

Thus did the Internet and the tools required to access it evolve. As it became accessible to everyone, it offered more of what a general cross-section of the population wanted, so more of a cross-section of the population got online. A rather circular effect, in all.

With more people online comes a stronger disposition toward rowdy or anti-social behavior. If you doubt that, consider what happens when you put 50,000 people together in a sports stadium or concert venue. All bets are off in terms of civilized behavior.

But the simple presence of more people online doesn't fully explain the increased incidence of malevolent activity online. If that were the case, you wouldn't meet any more obnoxious people in a chat room than you would, say, hanging out at the mall. We must again look to technology for the rest of the explanation.

When Nobody Knows Who You Are, You Can Do Whatever You Want

The Internet itself bears no little responsibility for behavior online. This is because its very nature *encourages* anti-social activities. How? Why? Because it is so easy for someone with a little knowledge to be anonymous to most Internet users. Anonymity all too often brings out the worst in people.

Given anonymity, many people are tempted to turn totally obnoxious or abusive, if not criminal. In fact, it is almost compelling to some. To a practiced user, the Internet seems to offer total anonymity of the sort that would allow one to do almost anything without fear of reprisal. Anonymity encourages people to assume totally new identities and behave in ways they would never do otherwise.

Note that in the preceding paragraphs I made a point of saying it is easy to be anonymous to *most* Internet users, and that the Internet *seems* to offer anonymity to would-be criminals.

The truth is, *there is almost no anonymity on the Internet*—not to those who know their way around and are willing to do a little detective work. Tens of millions of Internet users are unaware of this fact—but hopefully you won't be among them for long.

By now, you have some idea of why the Internet and online services evolved as they did. Before we abandon the subject of origins, a quick look at the genesis and evolution of online dirty tricks and practical jokes is in order.

HACKERS AND CRACKERS AND SPOOFS—OH, MY!

In those halcyon days when the online world's population was smaller than that of Wyoming, long before an Al Gore speechwriter coined the term "Information Superhighway," and before we were inundated with reaching analogies like "on-ramp" and "surfing the Net," there were few threats connected with being online. All you had to worry about was being humiliated in a flame war. (A flame war is an extended exchange of argument and insult in a public message base, involving two or more people.) That, and the possibility that someone might get your password and embarrass you by posting goofy messages in your name, or run up charges on your account if you used an online service.

Those hazards were easy to avoid. Most of us didn't get into online arguments. (It was far more entertaining to watch flame wars than to be in them.) And most of us changed our passwords early and often.

Besides, BBSes and online services were so new and exciting that most of us were too busy assimilating what was offered to even think about trying to go behind the scenes. *Hacking* was something that boring mainframe computer operators did to improve performance and battle boredom.

Consider: Publicly accessible online computer systems didn't exist before 1978. Early that year, Ward Christensen and Randy Suess put the world's first computer bulletin board system online in Illinois. Prior to that, the only way to get online was via a terminal connection to a mainframe or mini-computer. Or, if you had a friend with a modem, you might thrill to dialing up one another, typing one-line messages back and forth, and maybe transferring a file or two.

Within months of the debut of that first BBS, dozens sprang up across the country. Computing was no longer a solitary experience. The world's first online services—CompuServe (see MicroNET) and The Source—showed up in 1979, and there was no turning back.

There was no anticipating where things would end up, either.

Practical Jokes And People Hacks

The late '70s and early '80s comprised an era of relative calm online, but it wasn't without practical jokes and experimentation. That was inevitable; link thousands, hundreds, or even dozens of bright people through sophisticated computer communications systems, and you get a lot of exploring and testing of limits.

So it was that users quickly discovered clever and sometimes surprising ways to use system resources and capabilities. The result was a seemingly endless series of entertaining and largely harmless online pranks. Most of the time, the only people who knew about the pranks were the jokester and the "victim," and maybe a few of their online acquaintances.

The overwhelming majority of pranks were benign and, interestingly, did not really affect the host system. Rather, they played on human perception. For example, a user who had the name "ROGER" could easily be *spoofed*, or imitated by another user taking on the name. "R0GER." (Simply replace the capital "O" with a zero.) Most folks, seeing "R0GER" (with a zero) in a message header or a realtime conference line would see it as "ROGER," and assume it was the original "ROGER" (with an "O").

This was particularly popular in areas where a user could assume an alias, or nickname, such as in a realtime conference. This presaged the contemporary problems of fake email.

Spoofing system messages was also popular in realtime conferences in which a user could assume a nickname *and* send one-line "whispers," or private comments, to one or more users in of a group. When a new user popped into an online chat, someone would change his name to "." and send the new user an unattributed private comment that appeared to be a system message. The result—what the user would see—would be something like this:

> .Attention: Your account will be terminated in 5
> minutes.

Usually the object of the joke would realize he or she was being spoofed; if not, the perpetrator would confess soon enough. It was harmless fun. A variation on this joke was to make people in a private conference group think someone had entered their password-protected chat.

These practical jokes evolved into something else before long, however. Rather than prank messages, a new user in a conference or anywhere on a system that allowed one-to-one realtime private messages might receive a message like this:

> .SysAdmin: A hacker has broken into your account,
> and we need help tracking him down. Please reply
> with your password so we know it is you.

I first saw this sort of "people hacking" tried in 1984 on DELPHI. It still pops up today on DELPHI, AOL, and other services. Believe it or not, this trick occasionally works. So does a variation involving email. Online service managers are aware of such attempts to get users' passwords and are forced to issue frequent log-on or email reminders that their staff members do not ask users for passwords online, by phone, or otherwise.

Such activities are the direct ancestors of most of today's people hacks and many online scams. With few exceptions, any underhanded activity using email or public message postings involves spoofing a return address or system origin.

All the activities just described depend on the perpetrator being anonymous. This brings us to a major point of interest: Online crime is firmly rooted in and depends upon anonymity. This, in turn, points to the fact that stripping away the cloak of anonymity could well eliminate the majority of online crime. (Until that happens—which won't be soon—you need this book!)

Online Anonymity—Relative Or Real?

How much do you know about your online acquaintances? How much can you learn about the guy in the chat room last night or the woman who posted those interesting messages last week?

Very little, if they don't want you to know anything. Unless those people have posted details about themselves or put personal profiles online somewhere, you probably can know very little. If someone doesn't volunteer personal information in any way, all you really know is that person's ID and the system that provides their online connection. (Don't count on an ISP or online service giving you a user's information. Unless the user does something outrageous enough to draw the attention of law enforcement or courts, no ISP or online service employees will give you a customer's personal information. It's too much trouble, they can get fired, and the service can get sued.)

Let's assume the person you are interested in is a charlatan, totally bogus, for whatever reason. You know he or she uses the ID/email address, bxbitskozokl@toobogus.com. How much does that really tell you? Well, you know the person calls him- or herself "Bxbitskozokl" and has an account at toobogus.com. A little checking around can tell you whether "Bxbitskozokl" might be a really oddball first or last name, or maybe a literary allusion. You can also find out where toobogus.com is located. But that's about it.

You might infer that Bxbitskozokl lives in the city where toobogus.com has its offices, but don't count on it; packet-switching networks and long-distance phone service make it possible for Bxbitskozokl to log on to the Internet through toobogus.com from anywhere. On top of that, none of your online acquaintances knows who Bxbitskozokl is, either.

You find out that Bxbitskozokl is no sort of name and references nothing. It's a totally made-up (not to mention unpronounceable) string of letters. So, you have no real information. Bxbitskozokl is anonymous.

You know from what you've read thus far that this is not necessarily true. But consider how really anonymous Bxbitskozokl would be if you didn't have even the knowledge you've picked up thus far.

The point here is this: Unless you know what to look for, where to look, and how to get at it, you don't have any more information about another Internet user than he or she wants you to know. The vast majority of those using the Internet and online services are without a clue about what, where, or how to get information about someone else. Given that, online anonymity is a reality, and will continue to be until everyone knows how to break down anonymity using online resources. As I pointed out before, this anonymity is a large part of the allure of online misdeeds.

Hacking And Cracking: Computers Under Attack

While people hacking could be fun, system hacking was usually a more interesting activity for the technical elite, wannabes, and hangers-on who populated the early online world. It was also a time-honored activity— a rite of passage to some.

Hacking erupted in the early 1960s among mainframe computer freaks—computer professionals, actually. Many of the bright and curious among them often engaged in testing the limits of the systems entrusted to their care, an activity that included seeing how far you could take a computer beyond its nominal functions.

The term *hack* was originally used to describe an elegant or at least very clever programming trick that persuaded computer hardware to do things it wasn't intended to do. One who did hacks was a *hacker*. Later, because of the analogy between breaking into a system and safecracking, the term *cracker* came into use as well. (Both hacker and cracker have different meanings at different times, just as phone *freak* and phone *phreak* carry different connotations. But the idea is the same.)

Hacks were devised not only for the satisfaction of hacking, an intellectual exercise for some, but also to impress. In fact, it was more fun if others knew how clever a hack was. Thus the tradition of sharing hacks, or at least making them known to others, was born.

At some point, hacking grew to encompass software hacks that enabled someone to gain unauthorized access to a computer system—perhaps as an outgrowth of testing one's own system for weaknesses. That sort of hacking was, out of necessity, anonymous, but hackers still left their marks, in forms ranging from a message to the administrator of the hacked system, to disabling or altering some of the system's functions. Hacking on this level was largely harmless—which is to say it caused no irreversible damage. The early hackers were also, by tradition, law-abiding and generally avoided theft and destruction of any sort.

This tradition had become somewhat skewed by the late 1970s, however. A new, sometimes malicious breed of hackers hit the networks, and they wanted to do more than tiptoe into an online system and leave a calling card. For them, gaining unauthorized entry to a system was only the beginning.

If these new hackers wanted to leave a sign, they did it in a big way. They deleted or altered important data, or sometimes caused the system to crash. Later, malicious hackers got into spreading computer viruses—sort of a way to crash systems second-hand, although not very targeted.

The means of intrusion were no longer simple, elegant hacks. Entry often relied on an all-out attack on the system's password protection setup, or something equally straightforward. Brute force was the name of the game; guessing a system password or using a "back door" were things of the past. (A *back door* is a means of logging on to a system that is built in by the system's designers, usually designed to give a manufacturer's engineers quick access to a customer's computer system. It was often as simple as an ID/password combination such as "system/repair.")

If caught, some of these hackers made the news, and often ended up with high-paid jobs protecting systems from other hackers like themselves. If they weren't caught, perhaps they retired wealthy, or got bored and gave up.

Figure 1.2 Early computer hackers faced few barriers in illegally entering systems.

Not all hackers bore malicious intent toward the systems they infiltrated. Largely harmless pranksters of the old school continued to hack along with young Turks who were bent on causing as much cyber-havoc as possible.

Yet another style of hacker was emerging. Like their predecessors, these new hackers strove to remain anonymous. Quite *unlike* those who had gone before, they did not seek to draw attention to their activities. Rather, they wanted to remain unobserved as well as anonymous, because detection would mean their routes into a system would be closed.

This new breed of hacker broke into systems to use them and/or to view data they stored. This meant they weren't in there ripping up databases. Thus, the likelihood of detection was less, and this sort of hacker's intrusions could—and did—continue for months on end.

Some of these hackers were into stealing and accumulating data. Sensitive information about individuals or organizations might be sold or used for other nefarious purposes. (Some readers will recall the notorious German hacker ring that made headlines in the early '90s by breaking into NASA computers looking for salable defense secrets.) The hacker might have a personal interest in the data available. A few altered data for personal benefit—changing personal records in a system or perpetrating elaborate financial thefts (a popular theme in movies dealing with hackers).

Some hackers just browsed through information with no goal in mind—sort of like the software pirates of the early '80s, who accumulated illegal copies of programs but never sold or used them.

Most of those who broke into systems for specific purposes were after telephone outdialing links, which could then connect them to still more powerful systems, where they might browse, use, or abuse data of all sorts. One such hacker, a 14-year-old boy living in New England, had quite a run in the late 1980s. For nearly six months, he routinely dialed up a Digital Equipment Corp. (DEC) VAX mini-computer owned by Apple Computer in California. He had originally hacked his way into the system and set up "super-user" account status for himself—which enabled him to do whatever he wished on the system. Since this computer was linked to a network of DEC machines, he was able to use it to dial out to other systems and "look around" at no cost. Other computers he toured included one at a U.S. Naval weapons testing center and a Federal government system in Atlanta. He was finally caught and stopped, but it is difficult to know how many others were similarly occupied.

All of this was relatively innocuous as far as average computer users were concerned; after all, it wasn't *their* pockets being picked, nor their systems being trashed. The problem got a little closer to home with rumors of more elite hackers who went after users' accounts on online services by "tailgating." This involved linking with someone logging on to an online service through a packet-switching network so that everything the hapless online service user typed was echoed on the hacker's screen—including the user ID and password. The hacker could then use the account at will, often running up large bills and sometimes changing the password to lock out the real owner of the account. This wasn't as common as was once thought, but tales of this sort of hacking served to remind the newer online service users to safeguard their passwords.

Why Some Hackers Get Away With It

The incident, related in the accompanying text, involving the 14-year-old using a minicomputer to dial into other systems around the country, really happened. As it turned out, an employee who used the VAX computer the kid was hacking knew about him for months. The problem was, she was unable to convince her superiors to do anything about it. Why? Because nobody high-up at Apple wanted the news to get out. It was easier for Apple to bear the average $10,000 monthly phone charges the kid was running up than to take the bad publicity.

The boy was eventually nabbed, but not before a jurisdictional argument between one FBI office and another almost killed the legal end of the investigation.

The story was related to me, in some detail, by the employee who originally blew the whistle. I was a bit closer to another hacking incident in 1991. At the time, I lived near Cincinnati and had a credit card with a major Midwest department store chain called Lazarus. In July of that year, I noticed that the Lazarus bill had arrived 10 days late for the third month in a row. In looking over the bills in question, I discovered that they had been posted on time, but they bore the wrong zip code.

I telephoned the company's credit department, which changed my zip code back, and the August bill arrived on time. come September, though, my bill was late and bore the wrong zip code again.

This prompted me to see where that zip code originated, as the same zip code was on all four late bills. It turned out to be the zip code for Hicksville, Ohio (yes, the town really exists). "Hacker prank" came immediately to mind, so I telephoned Lazarus and after some delay reached the MIS manager.

"I think you may have a hacker getting into your system," I ventured, after giving her the story.

"That does not happen to us," was the reply, and the theme of the rest of the conversation—as well as another one in November, after I went through the same cycle of good zip code/bad zip code.

I mentioned this to the manager of my post office branch, hoping to get some action. No satisfaction there, but I did learn that Social Security recipients whose mail was delivered from that office and whose last name began with one of the first 13 letters of the alphabet had also had their monthly checks routed through Hicksville, thanks to the wrong zip code.

The only thing left to do was to contact the Secret Service, which counts among its duties any sort of "wire" or computer fraud involving government systems. The local agent was pleased to gain the information about Social Security recipients. I never did learn the final outcome of the matter, although I heard that someone had hacked their way into an Atlanta postal service computer that dispensed address information to government agencies and paying corporate customers. All I know for certain is that my Lazarus bill arrived on time and with the proper zip code ever after.

Both of these cases have hacking of some sort in common, along with denial on the part of the hacking victims. The aim was not just to deny that such a hack happened, but to deny that it ever could happen. Such is the sort of fear generated by hackers; to be a victim of one is to lose all credibility.

Computer Viruses

Computer viruses showed up in the 1980s. As was the case with hacking, viruses started as annoying practical jokes. They delivered humorous or political messages, then let you go on with your computing activities. Viruses eventually turned evil, though, destroying data and reformatting the hard drives of the unwary. So, we watched our downloads and took other necessary precautions.

That was as bad as it got until late in the decade when the online population explosion hit. Then things turned nasty, and data-destroying, system-disrupting, and hard-drive-reformatting viruses for PCs and Macs were showing up everywhere—or, they were at least rumored to be everywhere. We had quite a virus craze for a while, especially after the media publicized the Columbus Day Virus and other virus stories.

The truth was, few viruses actually made it into general circulation, thanks to the speed with which news travels online. Nowadays, counteracting features are added (as downloads) to virus-protection programs, or viruses are proven to be a hoax within days of the first rumors about them.

If you think about it, a virus is a hack—usually an elegant hack, but a vicious one. It's a way for hackers who are experts in one sort of system and/or software to exercise their knowledge. As is the case with most hackers, those who create viruses want to remain anonymous and enjoy the effect their work has on others. This is probably the ultimate intellectual exercise for most virus creators. A few have been known to launch viruses on specific systems for revenge or other personal reasons—but those are a minority, and, interestingly, the only ones who have been caught.

Computer viruses are yet another descendent of early hacker activities. They represent the sort of hacker activity most likely to affect you: impersonal attacks on computer systems.

The Internet Today

Which brings us to today, with nearly 50 million people online worldwide—in a largely lawless environment that provides the temptation as well as the means to scam, annoy, abuse, harass, and generally aggravate others with relative impunity.

Some have portrayed the Internet as a frontier, wild and lawless as the American frontier of the early 1800s, because of its newness. The metaphor certainly has

Figure 1.3   Modern times on the Web.

romantic appeal, but it doesn't hold up. A true frontier is undeveloped and largely unpopulated. These characteristics were true of the online world 15 years ago, but not today.

The online world and the Internet are well beyond the frontier stage. The trails have been blazed, settlers have staked their claims, and the settlements are growing. A more appropriate metaphor, in the same *genre*, might be the Industrial Revolution in America. This was a time when travel was cheap and easy, and people could leave a bad situation in one city and move on to another, there to reinvent themselves as they pleased. It was also a time of dazzling innovation and invention, which we are even now enjoying on the Internet.

That same period in American history was one of crime and lawlessness wherever there was civilization. Cities large and small harbored felons and other rude types who struck out in anonymity and disappeared the same way. Smaller towns and settlements were preyed upon by outlaws, who ventured from unknown hideouts to terrorize and take what they could. It was all possible because society was largely unprotected and unaware. People fell prey to con artists out of their own ignorance and were robbed, harassed, or terrorized by untraceable individuals who wore anonymity like armor.

(That era also boasted hucksters flogging all sorts of miracle medicines and devices that were utter fraud. You don't have to look too far to find the same hucksterism on the Internet today.)

But, why bother with metaphors? The truth is, today's Internet population pretty much reflects urban and suburban demographics nationwide. You have pretty much the same sort of people online as you find running loose anywhere in the real world (and some of them shouldn't be running loose at all—online or off!).

The big differences between the real world and the Internet are the ability for people to be anonymous and untraceable, and the fact that the technology that makes the Internet possible also engenders all sorts of errant behavior. Put those who are inclined to be miscreants in such an environment, and you have more than enough threats to match the promise of the Internet.

You'll notice that I've placed more than a little emphasis on personal privacy and retaining control of personal information in this chapter, as I did in the Introduction. This is because privacy and control of information are what so many would-be online criminals and scammers rely on for protection. You should always remember that, because you can use information in the same way: to protect yourself—*and* to neutralize the threats.

Now, on to Chapter 2, in which we take a hard look at exactly what *you* risk being online, and why.

Chapter 2

Security Overview—What You Need To Protect, And Why

Chapter 2

Security Overview— What You Need To Protect, And Why

Chapter 2

To the uninformed, to say you are risking anything by going online with your computer may seem a bit of an exaggeration. After all, it's nothing more than a mass of plastic, glass, silicon, and metal hooked to low-voltage telephone lines. It's all very nonthreatening (except, perhaps, when it comes to figuring out how to use it). Most of the time, all you're doing is clicking on and viewing pictures, and typing and reading words.

Of course, neither your computer nor its connections with other computers is the problem, which is to say the Internet is not the problem. Collectively, the Internet is nothing more than computers and telecommunications links and associated hardware and software. In short, tools. As is the case with most tools, it's what people *do* with this collection of tools that gives the Internet its form and content. Thus, the real risks to being online are associated with what actually shapes the Internet: People.

"Okay, fine," you say. "I knew that people cause most of life's problems. Now, what exactly am I risking by going online?"

My answer to that is this chapter, wherein I will define various categories of online risks and help you determine the specific risks you might want to avoid. Please note: If you think you have no reason to keep your personal information private online, read this chapter anyway. You will find that you do have reasons to guard your personal information.

Information Is Valuable, But Privacy Is Priceless

With the advent of the Information Age, information became one of the most valuable commodities in the world. Before the 1960s, information was not accumulated in the wholesale manner it is today. The market for it did not even exist, and—more importantly—neither did the technology to create, maintain, and transfer large databases. Most information gathering was extremely specialized—for law-enforcement, tax and census purposes, and a few large marketing operations. It was also done manually—including updating and copying records—and it was expensive.

Computers changed all that. Today, information about tens of millions of individuals is collected and used for profit and other reasons by governments, commercial operations, and organizations. "Information brokering" is a recognized, if not always legitimate, occupation. A whole economic sector is dedicated to accumulating and trading information on people—their financial, medical, and social backgrounds, interests and spending habits, and other personal information.

This goes on largely because the technology to do it—computers—is available. Ironically, the technology is available in part because of the demand for the technology.

Obviously, information about you and me has some value—or at least some *perceived* value. For example, marketing companies sell our names and addresses and the fact that we bought a new home or car to other companies, which figure this information has value because we might buy something from them. (Never mind why they think that. In my case, the information is of no value, because I toss out virtually all advertising that comes in the mail. Still, the companies buying mailing lists perceive a value—i.e., a sale—so they keep sending out the junk mail.)

As you might imagine, junk mail has an online counterpart, called *unsolicited commercial email,* or UCE. More frequently referred to as "spam" (I will explain that name in a later chapter), it is the plague of the Internet. Multilevel marketing types, and just about everyone else with a useless product or get-rich-quick scheme, flood the Internet with literally millions of unsolicited email messages daily. They are known collectively as "spammers."

Thus, even the most basic piece of information about you in the online world—your email address—has some perceived value. But the thirst for information doesn't stop with email addresses. For instance, a large market exists among computer manufacturers, software publishers, and online services for information about the sort of computer and software you use, and your computing interests and activities.

Such information is collected from hundreds of thousands of computer users every day. Sometimes, the information is provided by the users themselves when they complete online surveys. Almost as often, the information is collected without the knowledge of the person being "polled." (I will explain in Chapter 4—and I will tell you how to avoid it.)

The type of computer and software you use is not the only information that can be grabbed without your knowledge. Go to any of thousands of World Wide Web sites, and the person running that site can know these facts about you:

• Your computer and operating system type.

• Which Web browser you are using.

- The site and page you are coming from.

- Your Internet Service Provider (ISP) and what part of the country you're in (often the city and state).

- Your email address.

Figure 2.1 shows a bit of what can be learned about you from your browser. You won't have a clue the information is being gathered.

Try It For Yourself...

To see a sample of what I'm talking about, point your browser to the following URLs:

http://www.anonymizer.com/cgi-bin/snoop.pl

http://www.coriolis.com/webpsychos/files.htm

You'll see a bit about what can (and cannot) be learned about you—without your knowledge—as you innocently surf the Web. It may surprise you.

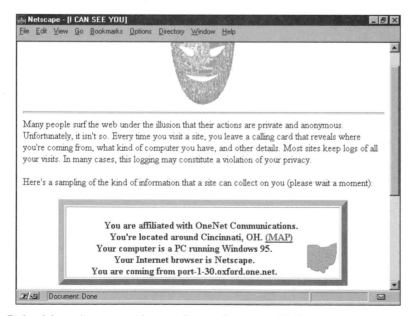

Figure 2.1   Many Internet sites collect all sorts of information about you.

That is only the beginning, and it is but one way that information about you gets online. People who know their way around online can find even more personal information about you. This is because, whether or not you willingly provided it, probably more information than you think is available (and publicly accessible) online.

The fact that someone has gleaned information about you without your knowledge is not in itself harmful. It may make you feel uncomfortable and that your privacy has been compromised—which it has.

That leads to an important point that I will reinforce throughout this book: While information is a valuable commodity to many, privacy is even more valuable to most of us. And, it's pretty rare—which makes it all the more valuable.

Privacy begins with controlling personal information. You cannot control what is in government, credit union, medical, military, and similar databases in the real world. But you can control a lot of what ends up in publicly accessible Internet databases and other online resources. This is possible because information is collected and stored differently in the online world, which means you can take steps to stop your information from getting out, and to get it removed from public access if it's already out there.

The Days Of Our Lives

Remember the editor I discussed in the Introduction—the fellow about whom I learned so much in half an hour? As I noted, he was not very active online. That may have started you thinking about how much more could be learned about someone who *is* active online. You, perhaps, or me.

I first went online in 1979, and have been using online services such as BBSes, and the Internet continually since 1982. Given that I've been active online for so long, you might expect that you could learn quite a bit about me from online resources. If you are willing to spend five or six hours searching several online services and various Internet resources, you can learn these things about me:

• My age, where I was born, and where I grew up.

• Where I currently live and my past three areas of residence.

- That I am divorced (and why I am divorced).

- Several medical conditions for which I have been treated.

- That I was in a bad auto accident in 1994 and could not work for 11 months.

- That I have been self-employed since 1983.

- The name and location of my last employer.

- My children's names and other information about them.

- Several email addresses I have or have had.

- Almost every place I traveled in the U.S. during the 1980s, exactly when, and for what purposes.

- My tastes in food, cars, music, literature, and many consumer goods.

- My political and religious views and affiliations.

- My military history.

- Whether I drink or use drugs (I do neither).

- Extensive details on my finances and tax status during much of the 1980s and '90s.

- My educational background.

It doesn't stop there. If you have the time and motivation, you can learn quite a bit more about me—including some odd and definitely frightening things about people and events on both sides of my family. Getting all this information would cost you next to nothing (the approximate value of said information), aside from your time and online service changes.

I don't really mind others knowing such things about me. But not everyone is that freewheeling about the facts of their lives. Some people have good reason for keeping a low profile.

Wherever you stand on the matter, how would *you* feel if someone was able to learn your medical and employment history, many of your personal habits and tastes, some of your financial history, your family status and makeup, age and place of birth, and other, similarly personal information? I suspect you would not like it—especially if you did not know you were being investigated, "researched," spied on, or however you might describe the process.

If you spend much time online—and don't take care with personal information offline—all of that information may well be out there about you someday. It may already be out there, and someone could be reading it right now.

If you knew someone were collecting such facts about you, you would want to know who it was and why they were interested in you. In the online world, the "who" can be literally anyone; as I just illustrated, even you can learn that much about someone you don't even know (me). As for the "why" of it, well, I leave that to your imagination or conscience.

The most important element at the moment, though, is not who is looking you up, or why or *how*. How can such information can be found? How did it get there?

As I've implied, if information about you is scattered around the Internet, you probably supplied a good deal of it yourself. The rest was gathered and placed there by others. This is certainly true of the information that is available about me, listed a few paragraphs back.

Given that you put a lot of that information out, you can also get it back—and along with it some of your privacy. Or, if you are new to the Internet, you can keep it from getting out in the first place. That, to telegraph later chapters yet again, is much of what this book is about...

...but we were talking about risks. So let's look at the risks in having personal information easily accessible by just anyone.

THREATS TO PRIVACY AND PERSON

Personal information can be a threat to your privacy. How it is a threat depends on the nature of the information and, more to the point, who has it. If, for instance, your telephone number or address is made public, just about anyone can telephone or visit you. Again, this doesn't bother some folks. The people who feel threatened by having this information public are those who fear being harassed, for whatever reason.

Does this mean that, if you don't have any mortal enemies and haven't offended the town psychopath, it's okay to have your home address and telephone number out on the Internet, where anyone can find it? Well, no. As you will learn, you can make enemies online by the simple act of speaking your mind. You can get into trouble without even knowing it, if you violate certain unwritten rules of the Internet, USENET Newsgroups, or online services. The rules, such as they are, are "enforced" at will by certain of the more forceful personalities in a given online society. Such enforcement can run the gamut from private (email) or public (public postings) reprimand, to online *and* offline harassment and/or threats. (For more information on these unwritten rules, see Chapters 3 and 5.)

Inviting Email Harassment?

Violating the unwritten rules of the Internet (which are sometimes known by the cutesy sobriquet, "netiquette") can get you into trouble. Violations can be as simple as posting a public reply to the wrong sort of USENET Newsgroup message.

If you doubt that, visit this URL:

http://hnet.hutton.com/~mredrain/metoo.html

You will find a page listing the email addresses of people who have posted a two-word reply to certain types of USENET messages. Once you see the page, the reason for the list being there will be clear, if not understandable: These people violated an unwritten rule against posting useless messages, thereby cluttering up the message threads.

When you visit the page (called "The Lamers Page"), you will see that the person who put the page together not only published the names of the offending parties, but also provided click-on email links. This makes it very easy for those who were offended by the postings of a given user to send harassing or at least annoying mail to that person.

While this sort of invitation to retaliation is rare, it gives you an idea of just how far some people will go when provoked by others who had no idea they were provoking anyone. (These people were foolish, though, as will be obvious when you look around the Lamers site.) Some people are willing to go much further than this when they are provoked, or think they have been provoked. Just imagine such a person having your home address and telephone number.

Similar pages are devoted to publishing information about the more odious bulk emailers, along with their email addresses. This is perhaps a more positive use, and it doesn't invite action against those listed. One such page is located at:

http://www-math.uni-paderborn.de/~axel/BL/archive.html

So, even if you do not now have reason to fear that the wrong person may know your telephone number or where you live, you might want to keep that information off the Internet. There are simply too many ways you can end up doing the wrong thing when interacting with others in public online venues.

When Trouble Comes To You

Sometimes, you can get into trouble without doing anything. Even if you don't offend someone directly, some people find or create offense where none exists. I've seen this type of person at work in public message bases more than once. One rather chilling example involved a disagreement between two participants in an online discussion group. An argument that spanned a half-dozen messages and replies ensued, and it predictably escalated into a flame war. The less-aggressive of the combatants eventually realized that they were arguing over something that had no "right" answer. (It was, in fact, a matter of personal tastes.) That fellow apologized, in public, and said he was through arguing. The other party fired back, "You

are not through with this until I am through with you. I have your home address...."
I don't know how far this went, but the implications are rather frightening.

You may draw unwanted attention without ever having had direct contact with the person who is bothering you. I have found this to be the case at times simply because I am a writer and public speaker. Someone may take issue with something I've said in a column or a quote from a speech or interview. Anyone who has even a minor public persona must expect a certain amount of this, but not to the point of stalking or harassment.

In cases where someone will not stop emailing you, the key to putting a halt to the bothersome email is contacting the sender's ISP. ISPs (and online services) are normally responsive to such complaints about their users. They will either warn the user or immediately terminate his or her service, as was the case with a series of ugly email messages I received on the old GEnie online service in 1988.

I was an invited participant in message-base discussion groups hosted by several of the service's RoundTables (GEnie's name for forums, or special-interest groups), mostly on the subject of writing. Out of nowhere, I began receiving strange messages from a GEnie user that had nothing to do with what I or anyone else had said in the message bases. Specifically, he wanted me to write about how the police were allegedly harassing poor citizens in his city. These included admonitions that I write about the pleasure and necessity, in his mind, of "killing all cops and Jews."

This wasn't really something I could reply to, so I didn't. The messages kept coming, getting uglier and uglier, including threats to my personal safety, since I obviously did not share his view of how things ought to be.

As it turned out, his online profile said essentially the same thing, in the same words. I handed that one over to the management at GEnie. They killed his account then and there, and advised law-enforcement officials in his city. Thankfully, I've not heard from or about this guy since. Nor do I wish to. I could have become the target of a stalker had I argued with him.

All of this is not to make you paranoid about being online. I just want to urge you to be cautious, particularly if you are new to the Internet.

Lest you think that the situation really can't be that dangerous, consider this: Sites devoted to safety on the Internet are becoming popular. Even the well-known Guardian Angels organization, which fights street crime, maintains a presence on the Web. As shown in Figure 2.2, the site is devoted to safety on the Internet, a theme reflected in the name: CyberAngels.

CyberAngels, about which I'll have more to say in later chapters, works to provide resources for victims of online harassment, stalking, and similar activities, as well as helping Internet users avoid such problems. Its very existence says something about the need for such guidance.

Email Revenge?

On October 21, 1996, a repulsive message showed up in the email boxes of thousands (perhaps tens or even hundreds of thousands) of Internet users. Apparently coming from one of two AOL addresses, the message offered child pornography for sale. The following is a quote from the first paragraph, in part:

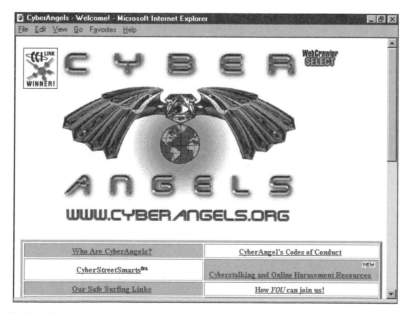

Figure 2.2   The CyberAngels Web site is devoted to safety on the Internet.

"Hi! I sent you this letter because your email address was on a list that fit this category. I am a fan of child pornography and for the past 4 years, I have been able to gather quite a collection of it. I have pictures, VHS tapes, posters, audio recordings, and games based on child pornography. I am now selling my products (or trading for other child pornography). I have a complete color catalog of all my products now available."

The message included a price list, name, and street address. Almost everyone who received it was outraged, and a number of people reported it to AOL and law-enforcement agencies in the city where the supposed perpetrator lived. The FBI investigated and found that the person named in the message was not the one who sent it. Nor were the two email addresses shown as the source of the message valid. Someone totally unknown sent the message, faking the return address and even the email headers.

This was apparently an attempt to seek revenge or for other reasons harm the person whose name and address appeared in the message. Certainly, the individual named became the object of a lot of hate mail and, for a brief time, an FBI investigation. This was certainly harmful in that it was an invasion of privacy, an embarrassment, and damaging to this person's reputation. It serves as an example of just how far some people might go in using the Internet to harm someone else, for whatever reasons.

True Names And Other Dangerous Information

Obviously, you have more than enough reason to guard your address and telephone number and other personal information when you are online. In some Internet venues, in fact, the prudent course may be to avoid giving your true name.

The same is true of the identity of your employer. In some incidents, sparked by arguments or flame wars, one party has complained to his or her enemy's employer. This is particularly effective if the target works for a computer or online services company.

It is possible, by the way, to keep your email address secret, yet still be able to receive email from those who want to look you up. I'll discuss this and other ways to control email in Chapter 10.

Public Interaction: Newsgroups And Other Message Bases

I hope that, by now, I have given you reason to be careful about giving out personal information. You should also be aware that you should avoid jumping right into any online discussion, whether it's in Newsgroups, an online service's message bases, or even a message base at a Web site. Until you understand the nature of the venue, the sorts of people who frequent the discussions, and the unwritten rules, you really need to keep a low profile.

If you will be voicing potentially controversial or inflammatory opinions, you may want to keep your email address private. You can do this by dedicating one email address to public messaging and not reading the email it receives, using an "anonymous remailer," or by other means discussed in Chapter 10.

This is also a useful service for those who wish to discuss very private issues with others who share an interest or experience. Note, however, that it is not a means of harassing others with impunity.

Getting The FAQs

Most USENET Newsgroups, as well as some message bases elsewhere, provide a guide for acceptable conduct within the group. This covers the range of topics that can be discussed, whether flames will be tolerated, and other important issues. Such a guide is usually called a FAQ, an acronym for Frequently Asked Questions. FAQs typically consist of the answers to questions that are often asked by new users, in a question-and-answer format.

Seek out a FAQ whenever you enter an area new to you. If you cannot find one, email one of the more active people in the group to ask whether a FAQ or some other guideline is available.

Examples of Newsgroup FAQs can be found at:

http://www.spirit-lake.k12.ia.us/html/jbolluyt/newsgrp.htm

http://www.ucsalf.ac.uk/usenet/computer-security/

ftp://ftp.cs.columbia.edu/archives/faq/news/announce/newusers

http://ancho.ucs.indiana.edu/FAQ/USAGN/

Your best approach in joining the discussion in a Newsgroup or message base is simply to read a few weeks' worth of messages, to get an idea of how the group works. If you do decide to participate, take care not to offend anyone. (If you do decide to give someone a hard time in a public forum, you will learn that anyone who has been around a while has friends there, and friends tend to stand up for one another. You could end up being the object of a lot of flames. This could turn everyone in the group against you.)

SUMMING UP

You run certain risks when you enter the online world. Most involve the usual problems you might expect when dealing with an unfamiliar society: committing a minor (or major) *faux pas*, stepping on others' toes, violating unwritten rules, or outraging one of the more influential or important locals. The risks are multiplied online, largely because online communities are so numerous and have so many variations in rules.

Also, because online contact is truly second-hand, without the sorts of physical references you get in the real world, you cannot rely on your normal means of evaluating people.

Therefore, you need to proceed cautiously in all online activities, but particularly those that involve contact with other people. Treat everyone as a stranger until you really get to know them. You also need to retain as much control as possible, which means controlling information about yourself and controlling communication.

Safeguarding The Obvious: Passwords And Credit Cards

Failure to control your personal information can result in a lot of aggravation and loss of time. You risk more serious losses if certain types of information, such as your password or credit card numbers, get out.

These are obvious items to safeguard for most readers, but some people are looser with passwords or credit card and PIN numbers than they ought to be. So, a few warnings about what can happen if your information does get out....

First, passwords. Do not trust anyone with your password, and don't use setups that let you log on without entering your password. If you are using an online service, you know that you stand to lose money if someone gets a hold of your password and starts logging on. Per-minute rates for some areas and surcharge rates for others can quickly run up your bill. So can online purchases; an online service sets you up to be billed by credit card for your monthly fee and/or per-minute charges, *plus* any purchases you may make from vendors hosted by the service.

The Case Of The Hacker Who Wasn't

An acquaintance of mine who has two teenage daughters found out the hard way that you can't trust anyone with your password. Early in 1995, she signed up for AOL, which at that time charged a per-minute rate. For convenience, she set up the software to "remember" her password so she could log on without entering it. Two months later she noticed that her AOL bill was exceptionally large—not only had the large number of free minutes that came with the account been used up, but she had an additional charge of more than $300.

She was certain that nobody outside the house had touched the machine, and that her daughters had definitely not signed on to AOL. That last was believable, since neither knew anything about nor had any interest in computers—let alone using an online service. She was convinced that a hacker had gotten into her account. I didn't think it was that simple; I was convinced that someone had come into her house and used the machine.

She checked her setup and found that a new AOL name had been added to her account (AOL permits five additional logon names for each account). Appropriately, the name was "Pirate" something-or-other. Of course no password was entered for the pirate; he was logging on elsewhere.

As it turned out, the pirate was a male friend of one of the teenage daughters. (We eventually learned that this boy had been visiting one of the girls when the mother was away, and he had, according to the daughter, just "taken a look at" the computer.) What he had actually done was logged on using the password conveniently in the machine, created an add-on name and password, and logged off. He knew this would eventually be discovered, but never identified. The worst that could happen was that my friend would sign on with the master account and delete the ID he had created. This is exactly what she did. She also changed her password and removed the automatic password entry.

In addition to the potential for financial loss, if someone else uses your account, you stand to lose your reputation and even the account. It can happen—and has—that someone using a stolen password logs on to a service and posts all sorts of embarrassing messages anywhere possible. This can incur the wrath of other users—expressed in your email box—and the online service, which may cancel your account if there is any doubt that your password wasn't stolen.

As for credit cards, we all know that we need to keep a tight rein on those. Even though your financial liability may be limited, stolen credit cards can cause a lot of headaches. When someone gets your credit-card number and expiration date online, the limit to liability may be irrelevant, because you will not know the card is being used for as long as a month. With this in mind, you may want to make sure any online credit-card transactions you do are through a secure Web server. (I'm rather suspicious of credit-card transactions on general principles, so I don't order anything online, nor do I use a credit card for telephone orders.)

Cautious Contacts And Bad Information

When you are online, you can, in the right situations, be anyone you want to be. More than a few people take advantage of this. Married men and women masquerade as singles, men masquerade as women, and other people pretend to be almost anything.

This is not a phenomenon that developed with the Internet. People have been pretending to be what they're not for many centuries. It's just easier to pull off a masquerade online, where quite often the general population knows nothing about you except what you say.

The first time I ran across a masquerade on the Internet was in 1985, when a fellow on DELPHI represented himself as a newly minted M.D. He was actually a college dropout living on unemployment. While, as far as I know, he did not give out any bad medical advice, he could have if he wanted to. Since the incident with the fake doctor, I have encountered many more masquerade cases: a woman who worked at a convenience store claiming to be a high-level employee of Tandy, handing out information on nonexistent new products from that company; a woman who presented herself as a psychologist or a lawyer, depending on the situation, but turned out to be a divorcee living on alimony, who had not passed her state's bar exam; and all sorts of other folks claiming to be doctors, lawyers, officers in large corporations, airline pilots, the founders of major software publishers, famous authors and TV personalities, actors, and just about anything else. (I even heard of someone on CompuServe purporting to be *me*, in 1987, but I was never able to track that one down.)

I'm sure you can imagine scenarios for each of these masquerades. You can also imagine the harm that could be done to people who receive bad advice from fake professionals. Or, when someone claims to be a specific person—famous or not— you can easily see where this could be damaging to the person being impersonated, as well as to the people being taken advantage of.

(Online masquerades often get strange. Several years before I encountered the fake doctor, an online journalist named Steve Roberts reported an instance of a man who masqueraded as a woman in order to have "virtual sex" online. He always revealed his true identity at the end of a "session." Or, did he? It's difficult to tell, online.)

The final word is: Don't take anyone you meet online at face value. Until you get to know a person, or unless others can vouch for him or her, be cautious about what you accept as truth.

Don't take any advice from a professional until you are sure that person is what he or she claims to be. Beware of great offers on merchandise and "business deals." More than a few would-be con artists are plying their trade on the Internet. As is the case in the real world, if it sounds too good to be true, it is.

BAD ADVICE, WORSE INFORMATION

Fraudulent users aren't the only sources of bad information online. Sometimes, the bad information is unintentional. Many Web sites on medical, political, and other popular topics tend to present opinion and unproved information as fact. The people responsible for this incorrect information on the Web are most often themselves misinformed, or just hoping that the information is true.

The Internet also has its fair share of offensive information—that is, offensive text and/or graphics that nobody wants their children to blunder into. This includes, but doesn't stop with, pornographic sites. (Note: The majority of the sites offering graphic pornography require a credit-card number to enter.) You can also find racist, strangely violent, anti-government, and even how-to-be-a-criminal Web sites. (The how-to sites include varied information, such as how to pick locks, build bombs, hack into computers, and so forth.)

USENET Newsgroups also present such information—including graphics. The main concern over such information being available is the potential for children being exposed to it. Some sites may well encourage behavior in adults that would not be considered otherwise.

Download Follies

Even if you're new to personal computing, you've heard of computer viruses. Most viruses are spread via software offered for download. Today, finding a virus is rather rare, but one can pop up at any time. If you download an "infected" program and run it, you risk losing literally everything on your hard drive. Be aware of what you are downloading and where you're downloading from. Whenever possible, I download shareware from a Web site belonging to the shareware author, and I scan downloads for viruses.

Also watch for incomplete software packages. Sometimes, people download a program and like it so much they want to share it with others. The problem is, they've deleted the download file that contained all of the program elements. So, they put one together on their own, which may or may not contain everything you need to run the program. This is why it's advisable to get a program from its creator. If you can't do that, at least check the downloaded package for a README file that lists the files that should come with the program.

In later chapters I will have more to say about each of the topics discussed here. My intent here was mainly to make you aware of the real dangers of being online. That accomplished, let's move on to Chapter 3. It's a hands-on chapter, in which I show you the basics of online security, provide tips and advice on staying safe, and explore more of the "why" behind the risks of the online world.

Chapter 3

Online Security Basics: A Bit Of Prevention Is Worth A Gigabyte Of Cure

Chapter 3

Online Security
Basics: A Bit Of Prevention Is Worth A Gigabyte Of Cure

Chapter 3

Now that you know something about what the online risks are for the unwary, the time has come to get active in protecting yourself from the Internet—that is, from Internet denizens who have anything but your best interests in mind. That includes anyone who might want to use your personal information to their benefit and your loss, thieves who want to use your ISP/online service account or credit-card numbers, con artists looking to relieve you of your money, soreheads, stalkers, and general Web psychos. (Never forget that such people are indeed online. The Internet makes it easy for people to become something they would not otherwise be, and the Internet attracts people you probably would not come into contact with anywhere else.)

Some of what you will learn in this chapter parallels many common-sense precautions you take in the real world, albeit translated into online terms. Much of what I have to say here, however, has to do with threats for which no offline counterparts exist. For these, you must take special precautions.

Either way, the goal here is to enable you to prevent online trouble, or at least avoid it, by controlling information.

Protecting Your Personal Information And Privacy

By now, I hope I have established the importance of protecting your personal information online, as well as the value of privacy. As indicated by some of the examples in Chapter 2, you can learn a surprising amount about someone who's active online. In fact, you may be able to find out more about someone online than you might about some people you see every day at work or school.

Some of what you have to do to keep your personal information safe online involves the same sorts of precautions you take in the real world. The online world, however, has some special considerations, largely because of the many different ways information is obtained, stored, cataloged, and distributed online. (Apropos of that, part of what this chapter does is help you identify where and how your information can get out.)

When thinking about information online, keep these two important facts in mind:

- Most information about you online is provided by you.

- While you can remove information by or about you from many Internet repositories, not everything can be erased. Personal information made public all too often stays public. So, your best defense is to keep it from getting out.

It Starts With Your Name...

The most basic piece of information about you is your name. Almost all other information about you is tied to your name in one way or another, and you are most readily identified by name. Where a name is duplicated or does not provide definite identification, other identifiers—such as location, date of birth, or Social Security number—provide *contextual* data by which you are known. Occupation, locales you frequent, recreational activities, and any of dozens of other pieces of information can also provide contextual data.

Thus, to know someone's true name is to be empowered to learn more about them. It may be argued that someone with the name John Smith would be difficult to track down, but this isn't necessarily so. If you are the only John Smith in a certain area, or your employer or similar information is known, a potential tracker has a *context* by which to identify you. Less-common names, such as Pierre Chastain or Jesse Bilderback, require very little context. Given a single reference point, such as locale, the owners of those names are easy to track down.

A name alone often says something about its owner. Most first names reveal gender, and some imply a regional or national origin. Surnames may also indicate a nationality. A distinctive first name or surname might indicate a tie to a specific group of people or act as a complete identifier in itself, depending on the context.

Since your name potentially has a good deal of information attached to it, you might consider protecting it from the online world at large. I'm not encouraging you to hide your name or assume a bogus identity. Just be careful about where you are identified and to whom.

Online, the most basic and important piece of information about you is your user ID. (*ID* was originally short for identifier. Depending on where you are, and where you sign on to the online world, your ID may also be known as your UID, nickname, alias, username, logon name, screen name, or several other terms.) Like your name, your ID can say a lot about you.

Your ISP or online service knows you by your ID; your real name, address, and other contact information, as well as your billing information, are tied to it. Certain records of your online activities having to do with your access level, logon times, and the like are linked to your ID.

The rest of the online world knows you by your ID, but in a different way. Others use your ID to send mail to you, reply to your public postings, and address you in lieu of any other identifier. It doesn't tell anyone your name (not directly, unless you use your name as your ID), but it can say a lot more about you than you think.

Let's look at some first-line defenses for protecting what may at times be your most valuable online asset: your true identity.

True Names And Other Dangers

Science fiction was exploring the Net in print long before it became the subject of fiction in Hollywood movies and on television news. Indeed, the science fictional imagery of "cyberpunks" seems to have been a model for many online venues, as well as for a good portion of the online population. But few science fiction writers accurately portrayed today's Internet—or even the virtual-reality Net looming on the horizon. Almost none showed the real day-to-day concerns of inhabitants of their fictional Nets.

Many readers will be familiar with the early cyberpunk novel Neuromancer, *by William Gibson (published in 1984). In it, as in many movies, the Net is portrayed as a monster video game populated by self-made superheroes. On a more realistic level, but still making dazzling use of virtual reality in cyberspace, is Vernor Vinge's novella,* True Names. *First published in 1980 and thus predating the Gibson work and other "cyberpunkia,"* True Names *focuses in part on the obsession online hacker communities have with keeping their real names—their true names—a secret. In Vinge's world of hackers, for someone else to know your true name was to lose all—to be at the mercy of those who knew your true name.*

As you know if you've read Chapter 1, anonymity is every bit as vital a concern to contemporary hackers as it was to the hackers in True Names. *It should be a vital concern to you, too, in certain situations.*

True Names *is a good starting point for understanding the hacker culture and related Web communities. It provides valuable information for anyone who uses the Internet. (Vinge's novella is included in his collection of stories,* True Names and Other Dangers. *The book is published by Baen Books, **http://www.baen.com**.)*

Your ID, Whois, And Finger

Unless you provide additional information, most people online know little more about you than your ID and the ISP or online service you use. But your choice of ID can say quite a bit about you. Anyone who knows your ISP can look up certain facts and glean still more information. Consider this ID, seen as an email address, or in the header of a USENET posting: **chevyman@toobogus.com**.

If I saw this name online, I would infer that this person is a male who is into cars— specifically, Chevrolets. That much is obvious. But I could also find factual information about this person, thanks to some easy-to-access Internet utilities known as *whois* and *finger*.

Whois is an Internet utility that provides information about ISPs. If I access one of the Web interfaces to whois (such as The Web Interface to Whois, located at this URL: **http://rs.internic.net/cgi-bin/whois**) and enter "toobogus.com," I can see a screenful of information like that shown in Figure 3.1.

The most important information gained from this particular research is the location of the ISP in question. As long as this is not a national ISP, such as Netcom or

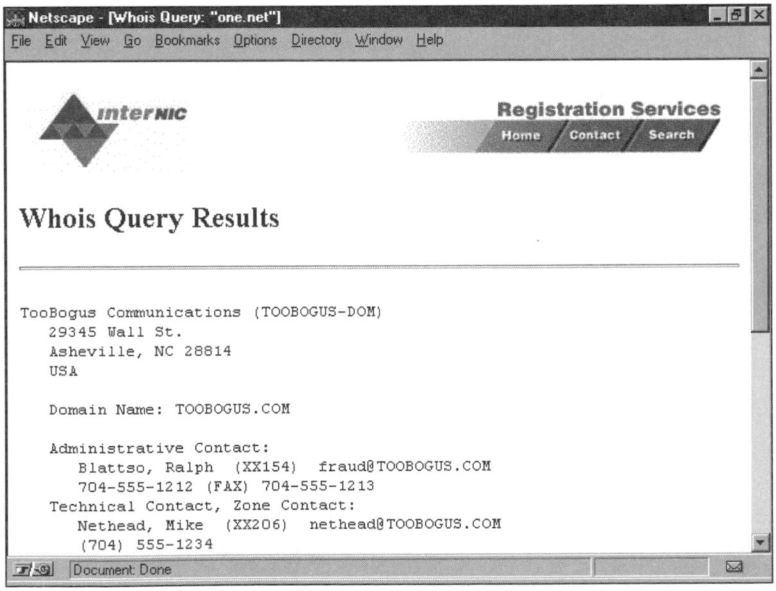

Figure 3.1   The Web Interface to Whois provides information about ISPs.

Mindspring, "chevyman" likely lives in or near the ISP's city—in this instance, Asheville, North Carolina.

So with this small effort, we have learned that this hypothetical person is a male fan of Chevrolets who lives within a local telephone call of Asheville. (Whois has other uses, which I'll discuss in later chapters.)

Now, let's take this a bit further and see what else we can learn, using finger. We'll use a finger gateway (**http://www.magibox.net/~unabest/finger/query.cgi**), as shown in Figure 3.2.

Continuing with our example, we type "chevyman@toobogus.com", and finger tells us that chevyman is really Mickey Bitsko. At least, that's what he told his ISP when he signed up—or what he changed his finger information to. (Yes, it can be changed.) Unless Mickey is an Internet techie or has read this book, the odds are that's his real name.

Finger can be quite informative. Depending on the version of the finger program that is operating on an ISP's server and how the user has set it up, it sometimes

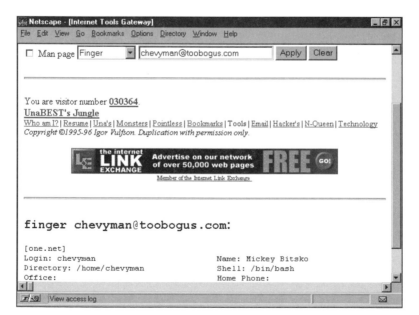

Figure 3.2   Finger provides information about specific users on an ISP.

contains not only a user's name, but also a company name, address, and/or telephone number. By the same token, finger often provides no information; many ISPs disable it.

As this hypothetical exercise demonstrates, your online ID can be an address, a license plate, and a name all rolled into one. It can make you easy to find—perhaps too easy. Let's say the fictional Mickey Bitsko happens to offend a true Web psycho who is an aficionado of Volkswagens. Mickey might come home from work the next day to find a deranged man in a VW bug waiting for him.

Okay, that's an exaggerated example. But you get the idea: If you don't like complete strangers knowing who you are and where you live, don't let your ID or your ISP give away too much personal information.

If you use a large national ISP or an online service, you probably don't have to worry about being fingered by finger. Nor will whois give an Internet sleuth any clues as to your whereabouts.

If you use a smaller ISP, you need to make sure finger will not provide your name. To do this, visit one of the Web finger interfaces (either **http://www.magibox.net/ ~unabest/finger/index.html** or **http://www.cs.indiana.edu:800/finger/gateway**). Enter your email address (**yourname@yourisp.com**) in the text box, and press Enter. If your ISP is running finger, you will see your name, as shown in Figure 3.2.

To remove or change your name, you can use the chfn (change finger) command while you are logged on to your shell account. Or, take the simpler approach: Look around the Help or Support section of your ISP's Web site for a Utilities or similar section. You should be able to find a screen much like that in Figure 3.3.

You will be required to enter your ID and password before accessing this screen. Once in, you can enter, change, or delete information as you please. It's up to you, but I recommend leaving all fields blank, or simply putting your user ID in the Name field.

Selecting An Online ID

Your choice in a user ID, and the information it provides about you, is completely under your control. This means you have a way of

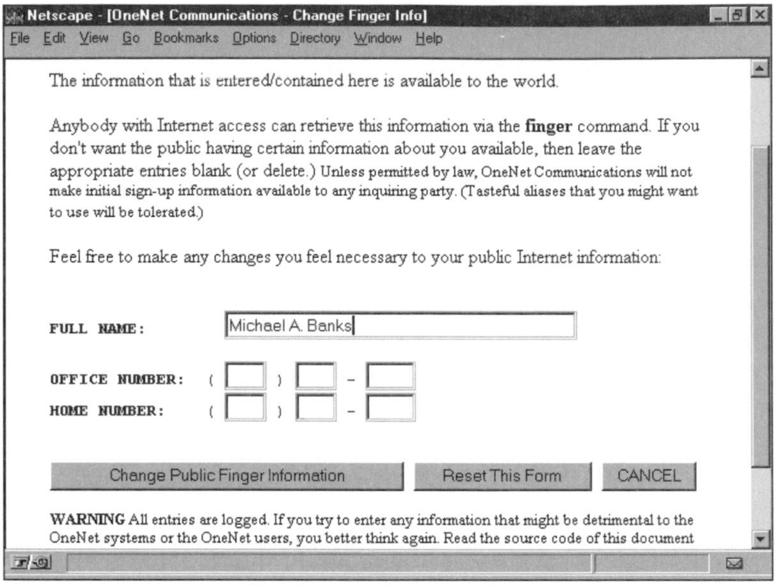

Figure 3.3   Most ISPs allow you to change your finger information.

controlling some of your personal information. Therefore, you probably want to take care in choosing your ID.

This is particularly important for women. For many reasons, women are often the object of online harassment and inappropriate activity that would not occur in a face-to-face situation. Thus, a woman might want to adopt a gender-neutral ID. (True, any woman ought to be able to go online using her real identity, but it's not practical in many online venues. For a more detailed range of information about the concerns of women online, stop by the Cybergrrl Webstation at this URL: **http://www.cybergrrl.com/**. *This site features a lot of solid content and an amazing array of links to related sites.)*

The majority of online IDs are some combination of initials and surname, or a word or word-combination that the user feels is representative of his or her interests, profession, or other important life element. You usually can't get into trouble with IDs based on these tenets.

Some new online-service and Internet users come with IDs that represent a passing enthusiasm or make what is at the time an important "statement." They later find their IDs embarrassing. Fortunately, IDs are easier to get rid of than tattoos; you just put in a request to your ISP for a change, or close down your current account and sign up for a new one.

Finally, unless you want to buy trouble, don't use a provocative ID. Such choices as "GoToHell," "ikillcats," "DerFuhrer," or similarly provocative words are guaranteed to make you unpopular in some circles. They might also draw negative attention of the type this book is intended to help you prevent.

The Walls Have Ears—And Memories!

From childhood, we're cautioned to watch what we say about certain topics, what we say around certain people, and how we say certain things. And we're always warned to watch what we say about others.

While following such advice is prudent in our daily dealings with people in the real world, it is almost vital when it comes to online communications. Online, the walls do indeed have ears—and memories that are perfect when invoked.

Saying It's Private Doesn't Make It So

Even the most "private" areas on the Web or an online service can have a pipeline to the outside world—or be accessible to people you wouldn't expect to find there. I observed a rather striking example of this on the old GEnie online service in 1990.

While I was not exactly a member of GEnie's staff, I was closely tied to certain GEnie services. So I had access to "background" areas that weren't open to the public. This included a closed, private BBS for staff members. Rather than announce my presence there, I occasionally lurked and read messages, to keep up with new developments on the service.

On one of my weekly forays into the area, I was surprised to learn that I was a topic of an extended conversation thread. The reason? I had recently written a magazine article about some new services on Prodigy, which GEnie staff members considered one of their arch-rivals.

I was a little surprised at some of the comments, which branded me a "traitor to GEnie," and worse. I stayed quiet and watched the thread evolve for a few days. As it turned out, several of the sysops thought that I should have included a statement that GEnie was somehow better than Prodigy—in an article about Prodigy.

Regardless of the lack of merit of my detractors' criticism, I am certain they never thought it would get back to me. And they definitely didn't think I would see what they had to say—particularly the insults.

I did see their comments, though. I also saw a good friend—a man everyone respected—go in and set them straight, even though he figured I would never see what he had to say, either. So, I kept silent. Until now nobody knew that I read what was said, all those years ago.

Of course, I haven't forgotten that incident. It was on my mind once when I was asked to provide references for a couple of my detractors. I declined the offer, saying neither good nor bad of them, for what it was worth. And I still owe my friend Jerry for standing up for me.

Because of the nature of online communications, literally everything you ever do online can be recorded and stored for future access. The majority of online communications are in the form of text: email; postings on USENET, online services, and Internet bulletin boards; realtime chats; entries on Web-page forms; and, sometimes, commands. In each case, the text you enter at your keyboard is transmitted to another computer. Depending on the nature of the text, it may be copied and passed on to still more computers. Sometimes the text is stored by the systems handling it, and sometimes it isn't—and sometimes it's stored by the person(s) to whom you sent it. The point is, it *can* be stored, and what is stored can be retrieved, copied, and transmitted to others.

Note that the concern here isn't over text you type being intercepted along the way. Rather, the potential for problems comes from communicating in a manner whereby *anything* you say or do can be recorded (and often is). In certain respects, this is like living in one of the totalitarian states that pops up every so often in science fiction, wherein everything said or done is observed and recorded.

Forever Yours, USENET

Early in 1996, a San Diego man was astonished to receive a three-page synopsis of his entire life via email from a woman he had met once, but didn't know.

According to news reports at the time, all sorts of private information had been gathered about writer John Kaufman by a woman who had apparently pieced together his life by searching out postings he had made in various USENET Newsgroups. Thanks to an Internet search tool called Deja News, the woman was able to zero in on every posting Kaufman, a frequent Newsgroup participant, had ever made. Presumably, she collected lots of information about him and inferred quite a bit more.

*With Deja News (located at: **http://www.dejanews.com/forms/ dnq.html**), you can find literally anything ever posted in Newsgroups. The search tool is so powerful that, once you've entered the appropriate keywords, you can view everything that's been posted by an individual, or everything ever posted on a given topic, by clicking on successive links. You can, of course, combine search criteria, so you might, for instance, find everything your former boss ever posted on the subject of illegal drug use—recently, or in the dim reaches of the 1980s. (Deja News intends to have available by 1998 not only contemporary postings, but also all USENET postings since 1979.)*

While the prospect of having your public commentary researched may not be intimidating, the amount of information that can be gleaned from Newsgroup postings is surprising. In Kaufman's case, the searcher was able to learn his childhood ambitions, his cat's name, facts about his family and personal life, and so much other personal information that the dossier probably rivaled what the FBI could have put together. The quantity and type of information were such that Kaufman was compelled to ask the woman to stop contacting him.

The moral: If you don't want something about yourself or your views known, don't even hint at it in an online post.

Fortunately, not *everything* you say and do online is recorded, but the possibility is there. Unless you've attracted the attention of law-enforcement organizations, you are probably not having your every move online recorded. Still, much of what you say and do online *is* recorded, and a lot of it is made available to the general public—some of it on a permanent basis.

Where are your words recorded? Anywhere that's public. That includes public postings and realtime conferencing. They're also recorded in private email—often saved by the recipient.

Public Postings

You should already be aware that anything you post in a public messaging system is recorded and kept available for others—sometimes in a searchable format. Public messaging systems include USENET Newsgroups; message bases or bulletin boards on AOL, CompuServe, and other online services; and Web page-based bulletin boards and guest books. Recording and retrieval of anything posted in such areas is a given; the only variables are how long postings are kept and how easily they can be searched.

Is this really a threat? If you read the sidebar headed, "Forever Yours, USENET," you know that such a massive collection of postings holds more personal information than some people would like to have available. What if someone had recordings or transcripts of every conversation you've had in the past month? Most of us would not want everything that is revealed in such a mass of information, directly or by implication, in any one person's hands.

Keep Your Postings (And Your Name) Out Of Deja News Archives

If you prefer not to have your USENET postings archived for future generations, add this line to your headers, or as the very first line in your postings: "x-no-archive: yes" (without the quotes).

On top of that, most of us tend to be far more candid in online postings than we are in person. The illusion of online anonymity leads many people to think nobody knows who they are, and nobody they know is going to read what they have to say. Anyone who thinks that way is wrong on both counts. As I've already demonstrated, and will again, your identity may already be public knowledge online. With the way the Internet is growing, the odds are good that even your Aunt Mary in Florida may be online next week (mine already is).

Or, your ex-wife, -husband, or other partner may show up and see what you've had to say about them. Maybe someone you've libeled will spot what you've said or be tipped off about it. Public postings have already been the basis for legal action, and many threats of same. Legal papers have even been served via USENET.

The stands we take and the statements we make may become embarrassing, or worse, years or sometimes only days later. Before the Internet, such foibles died a natural death and were forgotten soon enough. Online, they become a matter of public record.

Any way you look at it, baring your soul in a USENET Newsgroup or other public forum can have negative consequences. If nothing else, it invites an invasion of your privacy by anyone with Internet access and the time and inclination to sift through your rambles and rants. (On top of everything else, email addresses attached to public postings are regularly "harvested" by spammers seeking new victims.)

Just how long do public postings stay online? Messages posted in some areas disappear remarkably fast. In CompuServe Forums, messages "scroll off" in a matter of weeks, or less. This is because the message traffic is so high that the service would have to spend a fortune on storage space to keep everything. Fortunately, the messages are more ephemeral than not.

Other online service message areas may retain postings much longer. A few online services, including DELPHI, "prune" and archive messages only when necessary to free up storage space and other system resources. Prodigy seems to be somewhere between CompuServe and DELPHI. On AOL, some postings stay up for a year or longer before they go away. (This has undoubtedly caused more than a few red faces among those who post in the "Romance" area.)

Web-site bulletin board postings remain for an indefinite length of time—depending on how efficient or lax the Webmaster might be.

USENET posts are probably going to be around until the sun goes nova— or until our technological civilization fails. As noted in the sidebar, the folks behind Deja News intend to make everything posted on USENET since 1979 available to anyone who wants to read it—all in a conveniently searchable format with backups.

Accessibility varies. If you want to find something on Prodigy and AOL message bases, you may have to browse through hundreds or thousands of messages; once you find the proper category, you can specify a date range, and that's it. Public message bases on CompuServe and DELPHI are searchable by just about any set of criteria—provided you know which message areas to search.

As for messages on Web-site bulletin boards, you can use an Internet search engine. It may be tedious, but you can probably find just about any public posting at any Web site. Deja News is ready and willing to find anything USENET's Newsgroups may contain. Other search engines collect USENET postings, too.

You may wonder if providing all this information is illegal. It isn't. As with a letter to a newspaper, you provide tacit agreement for your public postings to be made public by the very act of posting them. (Deja News does plan to provide a means to keep your future posts out of its USENET database if you want them excluded. Watch your favorite Newsgroup for complete information.)

A good policy to follow for public postings might be to temper your words with the knowledge that your worst enemy may be reading them, or that an anonymous person might be behind the scenes compiling a profile on you—which just might be true.

Realtime Conferencing

If anything about the online world can be said to be truly addictive, it is realtime conferencing. No one knows exactly how many people participate in realtime chats on a given day. If the tens of thousands of chat-room and CB simulator participants that can be counted on AOL and CompuServe every night are any indication, the number must be upward of a million. In addition to those two online services, you have chat rooms on other online services, local BBSes that offer realtime conversation for their customers, private Web sites with chat features, and the ever-growing Internet Relay Chat (IRC) groups that dot the Web.

No matter what the venue, all chats have one characteristic in common: What everyone says can be recorded by anyone present. Sometimes you are aware that a chat is being recorded, as is the case when an online service hosts a celebrity guest in a realtime conference, or when someone decides to record a group's regular Tuesday-night chat for a member who's absent. The proceedings, edited or not, are made available for downloading or are emailed to others.

Most of the time, though, you don't know if a chat is being recorded. Chat rooms have no indicator that tells you someone is recording. This is done at a person's computer, and we have no way of seeing what a participant is doing at his or her end of the line.

The Case Of The Crusading Chat-Room Teacher

In 1987, the DELPHI online service was experiencing a growth spurt, along with online services in general. This brought all sorts of new people online, and they naturally gravitated to the chat rooms (or conference rooms, as they were known on DELPHI).

One person who stood out represented him- or herself (you never know) as a female teacher. She had a habit of cruising conference rooms and "lurking," or listening to conversations without participating. Whenever the talk turned to sex, however, she would admonish the participants for "talking that way" in public.

She quickly became something of a fixture in the conference rooms. If you were in a chat room in the evening, you could count on a visit from "The Teacher." The regulars shrugged and avoided references to sex when she was present. (There was a lot more tolerance in those days.)

The Teacher didn't last long, however. As it turned out, she had a Jekyll and Hyde personality. As the conference rooms thinned out every night around midnight, you would usually find The Teacher in a private conference with another DELPHI member, not one of the regulars. No one had any idea what that was about, but judging from her behavior in public chats, we figured she was probably tutoring someone.

As it turned out, The Teacher wasn't tutoring—at least, not in the conventional sense. Her cover was blown after only a few weeks when she roped Rick, one of the regulars, into a solo chat. The next day, Rick sent several dozen of us an email copy of the last couple minutes of their chat.

That log revealed a private agenda quite at odds with The Teacher's public persona. After an evening of chastising those who were talking about sex in public, she (or he—again you can't tell online) enjoyed slipping away to talk about sex in private—to be specific, to have a "hot chat" (more or less simulating sex by typing actions and reactions back and forth).

We never saw The Teacher again after that. Apparently, someone forwarded a copy of Rick's conference log to her.

The Teacher may even today be cruising the Net. If so, you can count on her (or him) being careful about what she types in a chat room, public or private.

You are probably safe if you conduct yourself in an online-service chat room or an IRC as if every session were being recorded and sent to just about anyone. As with Newsgroup postings, you never know who might end up reading a chat transcript—months, years, or even decades from now.

Even in talking with only one or two "close" online friends, you are at risk. Again, you cannot know if your words are being recorded, nor if the friend doing the recording might turn into a foe down the line. Blurt out too much personal information of the sort you don't want to get around, and it could come back to haunt you later. The online world has a perfect memory—and a long one.

How Much Can System Operators See?

You may think that, if you don't see anyone else online, you are alone. This isn't always true. System operators—and others with the proper privileges—on some ISPs and online services may be watching you. In fact, it is possible to watch and record everything you do. Or, as one of my ISPs' system administrator told me, "We can see literally every keystroke you make."

Of course, no system staff or administrators go to the trouble of watching people without good reason; they have too many other things to do. But it is possible—read Clifford Stoll's The Cuckoo's Egg for revealing examples.

Email And Privacy

The most-often-cited danger of using email is the possibility that someone may intercept your mail along the way. I don't worry about that with my own email. I don't say things in email messages that I wouldn't want anyone else to read. With regard to the actual transmission, all that concerns me is whether my messages arrive. Most of them would be fairly boring to a stranger.

You may have additional concerns, of course. If you work for a government agency or large corporation, you may be sending information in email that you do not want anyone else to read, with good reason. If that is the case, you had better be using public-key encryption or another strong encryption scheme, as described in Chapter 10.

By and large, intercepting email messages on the Internet requires quite a bit of effort and planning. Data—including email—are transmitted on the Internet in packets, which means a typical email message is sent in several pieces. Not every packet is sent over the same route every time, so anyone who wants to intercept your email must have considerable technical expertise and go to a lot of trouble to track the packets, then intercept and reassemble them. These requirements almost preclude it being done, but it is possible.

Email poses two realistic dangers. These have to do not with interception, but with how recipients and senders handle email. The first of these dangers is simply described: A recipient could forward your private email to others (as happened in "The Case Of The Crusading Chat-Room Teacher"). You either have to trust your recipients or refrain from putting information in email that you wouldn't want shared.

The second danger involves you *violating your own privacy* by sending email to people you didn't intend to. I've done this once or twice, usually because I was distracted and typed the email address of someone I was thinking about or to whom I'd just sent mail, instead of the intended addressee.

I once sent by mistake a strong message about a certain sysop to that sysop. This was more than a little embarrassing and had some unpleasant repercussions. That was years ago, but I still remember exactly what happened: I was so steamed at the person about whom I was writing, that her email address popped into my mind when I was addressing the message, and I duly entered it in the To field. I suppose the moral is, don't write or address email when you are upset or distracted.

You need to pay close attention to addresses, too. Remember the example of "ROGER" versus "R0GER" as an email address in Chapter 1? I was tripped up by that sort of problem with on-screen similarities of letters and numerals on a couple of occasions. This happened once when I was telling an old friend about a woman I was dating. My friend Teena's address ended in "T00." I typed the last three letters as "TOO." I was surprised when Teena didn't answer for several days, and even more surprised when I received a letter from a minister suggesting that I might not want the details of my romance to go to a total stranger.

I've also received more than my share of mis-sent email messages. These have included apparent replies to questions about UFOs, communications from members of a secret group on GEnie who were trying to force the management to dump a RoundTable sysop, an RSVP to an invitation to the Governor of Ohio's inauguration, and a couple of love letters.

The Insecure Security Department

At one time or another in the mid-1980s I was on almost every online service in existence. Among the more interesting was AT&T Mail. The most powerful and undermarketed email service in history, AT&T Mail bristled with features of all sorts. Its online mailing lists, user directory, and list-management software were among its stronger features. As it turned out, they also served as a reminder to me and AT&T's security department that the greatest software in the world is useless if nobody uses it.

I had been on the system maybe two months when I started receiving email obviously meant for someone else: a Peter Banks. I would get announcements of departmental meetings and training sessions within AT&T, company newsletters, and lots more. When I checked the AT&T directory, I found more than 30 people named Banks working for AT&T, including the Banks whose mail I was receiving.

In less than a minute of scanning the directory I could see the problem: My ID was "banks," while his was "pbanks." The people who sent the errant mail had probably not bothered to check the directory. He was likely the only person named "Banks" that they knew, and because user IDs on the system are assigned based on last name, they all assumed that his address had to be "banks."

I began forwarding misdirected mail to its rightful recipient, always with a copy and a note to the senders, informing them that they should edit their mailing lists. Most people corrected the error, but some didn't. Worse, more and more people were making the same mistake. Apparently, some of the departments were sharing their mailing lists. Each time a list with my name was copied, the errors multiplied; it was almost as if I were a virus on the system, replicating through shared lists.

This went on for several years, peaking in 1989 when I received a message from AT&T Security. The message was an alert for employees traveling in Europe. It urged them to guard data on their laptop computers in France, because the French Suarte were conducting industrial espionage, and to take special care with email.

I felt like I'd just come to the punch line of a long joke. I informed the security department of the gaff. They studiously ignored the irony of the situation, but did begin taking their own advice regarding email.

This anecdote illustrates a couple of important points. First, it bears out the oft-cited maxim that computers do exactly what you tell them to do. Second, it proves that computers can multiply errors as efficiently as they do anything else.

The message here is simple: Know your recipients. Think before sending potentially sensitive information to a given party. If you have any doubt that certain people can be trusted with the information, don't hand it to them in writing. Also, watch the address field. To minimize addressing errors, use your software's address book. Triple-check each entry. No two addressing shortcuts or nicknames should be similar. If you have two people named Will on your list, use the name "Will" as the nickname for the address-book entry for one, and use the last name of the other Will.

Following those simple cautions will make sure you never put private, personal information into the hands of someone who shouldn't have it. As illustrated in the "Insecure Security Department" sidebar, just a one-letter error can send your mail to the wrong person. Don't make the error.

Your Password: The Key To Everything

I noted earlier that your online user ID is like a combination address, license plate, and name. Continuing the analogy, you can think of your password as the keys to your house and car, along with directions for finding them.

Anyone who has your password can do anything you do online. He or she can become you—and probably do things you wouldn't do. The thief can surf the Web until he or she is bored, then spend time impersonating you. That latter activity has lots of possibilities. For openers, imagine someone in a chat room pretending to be you, and think about the worst the impersonator could do.

Along the way, the thief might change your password, meaning you can no longer log on. For that matter, depending on what the thief does, you may never log on with that account again. (Password thieves often press terms-of-service rules beyond the limit.)

All that is possible if you use an ISP. It can be worse if you use an online service. CompuServe, for example, has certain surcharged areas that carry high per-minute rates. CompuServe, AOL, Prodigy, DELPHI, and other services host vendors who take orders online. An impostor with your password can order all sorts of merchandise in your name and have it shipped to a pickup point rather than to you. It all gets charged to your credit card—online time, orders from online merchants, and whatever else the thief might stumble into to run up charges. The thief doesn't even have to have your credit-card number. (Beware that certain online services display your credit-card information in their "change payment method" utilities.)

If you have a Web site, someone with your password can really do a job on you there, too.

The Case Of The Purloined Web Page

My friend, Chuck, found out the hard way that loaning your password, even to a family member, can be a bad idea.

Chuck and his family, who live in Indianapolis, were visiting relatives in Florida over the Christmas holidays. A brother-in-law asked to use Chuck's ISP account because the brother-in-law's ISP didn't provide USENET access. Chuck agreed, and provided the usual warnings about not doing anything stupid with his account.

Some two weeks after Chuck's return from Florida, I happened to pay a visit to Chuck's Web site. I was more than a little surprised to find a strange punk-rock page, where I was accustomed to seeing pages dedicated to family and personal interests. This was definitely not Chuck!

Had the server somehow gone berserk, or had someone hacked into his account? I told Chuck about it immediately.

It didn't take Chuck long to solve the mystery. Someone had indeed replaced the home page, and a check of the server log revealed an entry from Florida on the day Chuck was traveling home. It all pointed to the brother-in-law with the borrowed password. When confronted, the brother-in-law admitted copying the new Web page from a stranger's site, and replacing Chuck's home page with it. He assumed that Chuck would find it in a day or two. Which of course was not the case; it was more than two weeks before anyone spotted the switch.

Fortunately, there was no real harm done. As Chuck put it, though, it was a good thing that the brother-in-law wasn't more technologically advanced. He might have done some things that were more difficult to undo.

The possibilities are numerous, but I'll leave it at this: Someone with your password can ruin your reputation, get a lot of people angry at you, cost you your online access, and cost you a lot of money.

Obviously, your password is valuable, not to mention a direct path to some of your most important personal information. Someone who knows your password can become you online—and that is not stretching the point.

DOES SOMEONE HAVE YOUR PASSWORD?

Until and unless the thief changes your password or does something particularly noticeable in messaging or chats, you won't know that your password has been compromised. If you use an online service where you can add charges to your card, you may not know you have a problem until the bills come in. You can try the following ways to check whether your password has been stolen:

- If your ISP or online service provides a means of checking your most recent logon and -off times, use it occasionally. You may find that "you" were online when you really weren't.

- Strange email referring to subjects about which you have no knowledge, especially from people you don't know, can be an indication that someone else is using your account (and perhaps emailing or posting messages).

- Trying to log on to some systems (such as AOL) and getting a message that you are already logged on could be a warning flag. (This doesn't always mean someone else is online in your name, however. If you get this sort of message when you try to log on after being knocked offline, it probably means the system hasn't yet realized that you are offline.)

- You may be alerted to a problem when your ISP complains that you are logging on with multiple sessions. (Of course, if you really are doing that, you're going to get complaints; ISPs don't like any one user hogging more system resources than necessary.)

- In Newsgroups or bulletin board areas, if you find messages you didn't post—or replies to messages you didn't post—someone may be using your password.

- If you get a message from your ISP about excessive failures at logon, this may well be an indication that someone is trying to hack their way into your account by guessing your password.

- If you use an online service, you can watch for a banner at logon that tells you the date and time of your last logon. Not all online services offer this, but if yours does, make a habit of watching for the notification. Compare it with your last online session. (This is how I discovered that someone was logging on as me with one of my DELPHI accounts. I changed my password, and that was that. Apparently, someone had guessed my password, and rather quickly. I was using a password that was only four characters long, so I was partly responsible.)

What To Do If Your Password Is Compromised

Ideally, no one will ever get your password, because you will be following the advice in the next section. But if, by some unfortunate circumstance, someone does get your password, here's what you should do:

- If you can, immediately change your password. (Follow the guidelines in the next section.) If you can't log on, call your ISP or online service's customer service number. (Be prepared to identify yourself, usually by providing your mother's maiden name, as you did when you signed up.)

- If you were able to log on and change your password, call your ISP or online service's customer service number, and let them know what's happened. If extra charges have accrued to your account, you may be able to get an adjustment.

- Check message areas you frequent for new messages from your ID that you didn't post, as well as replies to same. If you find several such messages, post a notice that your password was stolen and that you were not responsible for messages posted between a specific date and the present.

- If you are on an online service that stores messages, check the folder or file for any unfamiliar messages you've read and sent. Keep an eye on your incoming email for strange messages, and be prepared to explain that someone else was using your account.

• Change your password again.

Of course, the best approach is to take measures to insure that nobody gets your password.

PROTECTING YOUR PASSWORD

Password protection begins with the password itself. Your password should *not* be something easy for others to guess. If your dog's name is "Woodrow," and you use that for a password, anyone who knows you can probably guess it (as can people who don't know you but have read your posts in the alt.dogs Newsgroup).

The best approach is to come up with a combination of letters and numbers that have no reference to anything in your life (meaning birth dates, names of friends and relatives—anything that someone else might guess). I usually type the first few letters and numerals that come to mind, or that my fingers hit, then generate a few more characters that way, until I have a lengthy password.

Most Internet servers are Unix-based machines, so they are case-sensitive. This means that if your password is "A2MXB49" and you type "a2mxb49", the machine will not recognize it as your password.

Don't store your passwords in a file. Memorize them. If necessary, write new passwords on a slip of paper and keep it in a safe place, away from the computer.

Here are some tips on keeping your password safe:

• If an ISP or online service assigns you a password when you first sign up, change it within a few days. Some systems assign passwords based on a sequence that's easy to follow. For example, if you sign up for a service on November 19, 1997, your password might be 9719NOV. Anyone who is aware of such a pattern and knows when you signed up has your password. Other password-assignment systems aren't quite so obvious at first glance, but you should change the assigned password even if it doesn't seem "guessable."

- Don't keep your password in a file on your computer, and don't tack it up on a piece of paper next to your computer. Unless you are a complete hermit, other people are going to be around your computer. Someone could pick up on your user ID and password, and put them to use.

- If your software lets you store a password so you can log on without using it, don't use that feature. Do not use it even if your password is stored "invisibly," as is the case with AOL software and some CompuServe front ends, as well as the Windows 95 dialer. (Remember the example in Chapter 2 of the woman whose daughter's friend set up his own AOL account courtesy of this feature.)

- Don't give your password to anyone, for any reason.

- If for some reason you must loan your online account to someone at another location, set a limit on the time and find out what time your friend or associate will log off. Wait five or ten minutes from that time, then log on and change the password.

- Change your password periodically.

Credit-Card Numbers

The companies and banks who sent your credit cards to you have already told you most of what you need to know about credit-card security. Most of what they told you applies to using your credit card in the online world as well, but you should know a few more special concerns about using credit cards online.

I must first tell you that I am biased against online credit-card transactions. I don't even like doing credit-card transactions by telephone. This has a bit to do with the fact that I once had a Visa/MasterCard merchant account and, back in the 1970s, did repairs on credit card transaction equipment. These things, and certain experiences, colored my view of electronic transactions. That said, here's my take on the whole business.

Credit-card numbers are more likely to be intercepted than email, because people have lots more motivation. Most—but not all—Web sites that offer credit-card transactions use encryption schemes. These are not impenetrable, however; those sites that do offer encryption are susceptible to hacking (even the CIA has suffered a break-in) or, more likely, breakdown—just about any system is.

But these dangers—interception, hacking, poor design, or physical breakdown—are less likely to cause your credit-card number to be compromised than plain old ineptitude. System administrators who are lax or uninformed have been responsible for several instances in which people browsing commercial Web sites were able to view credit-card numbers and other data left there by previous visitors. In each case, software was improperly configured, leaving a virtual mile-wide gap in security. (For what it's worth, several administrators who have made such mistakes blamed poor or incomprehensible software documentation for the problems. Considering the typical level of documentation, this is believable.)

If you still want to buy online, I offer this advice:

- If possible, consummate your purchase by mail, telephone, or in person. I shop online to find items or compare prices, but buy by mail or in person.

- *Never* enter your credit-card number at a site that isn't secure. Sites that offer secure systems say so, up front. Your Web browser should be able to tell you if you are dealing with a secure server—Netscape and Microsoft's Internet Explorer even let you enable warnings that pop up if you are about to send information to a system that isn't secure. (The security involves encryption schemes that prevent anyone who may be intercepting communications from seeing your information "in clear.")

- Look into the feasibility of using one or another of the "E-cash" online payment systems. These involve placing money on deposit with a real or virtual bank, then presenting a code as payment. The setup is basically a virtual debit card. You can limit your losses to the amount you have on deposit. In contrast, if your credit-card number is stolen, your credit card might be maxed out long before you report the theft. (Here are a couple of starting points for more information on E-cash systems and providers: the Web sites of First Virtual Bank and NetChex at, respectively, **http://www.fv.com/demo/** and **http://www.netchex.com/ index.html**.)

Your Address And Telephone Number

You may have noticed that I haven't warned you against giving out your address and telephone number online. I figure you already know better than to tell strangers how to find you, and everyone you meet online is a stranger until you establish that they are exactly who and what they say they are. Also, keeping your real name off the Net at large precludes the possibility that you will be handing out your address and phone number online.

Your address and telephone number may well be available online, however. Several online resources provide such information. To track down the address and phone of the editor I mentioned in the Introduction, I used a low-cost database on CompuServe called Phone*File. With it, I learned not only the editor's address, but also that he had moved recently—Phone*File tells you how long a person has had their phone number, and his was a fairly recent change. Phone*File also gave me his wife's name.

All of that information cost me 75 cents. Not bad.

The reason I was able to find his address and telephone number online was because they are listed. Phone*File carries few unlisted telephone numbers, though it does have some.

The Internet offers quite a few free sources of address and phone number information, and a lot of the numbers are unlisted. Some of the information available at these resources is provided by those listed, but much of it is from "other sources," which vary, depending on the site you're using. Some buy information from companies whose business is to compile it—publishers of phone books and city directories, marketing companies, and so on.

You can look at a some of these resources by going to the Yahoo People Search page at: **http://www.yahoo.com/Reference/White_Pages/Individuals/**. This is a search engine that can find someone by name, as well as provide links to a number of white pages and similar search engines. If you haven't spent any time with this sort of resource, I think you'll be surprised at what's available.

I'll have more to say about online resources for tracking down addresses (physical and email) and telephone numbers in upcoming chapters. For now, be aware that, if you can be found in such resources, the odds are that you provided the information.

With that in mind, let's move on to Chapter 4, where we take a closer look at the many places online where you can hand out your personal information—often without knowing it.

Chapter 4

Where Do They Get My Information?

Chapter 4

Where Do They Get My Information?

Chapter 4

Information And Privacy

Someone is keeping files on you. The following information has been compiled:

- Your full name, address, telephone number(s), and previous addresses.

- Your birth date.

- Your Social Security and other identifying numbers.

- The name of your employer, and your employment history.

- Your marital status.

- Details of your criminal record (if any).

- Your medical history.

- A history of your credit transactions.

- The names and ages of your children (if any).

- Your credit card, checking, and savings account numbers.

Virtually all of that information (and lots more) has been compiled by these entities, among others:

- Your auto, home, or life insurance company.

- Your employer.

- Your bank and other credit grantors.

- Your doctor or a hospital where you have been treated.

- The bureau of motor vehicles in your home state.

Having read this far, you realize that you knew all this. It's no big deal, unless it's taken out of context. You have every right to believe that the information will be kept confidential by those agencies and companies. Besides, you're compelled to provide it, if you want to avail yourself of even the most basic benefits of our society—employment, a driver's license, and so on.

CONFIDENTIAL, BUT AVAILABLE

Fortunately, personal information *is* kept confidential, thanks in part to privacy laws. But that's not the only reason. Information about individuals is marketable. This means commercial interests that have such information—credit reporting agencies, marketing organizations, health-provider associations, insurance information pools, and similar operations—keep control of the information they amass. In doing so, they protect its value.

What if information such as that listed previously was not confidential? What if your employer had your complete medical history, including the fact that you had undergone psychiatric treatment 10 years ago? What if your auto insurance company learned from your employer that you aren't very conscientious when using a company vehicle? Depending on your occupation and driving record, either of those scenarios could cost you.

Let's open it up even more. Would you want your friends, relatives, neighbors, and employer to know how many times you were late with your house and credit-card payments, that you had been arrested for shoplifting on a dare when you were in college, that you had been a plaintiff in a civil lawsuit, that you had been denied a department store credit card because you were too heavily in debt, or that your car was about to be repossessed? Probably not.

But, again, your personal information is not going to be spread very far. Not in the real world.

WHERE DID THEY GET THAT?

Still, let's consider where such potentially embarrassing or damaging information about you originates. Almost all of it comes from you, right? Just about everything listed at the beginning of this chapter could be included in the information you must supply when you apply for a job, health or auto insurance coverage, and/or credit of any sort.

Very little of your personal information on record wasn't supplied by you. Your military record, medical history, and driving record probably came from others (divulged with your permission). Any legal entanglements—criminal or civil—are matters of public record.

INFORMATION GOES PUBLIC ONLINE

Almost all information about you online comes from you, too. But that's where the similarities between personal information in the real and online worlds ends— at the source.

Information flow online is unlike that in the real world. Virtually all information online is available to anyone. (This can be the source of many problems, as you have learned.) Also, while you must provide information about yourself to various real-world institutions, nothing compels you to provide information about yourself online.

Nonetheless, people often give out personal information online, sometimes without realizing it. Perhaps this is because they are accustomed to handing out personal information in the real world. Or maybe false feelings of anonymity and seeming one-to-one communication lull some people into thinking their information won't be spread across the Net.

Knowing or unknowing, no matter what the reason or motivation, too many people are too free with their personal information online. Hence, this chapter will show you where not to put your information if you don't want it to go public. It's basically a matter of keeping your information under your control, which means not letting it get out.

Before we get into that, though, I have a few words on a special reason you need to keep not only your real-world information private, but also your email address.

Harvesting Names On The Net

The compilation and management of mailing lists was one of the first tasks to be automated with computers. I'm speaking here of *hard-copy* mailing lists, of course—those that are used to print out mailing labels for magazine and catalog mailings, junk mail, and so forth. This was going on in the 1960s, about the time the term *junk mail* was invented. In fact, without the computerization of mailing lists, junk mail as we know it could not exist (for that matter, nor could the databases containing so much information on each of us that I referred to a few paragraphs back).

With the advent of the Internet, junk mail took on new dimensions. As I will explain in detail in Chapter 7, the explosive growth of the Internet in the early 1990s fostered the growth of a group of be entrepreneurs referred to as "spammers." Certain they will make a fortune by pressing a few keys and making the appropriate mouse clicks, spammers daily bombard the email boxes of tens of millions of people with sales pitches.

Junk email doesn't play well on the Internet. As opposed to being an effective sales tool, it usually drives people away from the few legitimate products that are offered. (The overwhelming majority of junk email offerings are get-rich-quick schemes.) Junk emailers enjoy very little success. What they are most adept at is angering recipients, wasting time, and hogging Internet bandwidth. It gets pretty bad some days, when you log on to find 10 new email messages waiting for you, 9 of which are junk email, or "spams." (If you've been online more than a few months, and posted anything in public, I'm not telling you anything new, of course.)

Junk email is the true plague of the Internet. Having your email address showing in the wrong places lands you right on spammers' lists.

The methods by which spammers compile their mailing lists are as intrusive and obnoxious as the spam itself. Programs have been created specifically to "harvest" email addresses from a number of online sources, including: member directories and profiles on all the major online services; USENET Newsgroups; BBSes on CompuServe, AOL, DELPHI, and Prodigy; and chat rooms on online services and the Internet. Some of these programs can also pull email addresses from guest books, BBSes, and mailing lists at Web sites.

The programs (I refuse to name them here) read email addresses in large chunks of downloaded or captured text from any of the above-mentioned sources and put them into a database. The database can then be used with any of several common email programs to send tens of thousands of messages per hour.

Although the majority of spammers seem to concentrate on AOL's several million members, they spam anyone whose email address falls into their greedy hands. Therefore, you may want to avoid letting your email address be seen in any of the public venues discussed here. Some of the advice in this chapter will help you to avoid specific places where spammers look for email addresses. Chapters 6 and 7 show you other ways to avoid spam (including alternate IDs and email filters), and Chapter 7 shows you some ways to deal with spammers.

Starting Points

The most common places you're likely to hand out information are also your first points of contact with the online world. These are your ISP, and online profiles or member directories.

Will My ISP Give Out My Information?

When you signed up for Internet access, you provided your name, address, telephone number(s), and probably a credit-card number. The only information that is routinely passed on are your name and credit card number, which the ISP provides to its bank to process charges against your account.

Other than that, the only time an ISP will give out your personal information is when requested by law enforcement or a court order.

An employee of an ISP or online service who has access to your information could conceivably give it out, but that is only a remote possibility. If found out, the employee would lose his or her job—and possibly end up as the defendant in a criminal or legal action. That's enough to stop most people.

Finger, Ph, Directories, And Profiles

Member directories have traditionally been a place for online-system users to make information about themselves available to other users. This made it easy for friends and others who shared your interests to find you, and added to the sense of community. These directories started as finger and ph listings on Internet servers and evolved into sometimes lengthy and complex mini-databases on online services.

Unfortunately, the online world isn't as friendly a place as it might be, so to be safe, you should keep your information out of these public directories.

Finger

Finger, which I described in Chapter 3, was designed to provide basic information about users. Depending on which version of finger is in use and how it is implemented, however, quite a bit more than a name and telephone number can be included in a finger listing. As you can see in Figure 4.1, a finger directory listing can include a lot of information.

To see this information, go to one of the Web finger interfaces (try **http://www.magibox.net/~unabest/finger/query.cgi**) and enter **nasanews@space.mit.edu**. You can do the same with your finger information, provided you are using a

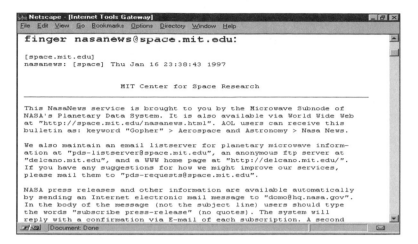

Figure 4.1   A finger directory can provide more than just a user ID.

standard ISP that provides you with a Unix shell account. All you have to do is create a text file called .plan in your directory. Its contents are displayed whenever anyone fingers you.

Given this sort of capability, finger was once popular as a tool for providing textual information—sort of a text-only Web site, which you could access without a browser. The more typical application for finger was to identify users, as was shown in Chapter 3.

Finger information is usually supplied as a part of the sign-up process, without your knowledge. As noted in Chapter 3, you can check to see if finger information about you is included on your server by going to a Web interface to finger and entering your email address. If your real name, along with any other information, is shown, and you do not want it to be, you will have to edit the finger listing.

Ph

Found at many college and university Web sites, *ph* (short for phonebook) serves as a directory of people affiliated with the organization. The listings are similar to finger listings, although a search page is usually provided. If you are affiliated with a server that has a ph directory, you may or may not be able to remove information, depending on the rules of the organization.

The ph system at a given institution may be searchable in any number of ways—by name, department, and so forth—or only by name. (Some universities are replacing ph with a new search engine, called an X.500 Directory Service. The idea is the same, no matter what it is called.)

Finger and ph listings were common back when the Internet wasn't so populated. Today, such information can be a liability if you want to retain privacy. Or, it can serve as an adjunct to or in lieu of a Web page.

Member Directories And Online Profiles

A member directory listing may consist of a one-line entry with your ID, real name, and perhaps the state in which you live, as is the case with the CompuServe directory. Profiles, on the other hand, can get quite involved, as shown by the example in Figure 4.2.

The example here is typical of what new online-service users put together when they discover the profile feature—often minutes after their first log-on. It contains rather more information than you might want some people to know. (I know, putting together a detailed profile is fun, but it's not prudent, particularly for women. Online profiles have, I'm sorry to say, joined a lot of fun things that you ought to be able to do, but can't—like walking around in a big city alone after midnight.)

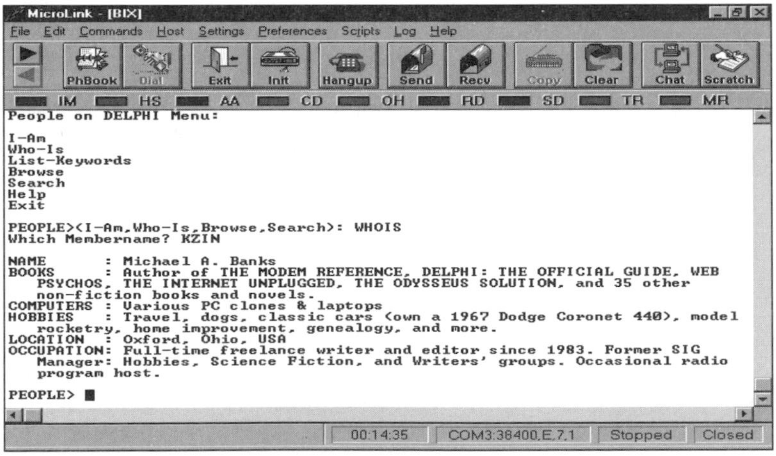

Figure 4.2   An example of an online profile.

Both member directories and profiles are searchable by keyword and user ID. Some, like AOL's, are searchable by content. Access is limited to members of the online service in question, but that's still quite a few people—including, of course, spammers who get temporary accounts on the online services to harvest names for their mailing lists.

Removing a directory listing or profile is fairly simple, once you know where to find it. Every online service lets you edit and/or delete a listing or profile entirely. You should be aware, however, that a service's main directory or profile listing isn't the only place you'll find information about yourself. On DELPHI and CompuServe, for example, each special-interest group or Forum you enter has a place for you to put information about yourself.

Even if you haven't put any personal information in a service's directory or profile area, it may by default contain your name and user ID. So, the best idea is to look yourself up to be sure you aren't on file. If you are, delete the entry.

Also worth noting is that, when you enter some online service groups or Forums for the first time, you are requested to provide your name. Since this information is available to everyone else who enters the area, it's probably a good idea to reveal only your first name, or perhaps use initials or a nickname.

Home Page Entries

Home pages are usually searchable, whether they're hosted by an ISP or an online service. You could argue that to have a home page is to want to be found, but how you are found is a different matter. If you have a business Web site with an identity that's not necessarily linked to your personal identity, you might not want to be found in your private *persona*. Or, as a private user, you may wish your home page to be found by your real name or user ID only.

With ISPs, this may or may not be controllable. Figure 4.3 shows a partial list of home pages on an ISP's server.

The list is searchable, but only by the name of the page, which is set by the user. Thus, if I wanted my home page to be searchable by my name, I would title it "Michael A. Banks," the title being the information this particular server uses to

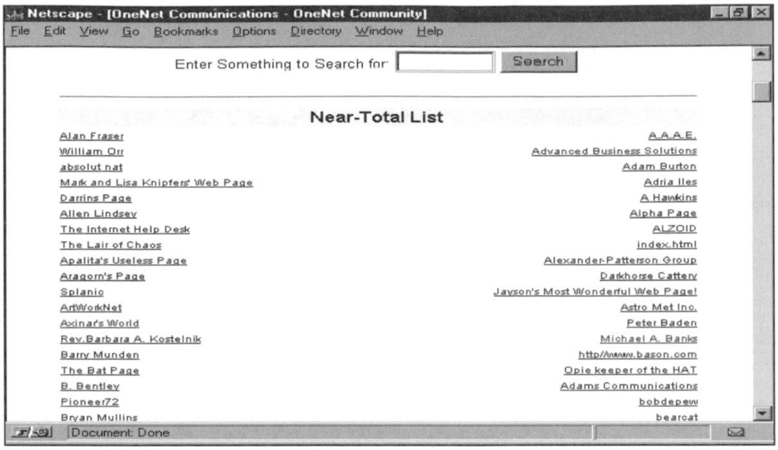

Figure 4.3   A searchable list of home pages.

find home pages. If I had a home page about Dodge cars, I would probably call it "The Dodge Page."

Online services—and some ISPs—set up their Web-page servers with more complex search capabilities. Figure 4.4 shows one example.

With this sort of search capability, others can locate your home pages by your user name, real name, keywords, and, in some instances, anything that's on any of the pages. (That last is rare, though.) If your pages are hosted by a server with such

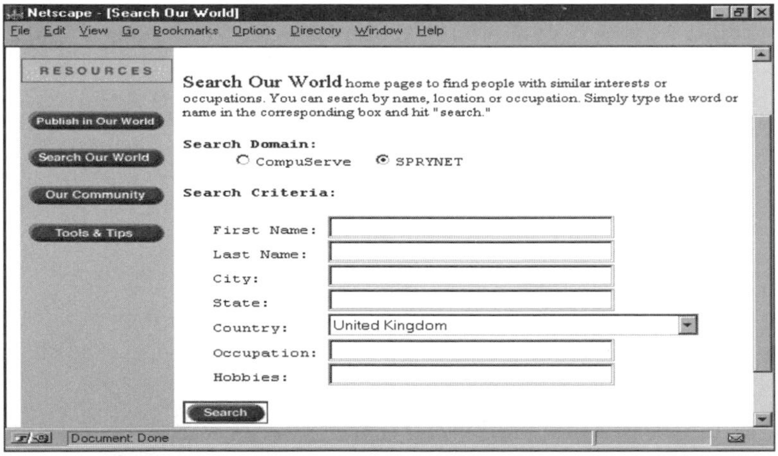

Figure 4.4   A more powerful approach to searching a server's home pages.

broad search capabilities, you may want to design your Web pages so they don't give away everything about you. Better yet, open a separate account—in the name of your business—for hosting your pages.

Putting Finger And Ph To Work For You

Finger, ph, and online-service directories can supply information about others as easily as they can reveal your personal information. For this reason, you should spend some time with them, as you never know when you will need to check up on someone—maybe the person who is sending you bothersome email or someone you met in a chat room.

While you might expect that anyone who seeks to harass, spam, or lie to others online would be sure to keep his or her information out of online directories, this is not always the case. Like most of the online population, some online malefactors just don't know that their information is out there. This is not to say that everything you find in a finger, ph, or member-directory entry is going to be true, but you may find useful information, offering up a real identify or exposing a fraud.

Whether you use an online service or an ISP for Internet access, you should also try out the Web interfaces to finger discussed in this book, and one or two college or university ph systems.

Here are several finger interfaces and ph systems you can practice with:

finger

http://www.magibox.net/~unabest/finger/query.cgi

http://www.cans.com/cgi-bin/cfa-finger

http://www.cs.indiana.edu:800/finger/gateway

ph

http://www.muohio.edu/directory/

http://www.cornell.edu/Direct/search_ph.html

http://msgwwww.ucs.indiana.edu/messaging/projects/addrbook/ph.html

Guest Books, Surveys, And Forms

You will find that many Web pages offer guest books, surveys, or forms. At first glance, these seem to be worthwhile endeavors. But you have to consider two questions: First, who are you providing this information to? Second, can visitors to the Web site see the information you leave?

Guest Books

Guest books are usually innocuous, friendly ways of saying hello to someone running a Web site that you enjoy. You're usually asked to enter your name, comments about the site, and maybe leave your email address and a link to your Web site or favorite site, as shown in Figure 4.5. Since most guest books are visible to anyone who visits a site that has one, putting your address in one is not a good idea.

Guest books are sometimes used to add email addresses to commercial mailing lists, which will result in endless spam. You can usually tell by the nature of the Web site if the person running it is using his or her guest book to build a mailing list. If the site is dedicated to selling you products you can't use (for example, those that will make you a millionaire in seven days), the guest book is probably being used as a device to get you to add your name to a mailing list. (This can be automated; all you see is the guest-book entry, while a program running on the server folds your email address into the list.)

Most guest books aren't run by spammers, but many are used by spammers who simply capture the email addresses of everyone who has "signed" the guest book.

If you leave comments in a guest book, stop with the comment. Or, you might leave your name, but not your email address. Better still, send your comments via email.

Figure 4.5 Web-site guest books can be used to add you to spammers' mailing lists.

SURVEYS AND FORMS

Surveys are usually interesting and often fun to fill out, but they offer the same risks as guest books. You may be providing yourself to a spammer's list, and others may be able to see your name and/or email address.

Legitimate companies use forms at Web sites to sign you up for a mailing (email or postal mail), often to send a free sample product as a "reward" for replying to a survey. Contests at Web sites are likewise handled by forms. These online forms, however, are sometimes poorly implemented and leave the information provided by you visible for the next person who comes along. That information might include not only your name and email address, but also your real address and phone number, and maybe even credit-card information (though it shouldn't). The best course of action before filling out such a form is to make sure it is blank when you first see it, like that shown in Figure 4.6.

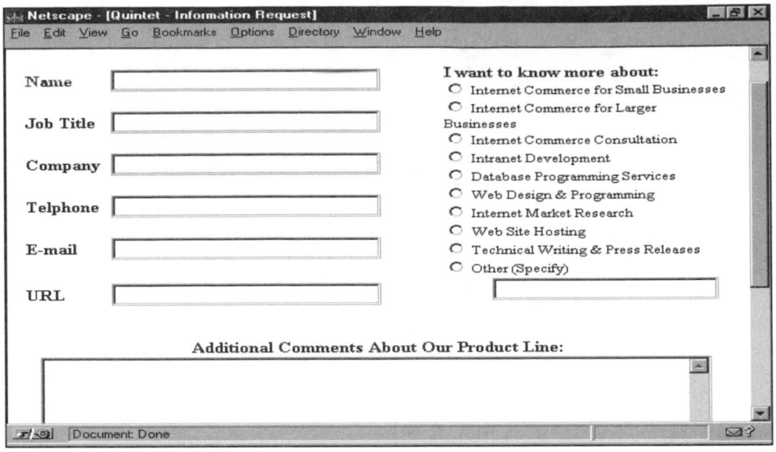

Figure 4.6   An online form, used to gather information.

If the form shows selections or information from the previous person who filled it out, don't use it. Use email to request information, enter a contest, provide feedback, or whatever else you were going to do with the form. This way, you know where your information is going.

Mailing Lists, Listserv, And Listproc

Internet mailing lists are excellent resources. They're an easy way for a large number of people to stay informed about special interests, products, or events. The basic mechanism is a regular message sent to the same group of people.

Some mailing lists, called *listservs,* allow participants to share their views, as well as receive information, creating a sort of interactive newsletter. Any email addressed to the list is forwarded to each member on the list.

You can sign up for any number of listserv mailing lists. The following site provides a sampling of some of these lists: **http://www.ttu.edu/~library/subject/listserv.htm**.

Mailing lists can be vulnerable. The recipients of a mailing show up as a part of the message if the list of recipients is not suppressed. This means everyone on the list will have your address. Listserv contents can be revealed to anyone who knows the proper command. Before you sign up for a mailing list, ask the person managing it whether the recipient list is suppressed. With listservs, ask the manager whether the **REVIEW=OWNER** and **STATS=OWNER** options are set. These options must be set in the manner shown so that unauthorized persons won't be able to see the list; the list manager should know what you mean. Also, ask if you need to do anything to keep your real identity off the list. (Sometimes, you have to ask to keep your address from being shown.)

On systems that use the Listproc mailing list program, you can hide your email address yourself. Send this command to the Listproc address: **SET listname CONCEAL YES.**

You should also keep your real name off of email headers, if you don't want your comments to a listserv to be associated with your real name. (For more information on changing email headers, see the section headed "Email," later in this chapter.)

Classified Ads

Classified ads permeate Web pages throughout the Internet. Placing a classified ad on the Internet seems like a great idea. After all, *millions* of people are on the Internet, which ought to mean millions of potential customers—but it doesn't. Thanks in large part to MLM mavens and other purveyors of bogus business opportunities, classified-ad sites on the Internet are clogged with junk nobody wants. It usually isn't worth wading through the garbage to get at what you might want to read.

As you might expect, then, posting a classified ad on the Web is not a good idea. You're not likely to get responses to your ad, other than endless pandering messages trying to get your attention. So, thousands of classified ad pages languish all over the Web. Some are paid ad sites, some are free. Almost all are useless, except to those spammers who harvest email addresses for their lists from such sites. Classified ad areas on online services are similarly public—and hit just as often by spammers pumping up their lists.

If you post a classified ad, consider using an account reserved for that purpose. Odds are you will get many more spams than legitimate responses to your ad.

Posting In Public

The major public venues for posting messages online are USENET Newsgroups, messaging systems on online services, and Web sites that offer bulletin boards. These are often prime targets for spammers, who use their automated "harvesting" programs to add the email address of each and every person who posts a message. You can protect against having your name added to spammers' lists just because you posted a public message—and to keep your email address out of the messages for other reasons. I'll touch on some here. Chapters 6, and 7 will offer more details.

A couple more reasons you should be careful about what you post: First, anyone who wants to do so can compile quite a profile or history of someone who posts a lot of material online. Remember the example, in Chapter 3, of the San Diego man who was emailed a detailed history of his life, based on USENET postings? Just a little information here and there adds up to quite a mountain of information.

Second, public postings can come back to haunt you months and, sometimes, years later. A comment made in haste or anger can be embarrassing, or worse, later. What if, for example, you were applying for a top job with a major corporation and learned that the human resources people routinely did Web searches for references to and by applicants? Would your month-long diatribe on the evils of capitalism and free-market economies be an embarrassment? Could it affect your chances of getting the job? It's something to think about.

USENET Newsgroups

USENET is the oldest component of the Internet, originating in 1979. More than 20,000 Newsgroups are out there, and spammers cruise each and every one of them—including the main anti-spammer Newsgroup, **news.admin.net-abuse**. Spammers post junk email in the Newsgroups and grab the addresses of everyone who posts there.

You can take several approaches to avoid spammers and other problems having to do with USENET. The most popular is to use a bogus name in the "From" header. This thwarts the email harvesting programs, because they recognize only the xxxx@yyyyyy.com address format. Of course, this runs the risk of someone accusing you of spoofing or hiding your identity for other reasons. You can get around this problem by including your real email address in a different format at the end of a message. Rather than "xxxx@yyyyyy.com", use this: "xxx at yyyyyy dot com." Spammers on the whole are a lazy lot (after all, they're here to get rich quick by pressing only a few keys), so they won't bother to enter your address manually. Others who want to email you still can. This does not make you completely anonymous, by the way; the headers that remain can still pinpoint the source of your message.

See Chapter 7 for details on how to set up your browser or email program to include a fake name in the message headers.

Alternatively, you can create a special account for posting in USENET, but never retrieve the email to that account. This is the only option available to users of some online services, since these services do not allow you to change the header information on your posted messages.

Unread email over a certain number of days old is deleted automatically on online services. ISPs sometimes handle email differently; check with your ISP to see whether this will be a problem. The ISP may be able to set up an account in such a way that all email to that account is rejected or deleted. Either way, you can always log on once a week or so to delete the dozens of spam messages waiting for you.

If you are more interested in maintaining your privacy, and not leaving any way for someone to identify you, you might look into an *anonymous remailer* service. As will be discussed in Chapter 10, anonymous remailers receive email or Newsgroup postings from your normal address, remove all the headers, and forward messages to their intended destinations. The only identifying headers belong to the remailer, and your "address," such as it is, is coded. Incoming email works the same way: The remailer receives email addressed to your confidential address and forwards it to you. This system is particularly useful for those who will be discussing confidential subjects in public or who for any other legitimate reason do not want to be identified. (Anonymous remailers do not provide service to spammers or anyone who wants to send harassing, threatening, or illegal email.)

Beyond all that, keep this in mind: Search engines can find almost anything that has been posted in USENET Newsgroups. Take a look at the Deja News search engine at **http://www.dejanews.com/forms/dnq.html**, and you'll see what I mean.

Keeping Your Name Out Of USENET Archives

As noted elsewhere in this book, but worth repeating, Deja News offers the ability to exclude your postings from its archives—which one day will include literally everything from 1979 on. You must add this line to your headers: "x-no-archive: yes". Alternatively, you can place "x-no-archive: yes" as the first line in a posting. (Omit the quotes in each case.)

Even without Deja News archiving your posted messages, they can still be found days, months, or even years later by other search engines that turn up USENET postings. Alta Vista (at **http://www.altavista.digital.com/**), for example, allows you the option of searching either Web pages or USENET postings. In addition, continuing archives of specific Newsgroups are available via FTP from UUNet and other sources.

The bottom line: If you say it in a Newsgroup, it won't go away. So, don't make any comments that you wouldn't want to return to haunt you years from now. Don't post with identifying headers if you don't want to get on spammers' lists or receive email about your postings.

Another possibility is that anything you post that's sufficiently entertaining could end up being compiled with similar postings. Several Web sites are devoted to just that. Among the more interesting is "The Lamer Page" (mentioned in Chapter 2), at these addresses: **http://hnet.hutton.com/~mredrain/metoo.html** and **http://hnet.hutton.com/~mredrain/aolmr.html**.

These pages will entertain and educate you as to certain unwritten USENET rules (in this case, not to waste space by posting useless material). They should also remind you that the strangest things can happen to your words on the Internet.

PUBLIC MESSAGING ON ONLINE SERVICES

A large part of the culture of online services is derived from message bases of various types. AOL has scores of bulletin boards in Forums and elsewhere. The same is true of CompuServe. DELPHI, using a slightly different nomenclature, provides sophisticated BBSes, called Forums, with its special-interest groups and clubs. On Prodigy, the message bases are BBSes linked to various topics.

All of these messaging systems have this in common: They can be accessed by only those who are members of the service in question. But, you never know who is lurking in a message area, scanning what you have to say. Also, the content of many boards is archived and made available for years in databases. Since what you have to say can add to someone's knowledge about you, you might want to refrain from posting, or create a second account to use only for posting.

Note that on online services, email harassment from fellow members isn't tolerated. If someone doesn't like what you have to say in a posting and wants to bother you about it in email, you can put a stop to that immediately. Just mail a complaint to the service's customer service department, along with a copy of any offending messages. The harasser will stop, or lose his or her account. (This doesn't stop someone with accounts elsewhere from bothering you, but complaints to postmasters at other online services or ISPs work almost as well.)

The only other danger to posting in online-service message areas is the fact that spammers harvest email addresses from these areas almost as frequently as from USENET Newsgroups. The harvesting programs mentioned earlier are designed to work specifically with AOL, CompuServe, DELPHI, and Prodigy message bases.

A final note: Messages can stay around for a year or more in some areas—on AOL boards in particular.

BULLETIN BOARDS AT WEB SITES

Web-site bulletin boards can be fun. They usually serve an audience whose numbers are too small, or whose interests are too narrow, to support a Newsgroup. Some are dedicated to the products and services of the company hosting their Web site. Others serve towns, regions, or special interests, as is the case with the *New York Times* Cybertimes Forum, shown in Figure 4.7.

Note that this BBS uses a confidential emailing system. Your ID is displayed without the domain name, as with "demontel" at the lower left of the screen. People who click on it can send email to you without seeing your email address. When such a mailing system is used, you don't have to worry about your address being revealed.

You can determine whether email addresses are included with postings at Web-site BBSes. You can reveal email addresses by clicking on a name or by moving your cursor over the name. Your browser's status line will display the link in the latter case. If it shows **mailto:user@xxxxx.com**, IDs are revealed. If you see something like **http://bin/WebX?135@^177509@1512@.ee6b4b9**, the server is using an anonymous mail-forwarding system.

Obviously, you don't want to leave your email address at sites where it will be visible to anyone. Remember, you often don't have to leave your email address at all.

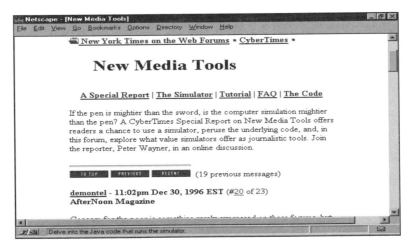

Figure 4.7   Online bulletin board entry.

Chat Rooms And IRC

Chat rooms on online services are strange places. IRC (Internet Relay Chat) sites on the Web are equally strange. You often encounter people whom you definitely would not like to have your email ID or know anything else about you. Among the mildest of the strange ones are spammers, who troll chat and IRC rooms for names to add to their lists.

I'll have more to say about the strangeness of realtime chats in the next couple of chapters. For now, you need to be aware that chat rooms on most online services provide little anonymity. Your real email address (your online service ID) is right out there for everyone to see on most systems. (One exception is CompuServe's CB Simulator, where you can adopt a "handle" that is separate from your ID.)

If you want to be anonymous in online service chat rooms, either create a separate ID for chatting, or use CompuServe. Note that if you use an alternate ID for chatting, people in chat rooms will still be able to email you, but you can always ignore the mail.

Being anonymous in IRC sites is a bit easier, although the system always knows your real ID. The Anonymizer (see Chapter 10) can help here, as can altering some elements of your browser's setup (also discussed in Chapter 10).

Email

Can you compromise yourself in email? Yes, in a couple of ways.

First, if you send a lot of email to people you do not know, you might want to leave your real name out of the headers. On online services where it is possible (AOL, CompuServe, and DELPHI), you usually have to search out a Preferences, Mail Settings, or similar area, where you can specify the personal name to be included in with your email. This is in effect with mail on the service itself, as well as email to Internet addresses.

If you use Pegasus, BeyondMail, Eudora, or the email system included with Netscape or Microsoft's Internet Explorer, go into the options or setup area and delete the personal name. This way, you are in control of who knows your full name.

The second way you can be compromised by your own email is similar to something that can happen with USENET postings. If you tend to fly off the handle and fire off outrageous comments to people you don't know, you may one day find one or two of your messages posted for the enjoyment of others. A few people cultivate the hobby of sharing the more outrageously entertaining email they receive, usually at a Web site. One such site is at: **http://phobos.illtel.denver.co.us/ pub/lamers/**. (Fortunately, the guy responsible for this page doesn't reveal the email addresses of his correspondents.)

Another way you can end up being one of the featured attractions at somebody's Web site is to spam. Where you spam doesn't matter; email and USENET spammers are hated equally by the majority of folks on the Net. So, if you're a budding entrepreneur who is tempted to seek early retirement by spamming, you had better think twice. For examples of what can happen to you if you spam, take a look at these pages:

http://www.ca-probate.com/aol_junk.htm

http://com.primenet.com/spamking/slatinfo.html

The first offers a list of notable spammers, with email addresses. The second focuses on one person—in rather intimate detail.

Now that you have a better awareness of where and how you give away personal information, it's time to get interactive. On to Chapter 5, and a look at just how strange some people can get online.

Chapter 5

Dealing With People Online

Chapter 5

Dealing With People OnLine

Chapter 5

In this chapter, we'll take a look at preventing trouble in some of the more popular online venues—and some ways to deal with problems in these areas.

Online Interactions: Where And Why?

People are everywhere on the Internet, but you don't have to interact with them if you don't want to. Some folks deal with the Internet on a one-way basis. They are content to read others' messages and conversation threads, rather than post messages in public.

You may be of a similar inclination—in which case you won't need some of the information in this book, nor most of what I have to say in this chapter. But if you are among the majority, you participate in online interaction in one or more venues.

Those venues include email, public postings, and chat rooms or IRCs. Each one has important considerations and rules, mostly dictated by online etiquette (also known as *netiquette*).

ONLINE ETIQUETTE

In overview, etiquette online is pretty much the same as etiquette in the real world. You treat people as you like to be treated, and you follow certain rules. Actually, the rules are based mostly on common sense, although you should make yourself familiar with some of the more important written and unwritten rules of online conduct.

Online etiquette is simple enough, but some people can't seem to grasp the concept. Others ignore it, and they are best ignored in turn, because you can't change them. It's usually fruitless—and frustrating—to try. Most people who need education in netiquette probably don't want to be educated, or can't be.

As noted, most online venues have special rules. We'll look at these now.

PUBLIC POSTINGS: "THERE'S NOTHING YOU CAN SAY THAT WON'T OFFEND SOMEBODY."

Public postings include BBSes on online services and at Web sites, and USENET Newsgroups. What you do in these areas is seen by more people than anywhere else, and it is in these areas—Newsgroups in particular—that etiquette should be most strictly observed. Not observing etiquette in a Newsgroup will result in almost instant criticism and reprimand, usually by more than one participant. (It's ironic that, in a self-purported bastion of free speech, you risk having what you say tromped on and censored, but there it is.)

While "criticism" and "reprimand" may seem mild threats, they are anything but. When you break the rules of etiquette in a Newsgroup, in front of thousands of participants, you can quickly become the object of public ridicule—and worse—by dozens or even hundreds of others. (And let us not forget that this sort of thing stays "on file" pretty much forever, thanks to such services as Deja News.) If you really annoy people, you might become the victim of a lot of hate mail, really fast—perhaps enough to fill your email box and stop other mail from being delivered.

Public online attacks are known as *flames*. Flames and flaming are a time-honored USENET tradition. They are a means of chastising errant newcomers and conducting extended arguments, also called *flame wars*. Flames are most often characterized by strong and emotional—and sometimes irrational—comments and responses.

Some Newsgroups have moderators. Annoying behavior in a moderated Newsgroup can result in your postings being canceled or deleted. (A moderator, who has complete control over a Newsgroup's content, usually has two goals: Keeping the conversations on the Newsgroup's topic and weeding out repeatedly annoying participants whose postings tend to disrupt the conversation threads.) If you persistently and knowingly violate a moderated Newsgroup's rules, your actions could result in all postings from anyone using your ISP being blocked (also known as a *USENET Death Sentence*, or UDS). This, of course, would result in you losing your account.

Learning The Ropes

So, what are the rules? You can get a feel for them if you "lurk" (read messages without posting) in a Newsgroup for a few weeks. Watch how the regulars communicate—and observe what sorts of behavior by newcomers results in an outcry from the old hands.

Many Newsgroups post FAQs (Frequently Asked Questions) that list the rules followed by participants. (I sometimes refer to these as the "rules of engagement," since so many Newsgroup—and BBS—conversation threads seem to involve battles of words at some point or other.)

A Newsgroup's FAQ often contains other useful information in addition to the rules. These may include, but are not limited to, explanations of acronyms or jargon used, and the history of the Newsgroup.

To find a Newsgroup's FAQ, look for postings with "FAQ" in the header or post a polite note asking the location of the FAQ. Another source of information about Newsgroups is, appropriately enough, a Newsgroup: **news.announce.newusers.**

In addition, you'll find a good number of general FAQs about Newsgroups scattered around the Net. Just about the best one going is Vince Zema's Netiquette Primer, located at **http://www.primenet.com/~vez/neti.html.** This brief document is a light, entertaining, and literate look at the peculiarities of online behavior and rules of same in public venues.

Zema points out an important truth about posting in Newsgroups—a truth that characterizes more Newsgroups than not: "There is nothing you can say that won't offend somebody."

That's almost literally true. Post a note that says it's a beautiful sunny day, as an example provided by Zema goes, and someone might call you a name and ask you what you have against Seattle.

As this example implies, some people are just looking for a reason to flame others online. Given that, and the fact that public venues online are so crowded, following the rules of online etiquette for public posting is critical.

For those who can't wait to check out the FAQs, here are some basic guidelines for posting in public:

- Do not use ALL CAPITAL LETTERS in your postings; it looks like you're shouting.

- In replies, always quote—or paraphrase—one or two relevant lines of the message to which you are replying. This gives people who may have missed the original message an idea of what you're talking about.

- Do not quote a message in its entirety; nobody wants to have to wade through endless repeats of the same message just to read the replies. Do this often, and people will start to ignore your postings—or maybe tell you in great detail exactly what you are doing wrong, in public.

- Don't say anything in a posting that you wouldn't say to the recipient in person.

- If provoked by a comment or a flame, ignore it. If you can't ignore it, give it a day and see whether you still feel like replying in kind.

- Even if you have a lot of knowledge on a given topic, don't try to come off as a know-it-all. On the Internet, attitudes often obscure meaning.

- Stay on-topic—that is, don't post irrelevant messages. Newsgroup topics are inviolate to most of their participants, who often react violently to attempts to discuss anything outside of a Newsgroup's professed subject area.

- Don't post commercial messages, except in the alt.business Newsgroups. (We'll examine this further in Chapter 7.)

- Remember that your posting will be seen by at least hundreds of people, and perhaps millions—and that, once written, it will not go away.

- Pay attention to how others communicate, and follow the general style.

If you follow these rules, avoiding trouble is easy. Again, search out the specific FAQ for any Newsgroup in which you intend to participate, and be sure to check out Zema's Netiquette Primer. The rules therein apply equally to BBSes and USENET Newsgroups.

Finally, remember that most Newsgroups and online BBSes have a group of regular participants who consider the area to be their online "home." These users are usually a tight little social group (clique, if you will). As is true for members of any social group, they probably view outsiders with suspicion and have little tolerance for someone violating their traditions and customs. You will probably have to wait a while (and wait for the advent of quite a few other newcomers) before you are considered one of the gang.

These group dynamics are often missed or ignored by newcomers, simply because they fail to recognize that groups of people online are exactly like groups in the real world. They exhibit the same behavior patterns and abide by rules—most unwritten and many unique to the group. Thus, if you treat a Newsgroup or BBS as an extended version of a real-world group or club, you won't be disappointed, and you will probably avoid flames.

Saying What You Mean: Enhancing The Written Word With Symbols

If you think about it, the written word might seem superior to the spoken word as a form of communication. After all, you have time to think over and change what you are saying, to ensure precision in meaning.

This is not really true, though. Half of the meaning is missing in written communication—there are no verbal cues to define nuances of meaning, such as sarcasm, humor, and all the rest of the additional meaning given to words by rising notes, changes in tone, and so forth.

Couple this with the fact that, in online communication, we're trying to adapt bare words to something that really requires the immediacy of voice communication. Online communication does indeed require the immediacy of voice communication—in chat rooms, postings, or email, we strive for the same sort of exchange as face-to-face communications.

I first saw evidence of the need for additional meaning in online communications in 1983 while watching a friend participate in an online conversation in a Q-Link chat room. (Q-Link, an online service for Commodore computer users, was the predecessor to America Online.) My friend was muttering as he typed, saying each word out loud as he typed it. I thought this was odd, but I later caught myself doing the same thing, and have since observed dozens of other people doing likewise.

I think this is a subconscious attempt to impart some additional meaning to the silent written word—or, at least to send it off with that meaning hanging in the air. Of course, the inflections of speech don't follow the words.

Fortunately, there are means of adding to words in order to clarify your meaning. Call it enriched communications, if you like. Adjuncts to written communications include a few typing effects, such as ALL CAPS to emphasize one or two words. The most common adjuncts are a few standard symbols consisting of keyboard characters arranged to look like a face, sideways. For example, look at this symbol:

:-)

If you lean your head 90 degrees to the left, you will see a rough approximation of two eyes (the colon), a nose (dash), and a smiling mouth (the close parenthesis). This usually signifies that the statement preceding it was humorous or ironic. Modified with a semicolon to:

;-)

it can be used to mean a smile and a wink.

These symbols are called smileys. More direct symbols, such as <smile>, <grin>, or just <g>, are also used, as are abbreviations. Examples of commonly used abbreviations are BTW (by the way), IMHO (in my humble opinion), and BRB (be right back).

These are used everywhere online: in public postings, realtime chatting, and email. Some people get a little carried away with online symbols and abbreviations, and you will discover literally hundreds of them, intended to represent every possible feeling, emotion, and nuance. But don't despair; you don't have to memorize scores of symbols and abbreviations. The few shown in Table 5.1 are among the most frequently used. You can usually pick up others in context.

You will find a large number of smileys defined at this URL: http:// cuisun9.unige.ch/eao/www/Internet/smileys.html. For additional definitions of abbreviations used online, check out the Free On-Line Computing Dictionary at http://wombat.doc.ic.ac.uk/ ?Free+On-line+Dictionary.

Table 5.1 Common symbols used in online communication.

Frequently used smileys and abbreviations:

:) or :-)	Smile
;-)	Smile with a wink
8-)	Smile with glasses
:D	Laughter
<g>	Grin
:-(	Frown or "sad"
:-O	"Oh, no!"
BRB	"Be right back."
FYI	"For your information…"
IMHO	"In my humble opinion…"
LMAO	"Laughing my ___ off."
ROTF	"Rolling on the floor…" (with laughter)
TIA	"Thanks in advance."
TTFN	"Ta ta for now." (note or message closing)

EMAIL

Email rules are pretty simple and mostly common sense. As with public postings, you want to be sure your meaning is clear. It's usually a good idea not to offend or insult anyone in email—at least no more than you would in a hardcopy letter.

Remember that email letters can be shown around, even posted publicly. Email you have sent is out of your control. The fact that any email message can be easily copied or forwarded means that you should exercise great care with what you say in an email message. As with Newsgroup or BBS postings, an email message might come back to haunt you years after you send it. (Email messages can also be forged—a subject we'll discuss later in the book.)

When replying to a message, copy a line from that message, or somehow refer to it in your reply. To do otherwise is rude. Folks who get a lot of email may well not be able to remember what you are replying to, especially if your reply is brief.

Finally, pay attention to whom you've addressed your email. One character different or missing in an address can send a message to someone you didn't intend to contact.

Chat Rooms And IRC

Realtime conversation is an addictive pastime for millions of people. The rules for participation haven't changed much since I first dropped into a realtime conference sometime in 1980. They basically boil down to not making a nuisance of yourself.

You will find FAQs or other guidelines for specific IRC systems at their respective sites. Guidelines for realtime conference areas on AOL, CompuServe, and other online services are available in the conference areas on those services.

You can also find IRC info at these URLs: **http://www.thenet.co.uk/~bvr/ index2.html**, **http://www.compusmart.ab.ca/aboutsmartnet/faqirc.htm** and **http:/ /lucy.swin.edu.au/csit/opax/userguide/irc.html**.

For now, here are some realtime conference guidelines:

- When you first enter a chat room, acknowledge greetings, but don't blurt out "What's happening?" or jump into the conversation until you get some idea of what people are talking about.

- Don't type in ALL CAPS. This is particularly distracting and disruptive in a chat.

- Don't use beeps. Some people who discover how to do this can't seem to leave it alone; if you make a practice of it, you may find yourself ejected and banned from a chat room.

- Don't try to get attention by pressing Enter repeatedly. Sometimes referred to as *flooding* (or *punting* or *scrolling*), this completely disrupts a conversation by making current conference lines scroll up and away.

- Don't flood the channel you're using with text or the same message (especially not advertising) over and over.

- Don't bug another user with repeated private messages (also known as /*whispers*).

- As with Newsgroups, stick with the topic at hand, if there is one.

Now that you have some idea of the sort of behavior that's expected in public online, let's look at how to deal with behavior that steps outside the invisible boundaries of online netiquette, common ethics, or the law.

Trouble In USENET Newsgroups And Online Service BBSes

As I noted earlier, whatever you post in a USENET Newsgroup is likely to be seen by hundreds, if not thousands of people. Given that the online world is populated by more than its share of somewhat twisted people, you can easily draw the ire or wrath of someone. This can take the form of flames in the Newsgroup or email harassment. If the person you've "offended" is one of a clique of participants in that Newsgroup, you may well find yourself hounded in public and private by more than one person.

A lot of USENET participants are simply hot-headed. They may act quite a bit differently when they are online (thanks to the phenomenon of anonymity). More than a few people come into Newsgroups looking for a fight. (If you doubt that, spend a couple of hours perusing just about any Newsgroup; you'll see exactly what I mean.) These people, often referred to as *trolls*, may post intentionally provocative messages or—more frequently—look for someone they can provoke with a reply to a message.

Some users have been driven away from Newsgroups entirely by flames. The emotional energy required to deal with repeated flaming is more than some people care to invest. Others waste a lot of time in extended arguments and flame wars, which, with the wrong person, might escalate beyond a Newsgroup. You might be "mailbombed," or even tracked down and harassed by phone or at home or work. All of these things have happened. (Mailbombing is a harassment technique that involves sending hundreds or even thousands of copies of the same message to one person. The intent is to fill up the recipient's emailbox and block legitimate messages.)

Think Before You Post

Given that most of the time you can avoid flames by thinking before you post, doing exactly that would seem to be the way to go. But you can't outguess every nutcase online. Trolls don't care whether you've really offended them, anyway; they flame over nothing, and some are quite good at manipulating people to get the sorts of reactions they want.

Here, again, if you ignore and don't respond to baiting, you shouldn't have a problem. If you respond, you might find yourself pulled into a flame war. Or, if you resist the flames after one response, the troll might decide to press again for still more responses. This can include email contact and abuse, in several forms, or real-world contact. It can and does happen that a real psycho might escalate immediately to email or other harassment.

Fighting Flames

If you are being flamed (or harassed, or however you might interpret it) in a USENET Newsgroup, you can do very little about it. As I stated a few chapters back, there are no "Internet Police," and much of the Internet is an anarchy. You do not want to fight fire with fire—that is, flame the flamers back. This almost invariably leads to escalation. Except in certain circumstances, your only choice is to ignore the heat.

Moderators And Managers: An Online Court Of Appeal?

If you are being harassed in a moderated group, you can appeal to the moderator, who has some power over Newsgroup participants. The same is true if the problem is taking place in a message area on an online service. A quick email note to the person responsible for the special-interest group (SIG), Forum, or other area where the problem is taking place usually puts an end to it.

Trolling For Dollars

Trolls who frequent USENET Newsgroups and online-service message boards are motivated by one of three things: They seek entertainment; they need somewhere they can take out their frustrations and feel in control; or a few are purely psychotic and are fulfilling some strange need by hassling others. Among all of these troll categories are those who realize some profit by manipulating others. Specifically, they seek to provoke someone into what might be called "actionable action."

An example of this was a person who was quite active on the major online services in the late 1980s. This person (who shall remain nameless and genderless) became quite adept at starting arguments over what he or she claimed was an area in which he or she enjoyed some expertise. As soon as a staffer of the online service in question could be drawn into such an argument, this person complained to the management and demanded unlimited free time for a given period in compensation for so-called damages involving defamation of character or similar claims. The management of the online services involved gave in to this rather than risk bad publicity.

This person also lobbied to have the service throw off some users who were critical of what he or she was doing. Nobody is sure if that tactic was successful. Either way, this person went to quite a bit of trouble to get free time—even back in the days when it really cost to be online.

Today, there is ample evidence that people are displaying the same type of behavior in USENET Newsgroups and, to a lesser extent, in online service message areas. Spend a little time in a few Newsgroups, and you'll see both actionable postings and threats of legal action over specific postings. Most such threats aren't followed up by action, to my knowledge, but a few have been.

The point? Get into a flame war, and you might find yourself on the wrong end of a civil lawsuit—or a tool in same.

Getting Personal: Email Harassment

When harassment moves to email, you have additional avenues open for dealing with the problem. First, ask the person to stop emailing you, and keep a copy of the message. (The best way is to cc: the message to yourself; date and time stamps from your system's email program will provide some authenticity.)

If harassment persists, contact the sysop or administrator of the system where the email originates. Forward a copy of any harassing messages you've received to the system administrator, along with a note requesting that the messages stop. (Be polite; odds are, this is the first the administrator has heard about the problem.)

Finding Out Who's Who Where

If you're at a loss as to where to direct a complaint to an online service or ISP about one of its users, use whois (as described in Chapter 3) to look up the ISP, and send your complaint to the person named as "Administrative Contact" in the ISP's listing. The system name to use with whois is the portion following the @ sign in the harasser's address (for example, the ISP for harassment@systhem.net would be systhem.net).

Or, you can send your complaint to the system's *postmaster*. Postmaster is a staff position and an address for nearly every ISP; the address format is postmaster@systhem.net.

If you feel that the harassment or threat you are receiving is serious enough, you might want to gather information on the person sending you the bothersome email. Begin with finger (detailed in Chapters 3 and 4) and continue on to some of the email-address and people finders discussed in Chapter 7.

THREATS AND LAW ENFORCEMENT

What, you may wonder, if harassment escalates to threats? Does that give you any additional recourse? The reaction of law enforcement to complaints of online threats or harassment used to be iffy. No more—public awareness of the Internet has increased a thousandfold over what it was even two years ago. With that has come recognition that online crimes can be as serious as those committed in the real world (and, indeed, can be followed by real-world crimes).

Although threats are most likely to be delivered via email, threats through any medium are taken seriously by most law-enforcement agencies. How they are dealt with varies from one department to another. According to Jack Banks—a long-time Internet user, lieutenant with the Boone County, Kentucky, Police Department, and police science instructor—complaints about online threats are indeed investigated. "Depending on which state you're in—and the results of an investigation—criminal harassment, terrorism, or similar charges might be filed," he says. The Portland, Oregon, Police Bureau routinely turns cases involving online threats over to the FBI, reports Jim Bellah, a detective sergeant in Portland. "The Feds have the best resources," he says. "If it's interstate, [the FBI has] the best laws to deal with it." Local departments then follow up.

If the harassment moves into the real world, the rules don't change, although the investigation will likely be faster.

The Usual Gang Of Idiots: Chat Rooms

Chat rooms are strange places. Anyone who has ever gone into one knows that. But what makes them strange? Realtime communication inspires really weird behavior in some people. The feeling of anonymity contributes to that, as does the sense of immediacy in realtime communications.

The problems that you run into in realtime chats echo in general the sorts of problems you find throughout the Internet. Some people claim to be a different age, gender, occupation, weight, or something else they're not.

I first participated in a realtime chat in 1980. It was interesting, fascinating, and addictive. Since then, I've burned up a few thousand hours in just about every online chatting venue in existence—and I was burned out on it years ago. (I should note that a good many of those hours were spent moderating weekly conferences in one or another of the online-service special-interest groups for which I was responsible.)

I've made two observations from my experiences in realtime chats:

• Realtime conversation is addictive. Some people participate just for the sake of doing it. This is probably why you see such insipid conversation in many chat rooms. ("What's new?"..."Same old same old. What's new with you?"..."Same old same old.")

• Many people are inspired to strange, and sometimes abusive, behavior in chat rooms. Why, I'm not sure. The easiest answer is that chat rooms attract strange people, and realtime communication seems to inspire weird behavior in some.

In overview, chat rooms are probably more of a game than a communications medium or a novelty to a lot of participants. (I'm excluding realtime role-playing gamers, of course.) In fact, I'm certain that more than a few people regard other people online as not-quite-real, and thus treat them as they might characters in a computer game. That may seem to be stretching things a bit, but it's not—not when you consider that when you're in chat rooms, you're dealing with the same sort of interface used in many text adventure games.

DON.MAC And Other Realtime Simulacrums

Back in 1988, I was finishing up the second edition of a book titled The Modem Reference. *This book was pretty much the only comprehensive guide to the online world back then—consisting of a half-dozen consumer online services and a host of specialized database and email services.*

With this edition, I had to include a disk full of programs and utilities to use with online services. Among the disk's contents were several scripts for use with PROCOMM PLUS and other popular PC communications programs. The scripts were designed to handle signing on, sending and receiving email, and other chores on CompuServe, DELPHI, and Genie. (AOL was excluded, because it used a specialized front end.)

In need of a few files to fill the disk, I came up with the idea of a fun script for use in chat rooms on CompuServe and DELPHI—a simulacrum of a human reading lines in a chat room and typing responses. The script logged on to a service, entered a chat room, and "conversed" with the people present. I dubbed the script "DON.MAC" after a more elaborate simulacrum that was the antagonist in Vernor Vinge's tale, "True Names" (see Chapter 3).

Though effective, the DON.MAC script was somewhat limited. After entering a chat room and adopting the nickname, "DON.MAC," the script greeted everyone with a cheery "Hello!" After that, it watched for phrases that almost invariably appear in questions within a few minutes of a new person entering a chat room—such questions as "Where are you located?" "How are you doing?" "What's happening?" and a few more similarly common queries. I included three or four responses for each question, to avoid repetition.

When a specific phrase appeared, DON.MAC sent one of the canned replies. An abbreviated version of a conference with DON.MAC might go like this:

```
DON.MAC> Hello, everyone!
KZIN> Hi, Don!
MODEMHEAD> Evening, donmac.
BARUKE> HI DON.
KZIN> Where are you from, Don?
DON.MAC> Cincinnati. And you?
MODEMHEAD> What's happening in Cincinnati?
DON.MAC> Oh, not much. You know—same old, same old.
KZIN> How about the Reds? Think they'll win the division?
DON.MAC> I don't follow sports much, sorry.
```

And so it would go. (I've omitted the typos in responses, intended to make DON.MAC more realistic.) After responding to four or five questions (the number was variable), DON.MAC would suddenly remember that he had to walk the dog or take out the trash. He would say so, bid everyone farewell, and make his departure.

Had I put some more time and effort into the DON.MAC script, he might have been quite a conversationalist. But he did a fine job of fooling people as he was. He often received email inviting him back to a chat, and sometimes when he entered a chat room he was warmly greeted by acquaintances who had "met" him in another chat room a few days earlier.

I retired DON.MAC after a couple of weeks. He was getting a little boring; everyone responded to him the same way—that is, when people "talked" with him, it was always the same idle chit-chat. I figured that one of his online "friends" would eventually catch on. While his comments were enough to fool people for a time, the sameness of his conversation was a bit robotic, to say the least.

*I'm not the only person to have thought of this. DON.MAC has several cousins who not only frequent online service chat rooms, but also surf the Web in search of interesting IRC sites. He wasn't difficult to put together. Given the proper knowledge, anyone can create a DON.MAC with a much wider range of conversation topics and the ability not only to answer questions, but to ask them, too. (For more information on IRC robots—also known as "chatterbots," as well as links to downloadable robots, visit "The BotSpot" at: **http://www.botspot.com/faqs/**.)*

It's something to consider when you enter a chat room. (But, remember: I retired my DON.MAC; if you run into him out there, it's not me.)

CHAT ROOM RULES AND REGULATIONS

The rules for participating in IRCs and online-service chat rooms, as I've already shown, can be boiled down to: Don't "shout" with all caps, don't make everyone's screen scroll by "flooding" it with text or empty lines, don't try to change the subject if the chat room has one, and don't use rude or crude language if others find it objectionable.

If everyone kept those guidelines in mind, about half the problems in chat rooms would be taken care of. Add to that "Don't waste time in chat rooms with sales pitches," and sum it up as "Don't be rude," and you have a complete guide to getting along in chat rooms.

With the exception of new users, idiots, clowns, and boneheads, most folks do follow the rules.

Some chats have additional special rules. A few—mainly those on online services—are monitored by online service staff or volunteers, who are usually able to put a stop to errant behavior. (If you don't like that sort of monitoring, remember that you have a choice; you can go elsewhere.)

Moderated Conferences And Chats

You'll find a special sort of realtime conference on online services and at a few IRC sites: those featuring a guest, who may be a celebrity, a politician, or other notable person. Because these conferences tend to be crowded, special software is used to control the group.

Basically, no one but the guest and the moderator can "talk" to the group as a whole unless the moderator permits it. Questions and comments are usually directed to the moderator, who previews them and releases them to the group at large if the guest wishes to respond. Any other comments from the audience are seen only by the rest of the audience (not by the moderator or guest). Knowing this in advance is helpful. Otherwise, you can make a complete fool of yourself if you join a chat with a guest without knowing the rules.

Read The Rules

Read all of the rules yourself before you enter a chat room. This way, you'll not only be able to distinguish between acceptable and unacceptable conference behavior, but you will also avoid breaking the rules yourself.

Moderators And Ops

Rules are enforced by chat-room moderators or, as they're more commonly known in Web IRC chat rooms, *ops* (*op* is short for *sysop*, in turn short for *system operator*). On some online services and at IRC sites, the ops have godlike control over a chat room and its participants. An op can throw a user out of a chat room, and/or ban the user from entering the room again.

Sometimes an op is present during a chat, and sometimes not. If the op isn't present, users can usually send a one-line message to alert him or her to a problem. (How that's done varies, depending on the service or IRC you're using.) If the op is present, the problem usually gets taken care of immediately.

How Does This Thing Work?

Your best course of action is to learn all of the commands for a realtime conferencing system *before* you ever enter a chat room. At least read the command list, and keep a copy handy in a window you can switch to when need be. Most conferencing systems have a large number of commands—some rarely used, and some vital.

On almost all systems, commands—such as those that change your nickname, send a one-liner to another user, or exit the system—are preceded by a slash (/) or dash (-). The commands, and how you enter them, will vary from system to system, but you can learn this from the system documentation.

Knowing a conferencing system's commands, or having them on hand, means you won't end up bugging people with questions about how to do this or that. (Most of the time, the people you ask will refer you to the command list, anyway.) It also means you'll be fully conversant with a system's capabilities—what is possible and what is not.

Taking Command Of The Situation: Protecting Yourself

If you find yourself in a chat room with a really obnoxious person or persons, you have several options. The obvious one is to leave. That tends to encourage miscreants, though, and it's inconvenient. The better option is always to report the problem to an online service staffer or IRC op, as the case may be, via a one-line send or email.

When there's no one to whom you can appeal immediately, you may have recourse through the system itself. Most conferencing systems provide a means of blocking lines sent by a given user—for example, **/block <username>** or **/ignore <username>**. (Personally, I find the command to block lines from a given user in DELPHI's conference rooms highly appropriate: **/gag <username>**.) Some versions of this command block only private one-line sends, while others block anything, public or private, coming from the person you're blocking.

If that invaluable command is unavailable, or impractical, you might consider going to another chat area with the few people you really want to talk with. Advise the others to meet elsewhere, using private online one-liners.

No matter what action you take to rid yourself of or escape an obnoxious or harassing chat-room participant, be sure to report that person to the online service management or, if you're at an IRC site, let the ops know.

If, for some reason, you can't rid yourself of a realtime jerk, you may have to abandon his or her haunts entirely—until, that is, you are able to track down the miscreant's identity and, if it is relevant to the situation, complain to a higher power. If you can't track down the identity and where the user is coming from, and/or the powers-that-be can't or won't do anything, you're out of luck. Without a way to trace the offender, realtime harassment is like having insults yelled at you from a passing car with no license plates; you have no recourse.

Who's Who?

You will need to know how to find out who someone is in a chat room, in case the system reveals only conference nicknames. Here again, you must rely on your knowledge of system commands to help you.

Depending on the conferencing system, you have two possible ways of finding out who someone really is. Some systems—particularly online-service conference systems—have a command that shows the real user IDs of everyone in a chat room. Other systems provide a command that you can use with a nickname to get the real user ID. Once you have the ID, you can get additional information using the techniques discussed in Chapters 3 and 7.

Sometimes, a hacker can hide his or her real ID. In rare instances, someone else in a chat room that's plagued by a jerk will know the jerk's real ID or other information about him or her. If you're otherwise frustrated, ask around after the problem user leaves, or get the email addresses of everyone else in the conference and ask if anyone knows anything about the problem person.

Dealing With Fools, Charlatans, And Idiots In Realtime

If you're creative, and clever enough to win a battle of words, you can try to overcome or even drive off the nuisance. Sometimes, people in chat rooms simply band together and ignore the problem. This often frustrates troublemakers, whose motivation, after all, is usually a response to their actions. If you ignore them, they give up, because they might as well be in a chat room alone.

In battling online harassers, you can use whatever tactics come to mind. An online acquaintance of mine who uses an ID that clearly identifies her as a woman often gets lewd one-line private messages. She finds that sending back a one-liner saying "Leave me alone! I'm a teacher" almost always ends the problem. She is a teacher, by the way, and speculates that most of the would-be sexual harassers are young teenage boys who don't like the idea of sending sexual remarks to a teacher. Of course, you have to have patience—and perhaps feel a little like playing games back at the game-players—to want to bother with this sort of thing.

Online Romance

Online romance enjoys more media coverage than anything else having to do with the Internet, or even computers—except, perhaps, computer crime. It's a guaranteed hot topic on a slow news day, and it has its own sort of charm.

But, as many others have wondered, is there anything to it, or is it just an over-reported novelty? I'm the last person to discredit the idea of meeting someone special online. I found my fiancée online, but that was a happy accident—we sort of bumped into one another when neither of us was looking. Similar online romances have happened to a few of my acquaintances, as well.

Before I met my fiancée, I dated a few women I met online. In contrast to other women I met in more conventional ways, most of those I met online had some sort of problem that made it difficult for them to meet men in the real world. (Problems or not, they all shared with me some interesting facts, which I'll impart in a few paragraphs.) The same was true of many men I knew who were trying to meet someone online—although with men it seemed to be a problem of expectations entirely different from the reality. (I'll explain that in a few paragraphs, as well.)

WHY LOOK ONLINE FOR A DATE?

As you probably figured out by now, I'm skeptical of online romance, despite my own happy ending. I really don't find the online world to be a special or magical venue where one is guaranteed to find a soulmate—at least, finding the man or woman of your dreams online is no more likely than it is offline. The idea of meeting a mate online is popular for the same reasons that telephone datelines are popular. Here's why:

- It's convenient; you don't have to leave home, get dressed up, or spend money. If you don't get a date, you're not out anything.

- You don't have to compete directly with anyone else; everyone is pretty much on the same footing.

- You can completely disguise your negative characteristics.

- It's a novelty. The Internet is new and not well understood, and, therefore, it just *might* be able to get you want you want.

None of those is really a good reason to rely on the Internet for a date. Consider: You have to go out to meet your dream date sometime, and you're going to compete against the last few people that person has dated—in his or her mind, anyway. Once you do meet in person, any discernible negatives will be out in the open. Finally, with regard to the Internet's novelty: 900-number chat lines were new and exciting once, too, but you won't find a lot of people who've had good experiences with dates they've found through that resource. (They probably remember their telephone bills more than any dates.)

Cautionary Tales

I know several women and men who have followed online romances to disasters of one sort or another. They offer anecdotal evidence of some of the typical perils of online love.

One young woman, who was in bad financial straits and had some other problems in her life, found escape in the people she met online. Eventually, she was inspired to travel more than 1,000 miles to meet a fellow she had become acquainted with online. The trip nearly exhausted her funds, and her car barely made it there and back. In the end, she was rejected by the man, who didn't like her physical appearance. This story, I am sure, has been repeated hundreds of times over the years. It's sad, but it says a lot about online expectations—and perhaps something about not disclosing everything about oneself to an online acquaintance.

Megan (not her real name), an English teacher, has a recurring problem with online dates. She's divorced, in her early 40s, attractive, talented in several fields, intelligent, rather charming, and financially stable. She lives in a small town, and having exhausted the supply of local eligible men, started dating a few men she met online. Without exception, each man turned out to be married. Unfortunately, her relationship with one was pretty far along before he revealed that he was married. I suspect the driving force here is the fact that they lived far from her and thus figured they could carry off a masquerade and hide their marital status as long as they liked.

A friend of mine (we'll call her Elinore) worked as a customer service manager for a major international online service in the mid-1980s. In those pre-Internet days, online communication with someone in another country was a real novelty. Through her job, Elinore met and fell in love with a man in another country. They carried on an online relationship for most of a year, and married shortly after meeting for the first time. He moved to the U.S. and, within months, became abusive. Elinore quickly divorced him, but not without suffering some material, as well as emotional, loss. This is an unhappy commentary on the peril of relying on email and realtime chats to get to know someone. As Elinore put it, "You really need to get to know someone in person before you make that kind of commitment."

Another acquaintance, Mick, has sworn off online dating completely because he was "shot down" two times in a row. The first time he went out with a woman he met online, she disappeared while they were in a movie theater. She later emailed him that she had had a panic attack, and didn't feel comfortable with another man so soon after her divorce. The second date ended before it started when the woman told him that he reminded her too much of a man with whom she'd had a bad relationship. She claimed he had the same looks, mannerisms, and personality as the fellow she'd just broke off with. He likes to think it wasn't him; whether it was or not, he says he has never had this sort of experience dating women he met or was introduced to in the real world.

Online romances aren't really new. Couples have been meeting and mating since consumer online services first came into existence. The first online wedding was either in 1980 or 1981, depending on whom you ask. The first book about online love (liberally sprinkled with online sex) appeared in 1985. Thus, meeting people online is not really new—but more people are trying it out. Quite a few folks, of course, are turning a profit on it, with online dating services.

Scores of magazine articles, TV reports, master's-degree theses, and books have been written about online romance. More than being a well-reported phenomenon, online romance is a phenomenon created by reporting—which is to say it's just too charming (or potentially profitable) not to exist, so it has been reported into existence.

You may well wonder why I am so skeptical of online romance. It's certainly not out of having endless bad experiences with women online. It's just that the reports of failed online romance far outnumber the successes. Many of those failures are sad, indeed. Online romance, more often than not, tends to be hollow, and it has a dark side for many.

Self-Delusions

The online world is filled with self-delusions. People sometimes think in terms of the online world as a virtual reality, as the repository of all the information in the world (if only they could find the password), or as a panacea for all of their problems. Many also think of the online world as having the solution to their romantic or sexual needs.

By thinking that way, you can all too easily project perfection on someone you've met online. But then the first face-to-face meeting occurs, and the Mr. or Ms. Perfection is anything but what he or she seemed to be online. Even though you may feel that you've gotten to know "the real person" or "the person inside" through hours of typing email and realtime messages, nothing matches meeting in-person and spending some time together to give you a feel for what someone is like. In more cases than not, one or both parties meeting in person are more than a little disappointed with the other.

I've heard about this happening so frequently that I feel confident in saying it's almost guaranteed to happen better than half the time. It's largely because of the expectations you build up when you're dealing with a potential romantic partner in an online venue. After all, if you are really seeking something as serious as a romantic relationship in the online world, you already have some notions to project. And it's very, very easy to make someone you meet online fit those notions—in your mind.

"No! Really, I'm 28, Thin, A Doctor, Rich, Have A Ferrari, And..."

Even worse, though, are the intentional lies some people use to dazzle potential dates. While I've never heard of anyone saying everything in the heading above, I've watched a lot of lies go by online, all in the name of "romance." The most common, from men, seems to be, "I'm not married." Men also seem to exaggerate many other aspects of their lives, including but not limited to financial status, age, appearance, education, and so on.

I suspect this tendency to stretch the truth—or lie outright—is, as is the case with certain other behavior online, the result of the feeling of anonymity and the certainty that you can be who and whatever you want. This tendency is not restricted to men, but they seem to be more blatant about it than women. The only truth-stretching I saw from women I met online had to do with weight and other personal-appearance issues.

Undoubtedly, most lies of the type mentioned here have something to do with the individual's dissatisfaction with personal appearance or circumstances. If not that, then a lack of confidence may drive someone to lie a bit, just to be sure to impress someone else.

The Biggest Lie In Online Dating

I've asked a number of women about their experiences with online dating, and found that they had one shared experience: An overwhelming majority of men they met online lied about their weight. This concern with weight has always been stereotyped as a trait of single women. Now the truth is out: Men probably lie about their weight as much as women.

Some people who are apparently seeking online romance are really after something else. Some are seeking sexual partners. If they have to fake a romantic interest, that's fine with them. As might be expected—or perhaps not—more men seek out this sort of thing, often with public postings, than women.

(To be fair to both sexes, there are women who seek the same thing. I had dinner with a woman I met online whose intent was the find the occasional sexual partner. Or, so she told me during dinner. She was a professional in her late 40s, single for 20 years, and otherwise unattached. For the curious: I didn't meet her criteria, as I was recovering from an automobile accident and was rather "wrecked," so to speak.)

Some people scam lonely hearts online for money (building a relationship, then claiming to need money for airfare to visit, or other reasons). There is also at least one documented instance of an online romance resulting in a murder, apparently planned.

Listen!

My friend Pat has dated several men she met online, and is good friends with several more. She notes that it is a good idea to suggest chatting over the phone with anyone who seems interested (and interesting), rather than meeting in person right away. This is a valuable tool in evaluating a potential date.

TAKE CARE WITH YOUR HEART

Proceed with caution in an online romance. Keep in mind that you usually do not know anything about someone online other than what he or she tells you. (Indeed, as some have learned to their chagrin, you can't even be certain about gender.)

This points to an important bit of advice: Don't believe everything you're told. Also, watch your own feelings, to be certain that you aren't doing a little wish-fulfillment by imagining your online partner to be more than he or she is. If everything checks out, you still need to take time to get to know the person offline before you make any important decisions.

Finally, don't pass out your phone number and address indiscriminately. If you think people are hard to get rid of online, imagine how they would be if they knew how to find you.

Summing Up: Prevention And Protection In Public

The best protection against online trouble is, of course, prevention. If you can avoid getting embroiled in public disputes online, and don't believe everything you're told, you're unlikely to have any problems.

Spending some time keeping the facts of your life private, as described in Chapters 3 and 4, is also a helpful preventive measure. If someone wants to harass or threaten you, they won't know how to get at you. This isn't limited to finding out your address, telephone number, and employer. The plain facts of your life can be used against you, as exemplified by the experience of the man in Chapter 3, who found the intimate details of his life compiled and emailed to him.

Before you dismiss the possibility of someone finding out very much about you, finish reading this book, then think about how much someone can learn about you in the real world, given a few important facts of the type that might be available online.

All of which is all the more reason to watch what you post and say online, and to keep your personal information offline and private.

Now, on to Chapter 6 for a look at some mechanized online threats: computer viruses and information-grabbing Web pages.

Chapter 6

Web-Page Treachery And Download Dangers

Chapter 6

Computer Viruses

Applet Viruses: A Potential Plague?

Will Your Web Browser Violate Your Privacy? (Yes!)

Protecting Your Information From Prying Web Sites

Web-Site Interrogations: Forms, Questionnaires, And Surveys

A View From The Other Side (Collecting Information Form Web-Site Visitors)

Can Your Web Pages Be Turned Against You?

Information Online—Good Or Bad?

Web-Page
Treachery
And
Download
Dangers

Chapter 6

This chapter focuses on several sorts of problems you can run into browsing or interacting with the Web itself.

Computer viruses are of particular interest here. As you'll learn, you don't necessarily have to do anything to get attacked by a virus. I'll show you how to avoid and deal with viruses. We'll also look at how some Web pages take information from your system without your knowing it, and what you can do to stop this. Finally, we give you a bit of advice about information on the Web—specifically, how a good deal of the information on the Web can be useless, misleading, or worse.

Computer Viruses

In the most basic sense, computer viruses are programs that take action—normally destructive action—

that you do not expect them to take. They may display political or insulting messages on your screen, delete files on the current disk, or wipe out your computer's operating system. Some virus programs operate on a time-delay basis, so that you'll use them and pass them on before they do any damage. Many are insidious, slowly altering selected files until one day—boom!—your system doesn't work. The variations are endless, but the end result is the same: disruption or destruction of your computer operations.

Most virus programs are disguised as Public Domain or shareware software, but a few have been passed around disguised as or embedded in legal and illegal copies of commercial software.

In the late 1980s, viruses became more widespread, passed along by personal computer users who enjoyed sharing software—by disk or modem—with other computer users. A sort of "living" virus made several appearances during this time as well, invading specialized public and corporate computer networks and disrupting email and other operations. (This was the famous IBM network virus, which was capable of replicating itself and moving through networks, almost as if it was a living, self-directed thing.)

As computer viruses started making the evening news in the late 1980s, even more of them popped up. At least one virus was publicly announced in advance by its perpetrator, who promised it would do nothing more than display a message about world peace on a certain date. A couple of particularly insidious viruses were disguised as virus-protection programs.

People create computer viruses for a number of reasons. Among them: revenge against a particular system or group of computer users, the desire for a noteworthy accomplishment (albeit in anonymous fashion), practical jokes, and experimentation ("to see if it can be done").

Actually, computer viruses are fairly infrequent nowadays, considering the number of potential exposures through downloads and disk-sharing. In nearly two decades of downloading thousands of files and getting freely distributed software on disk, I have experienced two virus attacks. One, built into a supposedly legitimate shareware database program, simply delivered a message, "Gotcha!" at periodic intervals. I got rid of that one by deleting the program. Another virus program was much worse; it concentrated on altering file sizes—specifically, the invisible system files on my hard drive—with the aim of filling up the drive. I had to reformat the drive to kill that one.

Rare though viruses may be, however, that hardly matters if *you* get one.

What Kinds Of Viruses Are Out There?

Viruses come in many different varieties. Some are activated only on certain dates (such as the infamous Columbus Day Virus). Others run only when you run a particular program or when certain system functions are invoked by any program. Still other viruses go into effect when you boot your system.

The actions viruses take varies widely. Some go happily to work, deleting all the files in a directory or on a hard drive—or corrupting or deleting system files—as soon as you run a program to which they are attached. Others create progressively larger junk files on your hard drive in an attempt to fill it up. Some subtly change a number of program or system files on your hard drive, perhaps replicating or copying themselves within each of those programs, until a certain goal has been achieved—at which point none of your programs works.

Self-replicating files are particularly nasty, as they can be lurking, dormant, in any of dozens or hundreds of files on your system, even after you get rid of one or two instances of them. Also, to assure they are spread, they may remain inactive until enough files on your hard drive are infected so as not only to insure that your system is trashed, but also to give you a chance to share one or more of the files they've infected.

Even the relatively "harmless" viruses are annoying. Imagine being greeted by a derisive or political message every time you start your computer. Worse, imagine seeing the same message after x number of keystrokes while you're using your word processor. Or, what if your system stopped every few minutes and required you to correctly guess a number between one and ten before you could continue working?

You get the idea, I'm sure. Viruses may be rare, but getting hit by one can ruin your day.

How Can A Virus Get Into My System?

A virus usually enters a system disguised as a program. For example, you may download a file called FUNVIRUS.EXE and run it. Then, while you're trying to figure out how to play the game, the program might be deleting all files in the current directory—or all directories—or attaching a virus to your boot file. (*Trojan horse* is another, older name for this sort of virus; it's quite appropriate, since many viruses sneak into computer systems disguised as "normal" programs.)

Downloads are the point of entry for most viruses, partly because so many files on individual PCs nowadays come in as downloads. The main reason, though, is because a virus-carrying file proliferates faster online than anywhere else. The quickest way to reach the most people is to circulate a file online—it can travel farther and faster online than by any other medium.

Viruses that spread online also have the best chance for longevity. It takes a long time from the initial discovery of a virus in a download before every last copy of it is stamped out. A good many people downloading it aren't plugged into online information sources, and some of them upload it elsewhere—with every new upload multiplying the potential number of computers exposed to the virus.

In contrast, viruses that spread on disk proliferate rather slowly. Computer owners don't share programs on disk the way they once did—now that everything you could want is right there online for the taking. In the rare instances that a virus sneaks onto a commercially produced disk or CD-ROM, every last copy of it can be quickly destroyed because software publishers keep close track of where their products go.

Virus Protection And Prevention

You should, of course, take care to check every program you get from *any* source before you use it. This goes double for anything you download—even ZIP files.

You can take certain precautions to reduce or eliminate risk, which I'll get to in a few paragraphs. First, let's take a quick look at the first line of defense against viruses: anti-virus software.

Anti-Virus Programs

A number of virus-protection programs are available. Some are commercial, and some are shareware or PD software. Here's a rundown of some of their functions:

- Searching suspected virus programs for embedded messages of the type frequently displayed by virus programs.

- Searching suspected virus programs for functions and operations that might damage your system or data (such as delete or disk-format commands).

- Blocking a suspected virus program from issuing potentially damaging commands of the types mentioned previously.

- Removing virus programs from your system.

- Repairing files damaged by a virus. (These include legitimate programs, which sometimes act as "hosts" for viruses, as well as data files.)

Among the worthwhile examples of virus-protection programs are Symantec's Norton Anti-Virus (NAV) for Windows and McAfee Associates' Webscan.

Norton Anti-Virus offers several levels of protection: You can do a manual check whenever you wish; the program can scan your system regularly, at preset times; or you can choose the Auto-Protect mode, which puts Norton Anti-Virus in memory, where it watches for viruses—even checking ZIP files as you open them. If it spots a virus, the program's pop-up window provides a warning and lets you decide whether it should delete, repair, or ignore the file containing the virus. Symantec offers automatic updates to the program at its Web site (**http://www.symantec.com/**).

McAfee's WebScan is designed to catch viruses in Web browser downloads and email attachments, providing constant, transparent virus detection. It can be integrated with all the major Web browsers. Among its options are the ability to scan some mail attachments for viruses before you open them and to scan downloads (including ZIP, ARC, and ARJ files, as well as self-extracting archives).

Another McAfee product, VirusScan, operates similarly to NAV, searching out and removing viruses. Updates are provided at the McAfee Web site (**http://www.mcafee.com**).

Yet another McAfee product, RomShield, deals with viruses that have infected a hard disk's boot sector (which normally locks you out of starting your system at all). A similar product, BootShield, eliminates and protects against boot-sector viruses.

Self-Protection Against Viruses

Prevention is always the best cure. You can do a lot to prevent a computer virus program from getting at your data or system.

Before proceeding, I should note that your computer cannot get a virus or be invaded just from the act of calling an online service or an ISP. Virus and Trojan horse programs that have been downloaded aren't dangerous unless you actually *run* them. (There is the possibility of a remote system sending commands to your system through certain kinds of communications software, but online services and ISPs aren't set up to damage your system.)

That said, here are some important virus-prevention tips:

- Be careful about what you download. If you have questions about a program in a download database, ask a sysop if he or she has used the program and found it safe. Ask other users about the program via a posting in a message base. (In general, if a program has a lot of downloads—download counts for programs in databases are visible on some systems—and you've seen no complaints about it in message bases, you are probably safe in downloading the program.)

- Copy all downloaded programs to floppy disks. If they are archived, unpack them onto a floppy disk. Before running a new program, carefully examine the files that come with it, and check any READ.ME or similar text files—the authors of PD and shareware programs often include a description, with file sizes, of the files accompanying the program. If you see any files that aren't included in the description, don't use the program.

- Even if a program is not suspect, scan it using one of the virus-prevention programs. If possible, run it from a floppy disk the first time.

- If you suspect a program may carry a virus, don't use it, check it with one or more virus-protection programs, and/or run it on a computer system that doesn't contain much valuable data (ideally, this would be a system without a hard disk).

- If you are suspicious of a program, but still want to run it, make sure you've made backup copies of all data and program files on your system's hard disk.

- If you suspect you have a program that is running on a time-delay basis, or gradually damaging your system, check the time and date stamps and the file sizes of your computer's operating-system files (both hidden and visible). Compare these with the original operating-system files. A frequent gimmick of viruses is to alter system files; changes in time/date stamps or file size indicate that this kind of virus is at work.

- When you buy a commercial program, make sure the factory seal hasn't been broken—neither on the external package nor the internal package containing the disk or CD-ROM.

You will also do well to visit the McAfee and Symantec Web sites frequently; each offers archives of information about computer viruses, as well as updates on the latest viruses threatening Internet users, online and off.

Other important resources for virus and anti-virus information can be found in these Newsgroups: **comp.virus** and **comp.lang.java.security**.

Don't Panic: Virus Hoaxes

Every year seems to bring at least one major virus hoax. Recent examples have included the Good Times virus (in late 1994); several viruses that were supposed to go into effect on a certain holiday and destroy all data files on PCs; some that were supposed to spread as attachments to email messages and destroy files if they were opened (not possible); and, in 1996 and 1997, viruses that were "hidden" in word-processor macros.

While none of those viruses proved to be real, they ate up a lot of time and bandwidth on the Internet. They had individuals wasting time looking for protection from or cures for problems that didn't exist. In the end, the rumors and hoaxes were often as effective as real viruses would have been in wasting time.

Whether each of the viruses was an intentional hoax, or just a kind of "urban myth," is impossible to say. Certainly, people perpetrate virus hoaxes for various reasons, and misinformed folks sometimes unintentionally start rumors.

While I don't advise taking the subject of viruses lightly, you might check around as to the authenticity of a virus scare before you take any action or waste a lot of time trying to find out what action to take. The sources mentioned earlier—McAfee, Symantec, and the USENET Newsgroups associated with virus issues—will usually have the latest information on any virus or virus rumor or hoax.

Applet Viruses: A Potential Plague?

The wildly growing popularity of Java applets and ActiveX controls has created a number of security issues. Perhaps the most-publicized case was in early 1997 when the members of a German hacker group announced a means of exploiting a weakness in Microsoft's ActiveX that would enable them to devise a way to hack into certain types of money transfers. That security hole has been filled, but there are and will be others.

Even ActiveX's one real security feature is rather useless, as most Microsoft Internet Explorer users don't know to use it. It uses digital signatures to verify that the person who created a given script or control is the same person sending it to you, but that can be worked around.

Digital signatures do not prevent someone from creating a destructive ActiveX control that might delete or corrupt important files. Java has a similar destructive potential, although it boasts a stronger approach to security.

All of this points to the fact that security holes are not the only potential dangers offered by ActiveX and Java. Both ActiveX and Java can transfer programs to your system, and what they do there is wide open, creating an inherent ability to host viruses. Symantec and other companies are developing or have recently introduced virus scanners that offer realtime detection and protection capability for such viruses.

Thus, sites that download ActiveX Controls or Java applets to you bear watching—as does the entire field of Internet applications. If you feel the least bit uncomfortable with a site or its applets, don't accept the downloads.

Microsoft Internet Explorer (MSIE) users: Early in 1997, Microsoft introduced a program to provide additional authentication security and other types of security to MSIE. To learn more about these efforts, visit this URL: **http://www.microsoft.com/security/**.

Netscape users: To stay abreast of information on hostile Java applets and protection against them, visit **http://www.netscapeworld.com/** *frequently.*

When "Free" Isn't Free: True Web-Page Treachery

In late 1996 and early 1997, quite a few people in search of cheap thrills in the form of "free" online pornography found that it was anything but free. Web sites advertised as offering "free" explicit pornographic images were liberally hyped in USENET Newsgroups and email by spammers. Thousands of excited Internet users headed for the "free" Web sites in question and downloaded the "free" special software required to view the images.

A few weeks after downloading their supposedly free software, they were shocked to find charges for hundreds of dollars for long-distance telephone calls to The Republic of Moldova near Romania.

As it turned out, the special software required to view the images had a few tricks up its sleeve. After it was installed and activated, it turned off users' modem speakers and surreptitiously dialed an international long-distance call, routed to Moldava. A server there apparently provided users with all the pornographic images they wanted—at $2 to $3 per minute.

Worse, some users continued paying the exorbitant rates after they left the porno site and surfed to other pages. In each case, the scammers—three people running two "companies" in the New York City vicinity—received approximately half the proceeds of the calls. In the end, they had taken Internet users for more than a quarter-million dollars.

The Federal Trade Commission shut down the operation in February 1997, apparently tipped off by AT&T, which noticed that an unusually large number of its subscribers were racking up large phone bills calling the same number in Moldova.

Unfortunately for the porn-seekers, they will have to pay their telephone bills to AT&T, despite the FTC's revelation that it was all a scam. They may eventually get all or part of their money back, as the U.S. Justice Department froze the assets of the companies involved.

The lessons here are both direct and subtle. Don't use a program if you don't understand completely what it does, and most things touted as "free" are anything but.

Will Your Web Browser Violate Your Privacy? (Yes!)

Maybe you've visited a Web site and seen a line like this (with your user ID and location, of course) after a brief pause:

```
Welcome bitsko, from Evansville, Indiana!
```

You were probably more than a little surprised; I know I was the first time it happened to me. The incident made me wonder: Just how much information about me does my browser give up?

Quite a bit. If you visit **http://www.anonymizer.com/cgi-bin/snoop.pl**, you will see information similar to that shown in Figure 6.1.

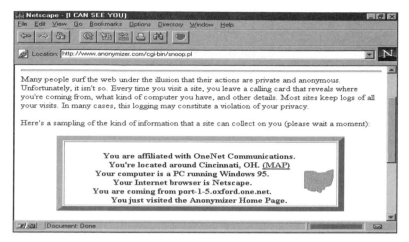

Figure 6.1   Your browser gives up more than a little information about you.

The server has this information:

- Your ISP.

- Your location (based on the ISP's location—usually a good indicator).

- The type of computer you're using.

- Your operating system.

- Your Web browser.

- The title of the Web page you just left.

A fairly simple CGI script can collect all this information. In the example in Figure 6.1, the script fed the information back to the server to use with the HTML page that displayed the information in Figure 6.1. It could just as easily write this information to a log file, to be compiled later, providing details about the equipment and software you use, the area you're from, and what other kinds of pages you tend to visit. This information is important to Web-site operators who need to have some idea of visitor demographics.

When you visit an anonymous FTP site, most Web browsers use your user ID and ISP for the ID and password.

Other approaches to gathering such information, and more, involve the Web server's logs directly. More elaborate setups can also get your email address—something you don't want to give some Web sites, such as those operated by spammers.

While I don't object to someone knowing where I'm coming from, in general, being able to grab so much detailed information is going a bit far. Sometimes, I wonder whether demographics for marketing purposes is all they're after. Indeed, this is most often the case, but it doesn't stop there; Web pages can take the information-gathering process even further.

WHEN COOKIES AREN'T SWEET

Web-site information gathering doesn't stop with grabbing information from your browser. Many Web pages can put information on your hard disk for later retrieval. A little innovation called a *browser cookie* can save all sorts of information about your habits and preferences at Web sites.

Most of the time, the information is used by the browser that places it on your disk. A file called cookies.txt in your browser's directory carries information that is fed to servers that request it. It is a standard 7-bit ASCII text file that you can open with a word processor or text editor. It looks like this:

```
# Netscape HTTP Cookie File# http://www.netscape.com/newsref/std/
cookie_spec.html# This is a generated file! Do not edit.
.realaudio.com    TRUE    /    FALSE  946684740    uid
20428837852776759403297.201.5.2   FALSE   /    FALSE  946511999
RoxenUserID0x9a8d4www.microsoft.com    FALSE   /    FALSE
937422000   MC1   GUID=6678311d08741a4df6410000f84a1409www.qualcomm.com
FALSE    /    FALSE  915148800    Am_UserId
ce738d21a4a930436.netscape.com   TRUE   /    FALSE  946684799
NETSCAPE_ID1000e010,13e3ac0b.infoseek.com      TRUE   /    FALSE
885340779   InfoseekUserId
8434353A128C8B8067D065AD77FC1047D81.hotbot.com   TRUE   /    FALSE
937396800   ink
IUOFW2PN41D1FDAA493E42EBD0F190C205CAF1A245.nytimes.com   TRUE   /
FALSE    946684799    PW    3$50·519+B.nytimes.com TRUE   /
FALSE    946684799    ID    3$50·5Bwww.harmony-central.com
FALSE    /    FALSE  946684799    s
2032762885388690574wc1.webcrawler.com    FALSE   /    FALSE
1011760174 AnonTrack    3A3F335432E7CA2E.timecast.com TRUE   /
FALSE    946684740    uid    2032539854681627251.hotwired.com
TRUE    /    FALSE  946684799    p_uniqid
```

```
yEPfCNoBxpdsu5EeJB.yahoo.com       TRUE    /       FALSE   883609200
GET_LOCAL   last=us/45/45003.html&ver=1wc1.webcrawler.com          FALSE
/   FALSE   862754912       wcchoice
"maxHits=100&mode=titles".excite.com       TRUE    /       FALSE
946641600   UID     76E5DAE832F586D2.film.com       TRUE    /       FALSE
944528400   FILMCOM testcookiewc2.webcrawler.com FALSE  /       FALSE
1012894703  AnonTrack       5BEB4EE432F919EFpegasus.usa.com          FALSE
/   FALSE   1293753600      EGSOFT_ID       206.112.208.14-
13973204856.29104889www.concentric.net     FALSE           FALSE
12972839999 beenhere        yup.techweb.com         TRUE            FALSE
942189160   TechWeb 206.112.208.44.852347461 path=/
```

This example is a small portion of the cookies.txt file in my Netscape directory. The information following each URL is, for the most part, meaningless except to data-collecting programs on the servers at their Web sites.

The meaning of some of the data is obvious, such as user IDs and passwords for some sites, and even the tongue-in-cheek affirmation of previous visits—beenhere yup—added by concentric.net. Some listings include network addresses for ISPs I used while visiting these sites.

The remainder of the data is either encoded—strings of letters and numerals that have significance to the sites that placed them there—or refers to elements or settings peculiar to a given site. The FALSE/TRUE strings, for instance, may indicate whether the visitor has been there before and has an ID at the site.

Some uses for cookies are obvious; for example, a user ID and password to a site can customize information presentation. Cookies are also used to keep items in virtual shopping carts. (If you have ever visited a shopping site and ordered items, but left without completing your order, then returned and found your list of items intact, you can thank information in your cookies.txt file.) Likewise, they might store the fact that you've been to certain pages at a site and thus prompt the server to provide access to new pages, and deny access to pages previously visited. Such a setup might be used to collect and store poll data (and prohibit anyone from taking the poll twice).

These are but a few possible uses for data stored in cookies. Another use involves statistics for marketing (or in support of a commercial Web site's advertising rates). As long as you don't mind freely giving information about your habits at a given Web site to the server at that site, you probably don't have any problem with cookies. Then, too, some information stored in cookies is to your benefit (user IDs and passwords, for example; with these in a cookie, you don't have to enter them every time you visit a favorite Web site).

If you think that storing information about you on your own computer and retrieving that information to use when you visit a Web site more than once is an invasion of your privacy, your appetite for information cookies is probably minimal. Ditto the idea of trusting information to a file that so many unknown entities can access. You probably won't much care for the idea of different Web sites trading cookies, either.

Trading Cookies

Some Web sites not only collect their own information, but they pick up information about previous Web sites, then interpret it to get even more information about your Web activities.

Here again, if you don't mind strangers being privy to your online habits, and using that information to your benefit, you're probably not concerned about what cookies do on your browser. But if you feel cookies, along with all the other information gathering that goes on online, are an invasion of your privacy, you may want to keep your information to yourself. If so, read on.

Protecting Your Information From Prying Web Sites

Your browser easily gives up certain information to servers that know how to get it. This includes all the "identity" information you provide in setting up your browser, and information about your mail servers.

Keeping Your Mail, ISP, And Related Information Private

If you want to avoid telling servers your email address, ISP, and other information, as shown in Figure 6.1, you have to delete email and server information in your browser's setup. *Note, however, that this will disable your email. The information must be replaced before you can send or receive mail using the browser.* Write it down, so you can replace the information when you want to use your browser to send or receive email.

To remove this information with Netscape and Microsoft Internet Explorer, follow these steps:

• Netscape—Select <u>M</u>ail and News Preferences on the Options menu. Click on the tab labeled Identity. Delete the information in the fields labeled Your Name, Your Email, and Reply-to Address. Next, click on the Servers tab and delete the information in the fields labeled Outgoing Mail (SMTP) Server, Incoming Mail (POP3) Server, and POP3 User Name.

• Internet Explorer—Open the Mail window (press the Mail button on the toolbar). Select <u>O</u>ptions on the Mail menu. Then click on the Server tab. You will see boxes labeled Name, Organization, Email address, Outgoing Mail (SMTP), Incoming Mail (POP), and POP3 Account. You must delete the information in these boxes if you don't want it available for querying servers.

Remember, copy down the information before you delete it, so you can redo the setup when you are back in known Web-site territory and want to use email.

Don't Let Your Web Page Give Your Email Address To Robots

You will learn more about the whys and wherefores of it in Chapter 7, but you want to protect your email address from programs that crawl the Web and extract email addresses from Web pages. There are two options you can use to thwart the list-compiling robot programs.

If you are conversant with CGI scripting—and your ISP permits it—you can set up an HTML email page, and funnel the output through a program that forwards it to your email address without revealing it.

A simpler approach is to not include a "mailto:" link on your pages. Instead, write your address as "me at myisp.net" or "me AT myisp.net" or something similar. Those who want to email you will have to enter your address by hand, but the address-gathering robots will ignore your address. (They look for email addresses in conventional format—that is, "me@myisp.net".)

Dealing With Cookies

Overall, the information that cookies collect and give up is not a great danger to you; it's not unlike filling out those consumer surveys that come with products (although, unlike surveys, cookies gather their information without your direct participation). Some of the information is beneficial to you—user IDs and passwords for Web sites, for instance.

Still, if you want to keep everything about your browsing habits private, you can delete the file, cookies.txt. It will be rewritten the next time a server sends a cookie to your system, however, so you will have to delete it periodically.

A simpler approach—which you can still augment by deleting the cookie file periodically, if you wish—is to turn on your browser's cookie alert to notify you when a server is sending a cookie to your system. With this set, you will see a dialog box that lets you accept or reject a cookie when a server tries to send it, as shown in Figure 6.2.

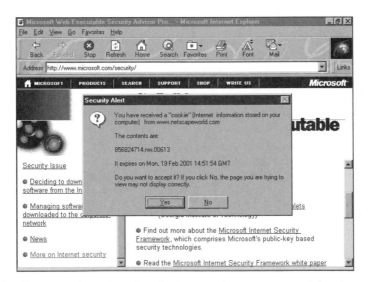

Figure 6.2   Set your browser to alert you when a server tries to send a cookie to your system.

Here's how to turn on the cookie alert with Netscape and Microsoft Internet Explorer:

• Netscape—Select Network Preferences on the Options menu. Click on the Protocols tab, and check the box labeled Accepting a Cookie.

• Internet Explorer—Select Options on the View menu, then click on the Advanced tab. Check the box that says, Warn before accepting cookies.

Web-Site Interrogations: Forms, Questionnaires, And Surveys

Forms, such as the one shown in Figure 6.3, are all over the Web. They're used by Web surfers to place orders, participate in polls, request information, subscribe to a service, get added to mailing lists, express opinions—just about anything you might do with a hardcopy form or questionnaire.

As is the case with hardcopy forms, you have no control over where the information you provide is going, or what is done with it. This is more than a little bothersome, because information provided on a form is usually used in some marketing scheme guaranteed to invade your privacy.

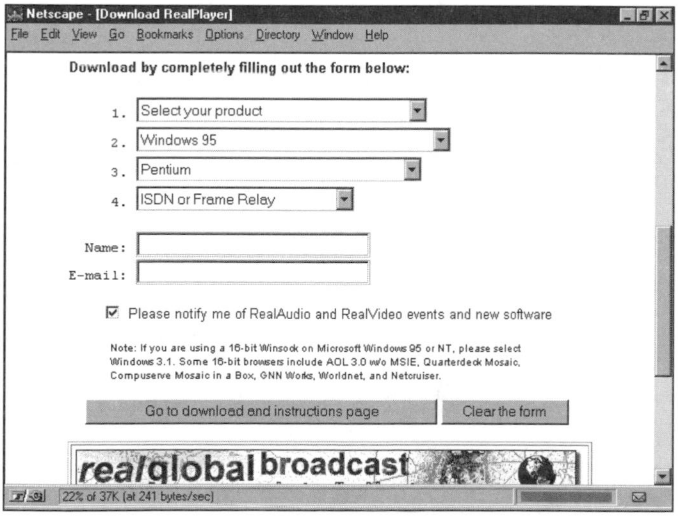

Figure 6.3   Forms are a means of getting you to give up information voluntarily.

The potential for your information being shared far and wide is about to get worse. As I write this, one major U.S. telecommunications company (*not* AT&T) is trying to organize manufacturers, publishers, resellers, and anyone else who markets computer products online, or even has a Web site, to let the telecommunications company handle all the online inquiries they get. The company also proposes to do mass mailings and coordinate everyone's mailing lists, sharing lists back and forth for a fee. This has the potential to significantly increase the quantity of junk email now clogging our systems.

Don't Tell 'Em Everything You Know

Here again, if you don't mind a slight invasion of privacy and the possibility of your email box filling up with special offers from manufacturers, you won't have a problem with forms. If you don't want to hand over your thoughts and habits to strangers, and you want to keep the junk mail down, don't fill out online forms.

In some instances, you must fill out forms to get to a specific Web page—say, to be admitted to a Web site or download an important program, such as the Adobe Acrobat PDF reader. When you run into one of these, provide the information you want to, but omit your email address and telephone numbers, and physical address. If the form won't go through without all of the blanks being filled in, fake the information. The same is true for online polls and other data interrogators that really *don't* need your email address.

On rare occasions, you will find Web sites that offer worthwhile content, but ask that you sign up. Not only that, they require a real email address to which to send you a password. (Among these are sites for *Wired* Magazine and the *Wall Street Journal*.)

When you run into this, you have to consider how likely it is that the operators of the Web site are going to put you on a mailing list and sell it. This, of course, means you'll be sold again and again as the list-buyers sell their lists to other companies. If they say they do not do this, do they offer any guarantees that they won't change their policy?

Does this mean you are left with the choice of either signing up or not? You have one other recourse: If you use a service that lets you create disposable screen names or IDs, create one to receive the password (or dedicate one for this purpose and keep it for all sites you run into that use the "we have to send you a password" trick to get your email address for a mailing list).

A View From The Other Side

Collecting information about Web-site visitors isn't an activity reserved for Webmasters proficient in the technical minutiae of Unix and servers. If you've ever wondered what it's like on the other side of the fence, you'll be interested to know that you, too, can gather all sorts of information about visitors to your Web site. ISPs often provide regular reports containing all sorts of information about the people who visit a site, when they visit, what systems they use, and more. These reports are based on information the server gathers and logs anyway, but it is an extra-cost service.

Rather than pay for the information, you might try writing a CGI or Java script that can collect and log information from Web browsers and cookies. Not that interested? For those who don't want to bother with all that, programs and services are available that can give you a lot of demographic information about visitors to your site.

One of my favorite services of this type (free for noncommercial Web sites) is FXWeb's Webtracker. It keeps track of the types of operating systems and browsers visiting the page I have designated, as shown in Figure 6.4. It also tells me what percentage of visitors return to my page. In addition, it provides a count of visits, and it turns information about the days and times of visits into graphs that show the comparative percentage of hits by day and hour. Webtracker also reveals what types of sites the visitors come from (.com, .net, .edu, .org, and so forth).

This is obviously quite a bit of useful information. I might use it to target the Web site more effectively by customizing it for the browser or operating system used by most visitors. I might add material for users who are bored at work, a fact I infer from the time of day I get a lot of hits—on Friday just after lunch time and just before going-home time.

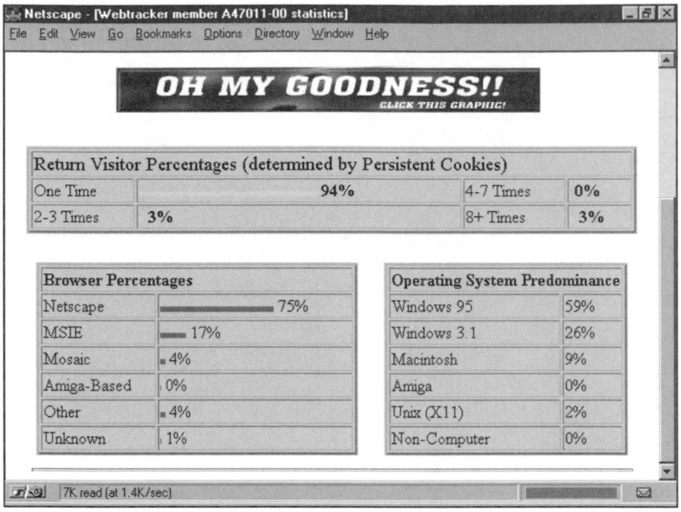

Figure 6.4   You can gather Web-site demographics yourself with tools, such as Webtracker.

If you're interested in setting up a page for Webtracker statistics, visit this URL: **http://www.fxweb.holowww.com/tracker/index.html.**

Many other services like this are available online, as well as software you can add to your site to gather and report information on visitors. Among the more useful software packages in this genre are Wusage (**http://www.boutell.com/wusage/**) and WebTrends (**http://www.egsoftware.com/**). For still more such services and tools, search Alta Vista (**http://www.altavista.digital.com/**) using the phrase "Web Site Tools."

Can Your Web Pages Be Turned Against You?

Ironically, the content of your Web pages can be turned against you. Thanks to the Web technology, and advanced image editing software, it's possible to alter photos. Photo alterations can range from simple practical jokes to the embarrassing and disgusting.

Someone can simply grab your photos for their Web page. These examples are a little odd, but relatively harmless. In one case, a man stole a head shot of his friend from the friend's Web site, and created a "wanted" poster that looked a lot like those FBI wanted posters you see in post offices. In another, a man grabbed a photo of an acquaintance's girlfriend, and posted it at his Web site, claiming this was his girlfriend (albeit with a name change). In each instance, the photos were placed on the prankster's Web site for any and all to view.

A skilled hobbyist with the right software can take a face or head from a photo, edit and resize it, and merge it into another image. There are hundreds of such hybrid images with definite pornographic themes floating around several alt.binary USENET Newsgroups. At least one person who creates such images offers to edit photos submitted to him for a fee. Others seem to be doing this for a hobby. The point is, a photo can be grabbed from any Web page, skillfully edited into something it's not, and spread around the Internet without the subject ever knowing it. (The same thing is frequently done with celebrity photos, by the way.)

There is no real defense against this sort of thing, short of not using personal photos on Web pages. You might try using only poor-quality photos, but a determined person with the right software can do "interesting" things with those, too.

Even if your photos are not grabbed and altered, they remain a target for another sort of misuse, in the form of links to your photos from other Web sites. While this seems innocent, it can be questionable—if not totally inappropriate—depending on your viewpoint. Consider several "babes of the Internet" Web sites that have been coming and going since 1995. These consist of links to women's home pages that include photos. While many might deem this flattering, it does have the potential for drawing unwanted attention from less-reputable Web surfers.

Information Online—Good Or Bad?

All too many Internet newcomers think of the Internet as the Ultimate Computer—a source for All Information on Everything. This isn't new to the online world; I saw the same behavior in the late 1980s when an influx of new modem users swelled the ranks of CompuServe, America Online, and other online services. Then, as now, many new users were irate that the information they wanted wasn't available. They bombarded the old hands with such questions as, "Where can I find unlisted phone numbers in Milwaukee?" and "Where is the complete genealogy of the Spleeb family?"

They wanted all sorts of information they couldn't get anywhere else, and they wanted it free and easy to find. Most newcomers were easily disabused of the notion that they could find literally anything online—although they retained a sense of outrage that anyone would dare charge for hard-to-find information (expensive demographics reports, for example).

The point of all this is simply to demonstrate the fact that our society has given online information an undeserved mystique. This could be the result of all those science fiction films that featured an all-knowing computer or robot, or it could be a simple attempt at wish fulfillment. It's probably a little of both.

Whatever the source or reason, many of us seem to expect computers to have all the knowledge we need on hand—or to be able to find it for us. Such desire for information can be seductive; it will make normally rational people believe that *any* information they find is valid if it seems to answer the question at hand. This is a trap.

You don't find many people passing judgment on the authenticity or veracity of online information. We may find Web sites with information that we call objectionable, crude, inappropriate, and even politically incorrect. But rarely is the information presented at a Web site judged as to its relationship with reality.

This is unfortunate, because a lot of bad information exists on the Web.

ONLINE INFORMATION: WHO IS RESPONSIBLE?

Just as the Internet has no police force, it has no central publishing house, library, or any other sort of information control or clearinghouse. Information can be placed online at will by anyone who wants to put up a Web site.

This means *anything* can be put online, without regard to factualness or even reality. Thus, you will find tales from self-purported UFO contactees, "true versions" of this or that historical event, and all sorts of other outrageous opinions or fiction being presented as fact.

This is quite unlike any other medium. Newspapers, TV and radio news reports, magazines, and book publishers are normally quite accurate because they check the facts and do not (*usually*) try to present opinion or theory as fact.

Nobody checks the facts for Web sites. This is probably an obvious truth to some readers. Still, it needs to be pointed out, because many Internet users regard the Internet the same as any other media. Much of the Internet only looks legitimate because of the information mystique I mentioned earlier, and thanks to the ease of making Web pages look like professional publications.

Literally anyone can put together a legitimate-looking Web site, every bit as professional and flashy as those maintained by *Time* magazine, ABC-TV, the *New York Times*, *Wired*, or other accepted media. Consider this: that Web site devoted to Mickey Bitsko's weekly trips to the heart of the sun with aliens from Venus and the Dog Star has the exact same distribution as *Time* and *Wired*.

Suddenly, *all information looks the same*. It all has the appearance of legitimacy. The Internet has no prerequisites for being legitimate—and no real way for information consumers to distinguish between accurate reporting and propaganda, between reality and imagination, between fact and fiction. It's really easy to present false or misleading information as fact on the Internet.

This goes for rumors, too—such as the virus hoaxes described earlier in this chapter.

Who's responsible then? Not a vast news organization or research team, but Mickey Bitsko—the interplanetary traveler—and thousands of others like him. Many will be more subtle, of course, merely slanting information or picking and choosing from the facts to support a viewpoint instead of reality. Some may present speculation as fact. Others may simply be ignorant of all the facts and believe the misleading or false information they're presenting. Such people answer to no one, and they're not going to lose their jobs for spreading false information, whether intentionally or out of ignorance. If you don't believe their information, you can't lead a boycott or protest in the media.

All of which points to two bits of advice:

- Don't view the Internet as media on a par with TV, radio, magazines, and newspapers; with few exceptions, it isn't.

- Don't accept everything you see on the Internet at face value.

Remember: Free speech is grand, but it doesn't make a lie true.

INTERNET INFORMATION STRATEGIES

A good strategy in dealing with information found online is to consider the source, as the old cliché goes. A report on the politics of drug dealing in *Time* online is far more likely to be factual than a similar report by a small, neopolitical organization whose agenda is served by the slanting of facts. This is largely because commercial Web sites operated by media organizations do have to answer to someone: their offline organization, their owners and investors, and their subscribers or viewers. Any news or information source on the Web that has a real-world counterpart is likely to be as reliable as that real-world counterpart.

Check information you find online. Errors sometimes creep into information that has been transcribed or otherwise altered for online presentation, and people make mistakes. In general, if it seems a little off, check it out.

Finally, consider this: Information, good or bad, is hard to erase from the Web. The ease with which information online can be copied or shared guarantees that it will propagate fast and far, indeed. But "unposting" is a far slower process. One bit of bad information can be multiplied by a thousand times within days, but retractions and corrections proceed far slower, or not at all.

Let's now take a hard look at a certain class of online scammers and their annoying online activities. On to Chapter 7, "Scams And Spam: The Plague Of The Internet!"

Chapter 7

Scams And Spam: The Plague Of The Internet

159

Chapter 7

Scams And Spam: The Plague Of The Internet

Chapter 7

This chapter examines two of the more bothersome issues of life on the Internet:

- First, we'll look at online frauds and con games. These are, by and large, the same old con games that have been around for a century or more, given new life by the Internet.

- Then, we'll take a close and sometimes entertaining look at certain online marketing techniques that are a real threat to online privacy—not to mention the efficiency of pubic postings and email.

First, however, some background on why the Internet is considered a big marketing operation by so many clueless "netrepreneurs."

The Myth Of The Internet As A "Market"

The Internet suffers from a persistent myth. It is portrayed over and over as a market with tens of millions of eager buyers—a market in which you can sell literally anything and everything.

But wait—exactly who says that? It's not the ISPs and online services. Nor will legitimate computer software and hardware manufacturers tell you that you can make your fortune on the Net. The truth is, no one who knows the Internet and business will tell you that offering a product or service on the Internet automatically and magically brings in thousands or millions of orders—not with any honesty, that is.

The only people pushing the Internet as the ultimate market are self-styled Internet "marketing experts"—that is, those who have a vested interest in making others *think* the Internet is the be-all and end-all marketplace. They fall into these categories:

- Those who sell online advertising—including but not limited to classified-ad sites and "newsletters."

- Mailing-list sellers.

- Many companies that provide autoresponder services. (An *autoresponder* is an email address that sends out the same canned text reply to anyone who sends mail to it.)

- Junk mailers—people who send junk email for others.

- A number of ISPs whose sole business is selling Web space for "business" sites.

These operations cater to amateurs—people with little or no sales or marketing expertise, but who want to believe that the Internet is a great source of easy money. The usual approach of the Internet marketing outfits is to provide a dizzying spiel of numbers and almost-promises designed to convince the amateur that the Internet's millions of users represent a like number of sales. Dozens fall for this approach every day, simply because it sounds good.

The whole thing has overtones of a con job—it succeeds because it appeals to a basic human motivation: greed.

Speaking of cons, would-be netpreneurs aren't the only ones certain that the Internet holds the key to their fortunes. Con artists of all descriptions flock to the Internet, knowing that this venue is likely to give them access to the largest number of potential suckers ever.

Interestingly, the con artists are the only ones who consistently make any money.

The Value Of An Online Presence

The majority of businesses that maintain online Web sites do so not to sell products directly, but to maintain a "presence." Although the worth of an online presence can't be measured directly, it is valuable—so much so that a major book publisher was willing to spend upward of $50,000 per year in the early 1980s just to have an area on CompuServe to publicize new titles and take requests for free catalogs. Not one book was sold through the "online store," but, as the publisher's marketing manager told me at the time, just having that presence was worth several times the investment. Today, thousands of corporations are finding an Internet presence equally valuable.

So, What Is The Market Potential?

If you stop to think about it, the potential for the Internet as a market isn't any greater than any other venue. The problem is that most would-be Internet millionaires ignore the facts. People don't log on just to shop, which is near the bottom of the list of online activities. Most people spend the majority of their online time communicating—by email, realtime chats, and public postings.

Next to communication in popularity is information-gathering—including comparison shopping. Shopping is largely restricted to small, specialized areas that have nothing to do with multilevel marketing (MLM), pyramid schemes, or any other easy-money plans that are what most amateur online marketers have to offer.

Products that sell well online include books and records, specialty merchandise, one-of-a-kind items, and computer products and services. Most come with a value-added element, in the form of a substantial discount or, at least, free shipping. Name-brand products have a definite edge.

Still, dozens of people are pulled into trying to make their fortune online every day—and many continue trying for months, throwing good money after bad. They don't understand that just placing an ad, catalog, or order form on the Internet guarantees that everyone on the Net automatically reads it. These people are often so blinded by the lure of fast money and absolutely certain that the Internet will yield customers by the millions, that they resort to desperate measures.

We'll take a close look at exactly what those desperate measures are. But first, let's see what sorts of scams are popular on the Net.

Con Games, Frauds, Swindles, And Rip-offs

Scams, frauds, cons, come-ons. By whatever name, schemes to relieve the unwary of their money are all over the Internet.

Some scams are perpetrated by knowledgeable con artists who use the Internet to do what they have been doing in the real world for years: defraud victims who expect to get something for an "investment" (most often, a very large return for a relatively small investment).

Other scams are the work of those who have bought into a con game and are trying desperately to recoup their investment. Still more are worked by people who think they are involved in a legitimate moneymaking enterprise, but are unwittingly making money for con artists who pulled them into a scam.

Internet Business Opportunities: The Same Old Scams, Or Something New?

Much of what's happening on the Internet is new, but not in the dozens of scams, schemes, and cons that force their way into your email box every month. Most of the "make money fast," "work at home," and similar offers pushed by spammers today have been around for years, offline.

About 15 years ago, I was working with a magazine that carried ads for the same types of schemes I see touted in email and USENET spams every day. My experience with the magazine gave me an informal but valuable education in the types of fast-money schemes people try to pass off as legitimate business opportunities.

Comparing the magazine ad scams with the Internet "business opportunities" reveals that many spammers offer the same old scams: envelope stuffing and multilevel marketing with home-cleaning products and vitamins—these are simply the old come-ons offered in a new venue. The only difference is that some of the products are new—free Web pages, pagers, or laptops instead of vitamins and miracle cures.

Whatever the product, taking advantage of these "business opportunities" still ends up costing you more than you can earn from them (if you make any money at all).

WHAT SORTS OF SCAMS ARE THERE?

Just about every sort of scam you've heard about offline has been translated to the Internet. While some scams may seem original, they're really just the same old, tired con games in a new venue, often dressed up in computer terms. I'll give you a sampling of the more popular online cons over the next few pages.

PYRAMID SCHEMES

Pyramid schemes are probably the most common scam going, online or off. They translate easily to the Web, where perpetrators can remain anonymous while reaching a large number of potential "recruits" with little effort.

Chain Letters: Pyramid Scheme #1

In the chain-letter scam, you receive a letter that has the names and addresses of five people at the end. The letter's text invites you to send a dollar to the first person on the list, remove his or her name, and add yours to the end. After this, you send the letter (with your name on the list of cash recipients) to 10 or more friends.

On the face of it, this looks great. If everyone down the line is sending a dollar to the person at the top of the list and then removing that name, your name will climb to the top of the list quickly. In theory, your name is at the top of the list on 10,000 letters—which means, in theory, you receive $10,000.

It doesn't work out that way.

Only a few people—the first ones to send out the letter—make a few dollars at this. The chain quickly breaks down. Because chain letters and similar pyramid schemes are illegal, most people who get them don't copy and send them on; nor will they send money to the person at the top of the list. They may even replace your name at the top with theirs.

Chain letters are popular on the Internet because they are so easy to copy, alter, and email to others—or to post in Newsgroups or other public areas. Internet chain letters differ little from the versions that have been making the rounds via the U.S. Postal Service for decades. Some perpetrators claim legality for their chain letters. The usual approach is to pretend you are ordering a product of some sort from the person to whom you send the letter. This doesn't change the illegal status, though.

The Internet Scam Hit List

The FTC keeps a close eye on Internet scams. Their Web site features bulletins on fraud, and provides background information on how the more popular con games work.

In the course of tracking Internet scams, the FTC developed a list of the top five Internet scams.

The pyramid scam is number one. According to the FTC, pyramid scams are found at Web sites, in Newsgroups and email, and even being promoted in chat rooms. Pyramids are often presented as legitimate "marketing" techniques.

Next on the list are scams offering Internet-related products and services at supposed bargain prices. These usually involve convoluted schemes that take the customer's money without handing over any products or services. The perpetrators disappear after making their kill. Close behind this are frauds involving computer equipment or software. Here again, the con artist takes the customer's money, then disappears.

Business opportunities hold fourth place. These include all sorts of Internet "jobs" and "businesses," including "Internet billboards" and other fraudulent advertising schemes. Work-at-home scams wrap up the list. Internet versions of these scams generally have in common the promise of big money, fast.

Bogus Marketing Schemes: Pyramid Scheme #2

Another example of a pyramid scheme has a few people at the top who recruit others, who, in turn, recruit still others, to "sell a program." As a recruit, you pay a registration, membership, or distributor's fee. This buys you the right to recruit others, and you receive a very tiny percentage of the money *they* pay the people at the top to buy into the program. You are that person's *sponsor*, and he or she is your *downline*. (The term comes from the idea that you make money from each person recruiting new members on down the line.)

You make less money on each level down, but this is, in theory, made up for by the tremendous numbers of people who are signed up by those in the levels below you. Recruits are promised a lot of money, fast. Impressive-looking charts and diagrams plot the recruit's progress through a *matrix* or other technical-sounding entity. In the end, though, only the founders—those at the top of the pyramid—make any real money. They pocket most of the registration or sign-up fees they collect from each new recruit.

When the cash flow starts to slow, the founders disappear, probably to start over elsewhere. At a certain critical point, the number of people involved makes the pyramid collapse. Some people don't send in their money or recruit friends. Only a few people dropping out makes the whole scheme collapse.

As with chain letters, these sham marketing operations may be accompanied by a token product. The product is often the "program" itself, but may also be a buyers' club, a contest, or a motivational session (to motivate the participants to bring in dozens of more recruits). Some of these operations call themselves multilevel marketing companies, but they are easily distinguished by the fact that they stress recruiting new, paying members, rather than selling a product. The real product is money, and only those at the top collect.

Easy Money

Among the boldest online con games I've seen is a pyramid scheme that relies on the lure of easy money and the anonymity of the perpetrator. This one is conducted by email. In a pitch full of hyperbole and offering the promise of financial independence, early retirement, or even millionaire status within a very short period of time, you are asked to sign up for a downline, matrix, or MLM scheme that doesn't require you to sell a product. Better still, you don't have to recruit a downline—the individual pushing the scheme promises that his or her organization will do it for you, using "powerful software" and the Internet.

It sounds great, right? You don't have to sell anything, and you don't have to recruit others. Your downline is created for you automatically, thanks to the magic of computers and the Internet. You make big money, and do nothing. If you have any questions, you can call a toll-free number where a recording will provide you with answers.

It sounds too good to be true—and it is. The clincher is that, to participate, you must fax a check or authorize your credit card to be charged by fax or email. The amount is usually in the neighborhood of $100. Amazingly, people fall for this, even though they never even speak with the person making this great offer.

Multilevel Marketing: Pyramid Scheme #3

MLM is an interesting method of selling and distributing products, to say the least. In brief, a manufacturer sells products not through retail stores, but only direct—which, of course, nets the manufacturer a higher per-unit amount. Buyers can be distributors, if they purchase a minimum quantity per month and pay a sign-up fee. This gives them the right to sell the product—and the distribution program—to others, who, in turn, can sell to still others, and on down the line, *ad infinitum*.

The theory here is that a distributor will recruit (usually referred to as *sponsoring*) a *downline* of sellers. These sellers must buy their products from the original distributor. In turn, each new distributor sponsors more people, who, in turn, sponsor more people, and so on. The manufacturer makes money by selling the products at inflated prices and from collecting the distributor fees.

As a distributor, you may or may not get a percentage of each of your downline members' sign-up fees. What you do get is increased sales. Each person you sponsor must, as you have done, commit to a minimum monthly purchase. Your downline in turn creates their own downlines, and you get a tiny percentage of the sales of each level beneath you. Success here depends on active participation by everyone in your downline.

This is probably beginning to sound like the pyramid scheme described in the preceding section—and it is. The difference is that MLM deals with a product, though it's usually not much of one—vitamins, food supplements, cleaning products, perhaps, that are no different from what you can buy in a retail store. Quite often, MLM distributors end up with a garage or basement full of products as their downline evaporates in the fashion of any pyramid scheme. Most people eventually drop out as they realize they are spending far too much time earning next to nothing. Those few who do succeed are constantly trying to recruit new members to replace those who drop out.

Often referred to by hip terms, such as *matrix marketing*, MLM has been applied to an absurd range of products—from the standard vitamins and cleaning product previously mentioned, to telephone cards, pagers, cellular telephones, laptop computers, Web sites, and even Internet access.

(Note that MLM schemes involving expensive hardware are quite often creative scams that end up with you buying the product, sometimes at an inflated price. The downline requirements are such that recruiting enough people to earn the free product is almost impossible.)

Reality Check

If you think an offer might be worth investigating, check it with another source. Never make a purchase or investment based on information from only one source. (Beware of strangers who email you about a great opportunity they've invested in. These are *shills*—people working with a con artist to draw in victims.)

Scan business opportunity Newsgroups for references to the offer. Use Deja News (**http://www.dejanews.com/forms/dnq.html**) to search for key phrases or names in the offer. You might find other people who have had experience with the offer and can share their opinions. You might find that 5,000 copies of the same offer have been posted in hundreds of Newsgroups—a sure indicator of a scam.

You can also use Web search engines to look for Web sites devoted to the general product being offered. Interestingly, many "exclusive" or "one-time" offers you receive in email are being hawked by hundreds of other people.

Consumer and government Web sites also contain information on Internet fraud. For starters, try the Federal Trade Commission (FTC) Web site at **http://www.ftc.gov** and the National Fraud Information Center (NFIC) at **http://www.fraud.org/**. The NFIC is a particularly good source of information about Internet fraud. As shown in Figure 7.1, it offers daily reports, updates on new frauds, and more.

INVESTMENT SCAMS

Investment scams vary widely, but like all cons, they appeal to greed, promising or implying returns that are inordinately high. The specific deal offered is often presented as being a "special offer," available only via the Internet.

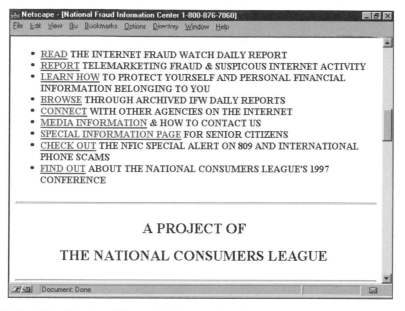

Figure 7.1   The National Fraud Information Center provides daily updates
on Internet fraud.

Ponzi Schemes

Ponzi schemes are named after a 19th-century con artist who promised large monthly returns to those who invested in his nonexistent company. Actually, there was no company. Only Mr. Ponzi, who collected large sums for investors, frittered the money away on an expensive lifestyle, and paid each investor a small amount each month out of the money he got from newer investors.   For example, Ponzi might collect $25,000 from three investors, each of whom he guaranteed a return on their principle of $5,000 per month. For the first few months, Ponzi paid each investor out of the original investments he collected. When the money started to run short, Ponzi signed on new investors. This continued until there were too many investors to pay, and the scheme collapsed.

Ponzi schemes are active on the Internet, and several have been and are being investigated. The most obvious indicator of a Ponzi scheme at work is an offer of inordinately high returns on alarge investment. The "investment opportunity" usually involves an unspecified "high-tech company," often outside the United States, so researching it is difficult. When details are provided, they are usually ambiguous.

Illegal Stock Or Investment Offerings

Online investment scams often involve illegal offerings—those not registered with the Securities and Exchange Commission (SEC) or not complying with the SEC's rules.

These offerings reach would-be or relatively unsophisticated investors who figure an Internet offering is as legitimate as any other. The opportunity is often touted as "new" or "exclusive to the Internet." The prospect of getting in on the ground floor is quite attractive to many, especially when the offer is compared with a well-known investment that had particularly high returns. As with the nonexistent offerings of Ponzi schemes, those making the offer are not forthcoming with details.

The SEC has prosecuted people behind several illegal and fraudulent Internet offerings, and others are being investigated. (The most successful of these illegal offerings fleeced Internet investors of several million dollars.)

FINANCIAL SCAMS

Illegal or unethical schemes are the basis for the most popular financial scams on the Internet. These involve credit-repair, offshore banking, credit cards, and guarantees of grants and loans.

- The concept of credit repair is attractive to many in today's economic environment, where all too many people find themselves overextended. The typical scam promises to remove negative items from your credit report. The credit-repair outfit offers—and often guarantees—that *everything* negative will be removed, whether it's true or not, including bankruptcy. This simply does not happen. Still, thousands of people fall for this offer every year. After spending several hundred dollars, they end up with little more than a credit report.

- Offshore banking involves an illegal activity: hiding funds and income in a foreign bank. Presumably, the bank hides information about its depositors from government agencies. Hiding money and income is illegal, and operations that offer offshore banking schemes are frequently investigated and shut down. Their "clients," having paid huge sum for what they were told was a "tax shelter," are left not only owing taxes, but often penalties and fines.

- Some operations guarantee they will get you a credit card, no matter what your credit history or financial status is. While not illegal, these operations are not exactly ethical either. All they are really selling is information about secured credit cards or banks that grant credit to poor risks. This information is available free—on the Web and off. Another credit card scam offers a card with a high line of credit, for a fee. It sounds good until the victim gets the card, and discovers that it is good only on overpriced goods from the catalog of the company that issued it.

- Companies and individuals who claim to be able to get grants, loans, and scholarships for a fee likewise sell information that is readily available elsewhere. These operations are often shut down by the FTC because, like credit-repair outfits, they lure in customers with promises that cannot be fulfilled.

- Email messages bearing news of a "prize" or threats of debt-collection action. These demand that you call a telephone number with an area code in the Caribbean, like 809. The person who answers the telephone pretends to not understand English, or keeps you on hold. The scam becomes apparent when you get your telephone bill—the call carries a rate of five dollars a minute, or more. The people behind the scam of course get a big cut of that expensive long-distance call. This is one that is likely to return, what with a large number of new, unfamiliar area codes being assigned to the U.S. and countries to the south.

OTHER SCAMS

Phony income opportunities and work-at-home schemes are really big. Now they, too, have been adapted to the Internet. One tried-and-true scam is envelope stuffing, in which you buy instructions on how to make money doing mailings. You may end up mailing out catalogs and order forms, but you will make money only if someone places an order—and the merchandise is usually less than appealing. You may also receive instructions on how to take out ads for stuffing envelopes and then sell the respondents the same instructions. On the Internet, the envelope-stuffing scam might translate into a catalog you email or post online.

Another long-time scam involves assembling products at home. You pay for parts and/or instructions for building an item. The company agrees to purchase all assembled items that meet its quality standards. The problem is, yours never do, so you've wasted your money. Home-product-assembly schemes adapted to the Internet might involve maintaining a database that requires you to buy expensive software.

Other categories of scams include phony health and medical products (weight-loss products are very popular). Web-based psychic scams have also been uncovered by the Better Business Bureau and other organizations, and phoney sweepstakes and "prize" offers are beginning to emerge online.

If These Schemes Are So Bad, Why Do They Succeed?

All scams have this in common: Whether the scam is an illegal pyramid scheme, outright investment fraud, so-called multilevel marketing business, or an offer to sell information with which the buyer can easily earn large sums of money, all offer the lure of easy money—fast and in large amounts.

Victims want to believe the con being pulled on them is a legitimate offer. Con artists are well aware of this and exploit it to the maximum. Their scams are easy to believe and are just complex enough that, on the face of it, they seem legitimate.

The hype that surrounds the Internet often contributes to the fog necessary for a con to succeed. For many, the Internet is an exotic place, where anything can happen. So, if an offer seems just a little too good to be true...well, so what? This is the Internet, where the possibilities are endless. In reality, the possibilities end when the victim's money runs out.

Why Do Con Artists Get Away With It?

Most cons endeavor to milk thousands of people out of a few dollars each, as opposed to stealing $10,000 each from 10 people. Those who are taken for $10, $20, or $50 usually won't squawk about it; in fact, most victims are too embarrassed to say anything. Then, too, the amount conned from any one person is usually not enough to interest law-enforcement agencies or prosecutors. (If, however,

10 or 100 people who were taken by the same person get together to complain, the indication of a large-scale fraud will get official attention.)

The FTC and SEC have prosecuted dozens of cases of online fraud, ranging from bogus credit repair and phony income opportunities, to illegal stock offerings and pyramid schemes. Still, the con jobs continue. This can be attributed in part to the lure of so many potential "suckers" in one place. Con artists see the Internet the way most other online criminals do: as a place where one is protected by anonymity.

For more information on online scams, visit the Web sites of the FTC (**http://www.ftc.gov/**) and the SEC (**http://www.sec.gov/**).

How To Spot An Internet Scam

Often, the most telling indicator that an offer is a scam is its presentation. An offer or ad that makes outrageous claims (provides extremely large returns on investments, cures incurable diseases, etc.) should be immediately suspect. "Special Internet offers" are likewise suspect, along with "limited time" offers or those that give you a discount if you order today.

Other fraud indicators include:

- The solicitation comes via email. Ignore it. Most "opportunities" presented via email are frauds. If the opportunity was so great, the scammers wouldn't have to force it on folks—everyone would be coming to them. The email hucksters are playing the odds: They send junk solicitations to 100,000 email addresses, and figure they will get 1/10th of 1 percent return—which is to say, 1,000 victims sending money. Don't be one of them.

- The netrepreneur offers no physical address that's not a mail drop, no voice telephone number, and no name. These are sure indicators that the scammer does not want you to find him or her later—and usually for good reason.

- The solicitation asks you for your credit-card number or—worse—to fax a check. Such demands for immediate cash are often the hallmarks of true fly-by-night operations. This is particularly true of those who offer only a fax number and email address (and many do).

- The con artist continually alludes to the "great potential for entrepreneurs" on the Internet—with frequent references to the tens of millions of customers online—yet can't show or explain the product you're supposed to sell. This clown is trying to sell you pie-in-the-sky; if he or she can't show you a product, can't show results, and tries to sell you on "potential" only, forget it. It's most likely an illegal pyramid scheme.

- The offer urges you to order before a certain deadline and/or claims to be available only to a limited number of people. This false urgency is a technique to get you to order before you have time to think things through or change your mind.

- It sounds too good to be true. It most likely is.

Spam: The Plague Of The Internet

If you've been online more than a few months, you've probably experienced this: You log on to check your email, and new messages are waiting—a lot of new messages, in fact, and none from anyone you know. The subject headers shout at you: "Make Money While You Sleep," "Earn a Thousand Dollars Every Time the Phone Rings," or "Retire Next Week!"

You may try to reply to some, or ask to be removed from the senders' mailing lists. If so, you will probably receive even more pandering email. Or, your message might be returned as undeliverable.

Needless to say, if you get a half-dozen or more such messages daily, this gets annoying—even more so when you are tricked into reading a message by a header, such as "Hi!", that implies the message is from someone you know.

For some, cost compounds annoyance. Junk email can be costly for those who use an online service at a per-minute rate or pay for Internet usage on a quantity basis. The same is true for those who dial up their email provider via long-distance connections. Even if you don't read the messages, you still use up valuable time displaying the headers, and sorting out and deleting the junk mail. In short, sending unwanted junk email is like sending mail with postage due—and it's mail you can't "return to sender." To see just how annoying junk email can get, take a look at The Blacklist of Internet Advertisers (for the address, see "For More Information" near the end of this chapter).

Finally, unsolicited commercial email (UCE) costs bandwidth on the Internet— that is, spam takes up computer processing power and other network resources that could be better used carrying legitimate Internet traffic.

WHERE DOES IT COME FROM—AND WHY?

Junk advertising in email—better known as spam—comes from many sources, almost none of them legitimate businesses. Typically, they operate with one person, a computer, Internet access, and a list of email addresses.

But, Why Do They Call It Spam?

*The spam moniker is an inside joke, having to do with an old Monty Python Flying Circus skit, in which a man attempting to order a meal in a restaurant is continually interrupted by a chorus of Vikings singing about spam. The term first appeared when scammers began filling up USENET Newsgroups with endless off-topic commercial postings. The term carried over to pandering email when spammers—largely defeated by Newsgroup moderators who deleted their postings—started turning to bulk email lists. (For more information on the history of spam, and Net abuse in general, check out The Net Abuse FAQ, maintained by J.D. Falk, located at **http://www.cybernothing.org/faqs/net-abuse-faq.html.**)*

Spamming is held in particular contempt in USENET circles. Finding spam messages posted in inappropriate places has been likened to trying to hold a conversation, only to be interrupted every few minutes by someone walking into the room with a bullhorn and reading an advertisement. In email, it's more like being forced to listen to ads in the middle of a telephone call.

> *Spammers rarely offer real names. Addresses are most often post office boxes or mail drops. Telephone numbers, if provided at all, usually lead to a recording with even more hype. Consider, then: Would you buy a computer, car, groceries, legal service, or anything from a person who wouldn't give you his name, real address or telephone number, and who had no retail location or office? Of course not.*

Address Checking

Thanks to several services on the Internet, you can sometimes check street addresses provided by spammers. I have found addresses used by several spammers to be mail drops, intended to make them look legitimate with a street address and suite number, but really serving to hide their location and identities. I discovered this by running street addresses through Web search engines. Since so many businesses have Web sites or are mentioned in city Web sites, I found matches with spammers' addresses in the addresses of private mail services. This didn't work every time, but it was useful when it did.

If a spammer uses a post office box and you want to learn his or her identity, you can write to the postmaster of the post office where the box is, informing him or her that the postal box customer is using it for business purposes and you wish to know the person's address, per postal regulations. (If the spammer falsely signed up for the box to use for private mail, notifying the postmaster might also have certain repercussions for the spammer.)

Finally, the Web has several look-up services for names, addresses, and telephone numbers. These include CompuServe's Phone•File, Biz•File, and several Web sites discussed in detail in Chapter 8.

Most tellingly, many spammers go to great lengths to disguise their origins. This is perhaps the ultimate tip-off that they have nothing worthwhile to offer. They don't want you to know where they're sending messages from, because they know that thousands—maybe millions—of Internet users are going to be angry at them, and they don't want a deluge of flaming email. Plus, the entrepreneur will likely lose his or her account if just a few people complain to the Internet access provider.

What Are They Selling?

A few spammers peddle real products, such as seasonal gift items, computer software or hardware, and CDs or tapes. The overwhelming (and they *are* overwhelming) majority offers scams, garbage, and junk—pitches for MLM schemes in various guises, get-rich-quick scams, and endless "free" offers that are anything but. Contrary to popular belief, the Internet does not level the playing field if you don't have a real product to sell

No matter what the "product" or "service," most spammers' offerings are characterized by one or more of these traits:

* If you wanted it, you would go to a store and buy it.

* If you knew what was really being offered, you wouldn't take it for free.

* What's being offered is priced well over its value, or more than what you would pay for it offline.

* When the product is information or a report, it is touted as "exclusive" or "secret." (This sort of offering is almost always information you can get at the library or online for free.)

* The product or service is an obvious scam or con.

Just the sorts of things you like seeing shoved in front of your face, on your nickel, right? I'm sure you'll order early and often.

What follows is a sampling of the "great offers" you can find in your email box. I've presented them in the order of frequency that they appear in my email boxes.

Mailing Lists, Software, And Spam Mailing Services

Mailing lists, software for sending junk mail to thousands of victims, and services to send spam for you comprise the biggest category of spam. In one six-month period, fully 40 percent of all the spam I received at various addresses—some 920 spam messages—were for this kind of junk. (There's a good reason for this, which I'll get to in a few pages.)

The ads for these products are most persuasive and often guarantee results, but I doubt that anyone has ever gotten a refund based on such a guarantee.

Multilevel Marketing

MLM schemes are the second-most-frequent spam offering. These include offers for free cell phones, pagers, Internet access, and laptop computers. Without fail, all of the "free" offers cost as much as buying the product from a legitimate source, if not more—unless, that is, you can endlessly "sell" the scam to others, and they, in turn, can sell it endlessly. It's a simple pyramid scam.

Make Money With Your Computer

How to earn big bucks with your computer (presumably while you sleep) is a perennial spammer favorite. This scam comes in two flavors. The most frequent is getting you to use your computer to advertise MLM schemes. The other method is to convince you to start a "business" (perhaps transcribing medical records) that requires you to spend hundreds or thousands of dollars for incredibly overpriced "special software."

Work-At-Home Opportunities

These schemes take the form of "reports" or offers guaranteed to help you make money at home by: assembling products, mailing catalogs, buying junk products to sell to your friends, reading books, clipping ads, and so on. The tired old envelope-stuffing scam—which always *costs* the would-be home worker—is at the top of the list of dozens of other "moneymaking opportunities" offered. Those few opportunities that don't require you to send money to get started are simple ideas that anyone could think of.

"Free" Telephone Calling Cards

The free phone-card offer goes through phases of almost overshadowing all other spams, then all but disappearing. This laughably simple con tries to suck you into accepting a "free" phone card that is not free. To make it work, you have to pay to have it charged up. You can earn a free hour, but you have to sell dozens of others on the scheme. (Note that to make money from most such schemes, the average person would have to put in 80 or more hours per week. Several friends have tried these schemes over the years, and learned to their regret that there was no way they could make any money without putting in twice as much as at a full-time job. At that, they made maybe $100.)

Internet Pornography Sites

Ads for Internet sex sites, disguised to look like letters from "female friends," abound. These sites require you to pay via credit card for the privilege of downloading pornographic photos, movies, and sound clips. Interestingly, the same things can be found in certain USENET Newsgroups at no charge.

"Free" Web Pages

Offers of an outright free Internet Web page with email service are almost always frauds. These offers come with small, confusing print that just barely informs you that the third year or the sixth month of service is free, with the preceding time period billed, due, and payable in advance. (Some of the providers offering this "service" disappeared after a few months, according to people who were stung by them.) A very few are MLM scams.

Secrets Of AOL And Free Email

The "secrets of AOL," how to get "free" email service and Web pages, and related offers of supposedly valuable technical or secret information are available—at $20 to $30 a pop. Most of these are nothing more than photocopied sheets with far less information or an entirely different sort of information than promised—usually a list of things you already know or could find on the Web yourself.

College Money, Seized Property, And Finder's Fees

These offers purport to tell you how to get college grants, buy seized property from the government for pennies, or get finder's fees for finding products that buyers want. I lump these together because they all require you to pay for information that is freely available from various institutions or government organizations.

Cure-Alls

Cures for incurable diseases, miracle plant extracts, and information as odd as how to keep the skin on your feet from crusting up invade Internet users' email boxes daily. All products and procedures are "guaranteed," of course, which means nothing.

Free Software

Offering free computer software is an easy way to get most computer users' attention. This is often a complex scam, though. It pulls you through several levels of promises before you get to the payoff (that is, you paying off the purveyors of the "free" software). Sometimes, programs are sold to you, represented as Beta-test software, and sometimes you are sold information about getting on Beta-test lists (usually difficult to do). This offer is sometimes a front for "software clubs." (Such "clubs" require you to pay in advance for non-returnable products that are discontinued products two years out of date, or collections of shareware on disk or CD-ROM.)

Telephone Chat And Date Lines

Spammers sometimes plug 800- or 900-number sex-chat lines and dating services. These are the same come-ons you see advertised on late-night television. Sometimes, the spammers own the services they're advertising, and sometimes they are paid to send the spam around by the service owners.

Own Your Own 900-Number Service

This one is a strong lure, apparently a great way to make lots of money without working. The scam requires you to buy/rent/lease a 900-number, with or without recorded "content." Once you're committed to that, the scammers are usually done with you. It's up to you to advertise and promote your "service." This is usually a losing proposition, because of the competition from established services. (Besides, you're not offering anything that hundreds of other would-be millionaires aren't offering; everyone who buys into this scheme gets the same recordings.) The scammers may offer to advertise and promote your service for you—for an additional fee.

A variation on this is to have you "invest" in a 900-number service. The promised returns somehow never materialize.

Chain Letters

As described earlier in this chapter, chain letters are losing propositions—and illegal. Still, spammers regularly send letters instructing you to: "Send five dollars to the five people on this list, and put your name on the bottom; in three weeks you will have $350,000!" Right.

"Lifetime" Reminder Services

This one is a favorite of newbie and amateur spammers. The deal is this: Supposedly you get email to remind you of birthdays, anniversaries, and other important dates for the rest of your life. You pay a one-time, flat fee of less than $50 for this "service."

The problem with this is that the so-called service providers disappear quickly. I'm not certain whether this is an intentional scam, or just spammers losing interest when they don't get thousands of people signing up. Either way, if you buy into this, you're throwing money away. Besides, there are *free* reminder services on the Web; to check out one, visit **http://www.hallmarkreminder.com**.

Secret Moneymaking Systems For Computer Users

This gag offers a moneymaking system that consists of disks loaded with "secret information." When you buy the disks, you also buy a license to copy and resell the disks and system. The "secret moneymaking system" is nothing more than a set of instructions on how to spam with ads offering the "secret moneymaking system."

That one is rather circular, but there you are. I imagine that those selling this garbage had themselves bought it and were merely trying to recoup their investments.

900-Number Technical Information Calls

These 900-number services, spammed extensively in email, offer "little-known" or "secret" technical information, such as how to hack into AOL, how to get free Internet access and Web pages, and so on.

Ambushes

Thus far, spams for Web pages that ambush you have been rare. The only instances on record are those described in Chapter 6, where ads for free porno Web sites pulled in people who downloaded special software that routed their telephone calls through another country at extremely high rates. This is worth mentioning again because I suspect this won't be the last time it happens. So, in addition to all the other advice thus far, be suspicious of anything labeled "free."

The full list is a bit longer, but those are the main categories.

Free: Secrets Of The Internet Spammers!

I've already spent time and/or money to find out what some spammers have to offer. So you don't have to duplicate my efforts, here's a mini-expose of a few of the more interesting spam offers I've encountered.

One of my favorites was a much-vaunted "find out anything about anyone on the Internet" guide. The spam promised information that you could use to "look up anyone/find anyone/get dirt and revenge on anyone" using the Internet. So, I sent off $20 to have the thing delivered to my front door.

*I figured there was an even chance that it wouldn't show up. The guy who pulled this was really good at hiding his electronic origins— none of the message headers offered useful information, so we couldn't track him down directly. A search on his address, using Alta Vista (**http://www.altavista.digital.com/**), revealed that the address to which buyers were to send checks was a mail drop—a private mailbox rental service. This person would be a little difficult to identify. (He can be traced, though, using some techniques that are beyond the scope of this book.)*

*I wasn't expecting much, anyway—which was a good thing, because I got less than nothing. The exciting secret information package consisted of six photocopied pages, each with poorly categorized lists of URLs. A good many of the URLs were simply online databases, such as Internet Address Finder (**http://www.iaf.net**) and FOUR11.COM (**http://www.four11.com**). Many more were URLs for government agencies, to which you have to submit requests for* *information by postal mail. Still others were Web sites for private investigators and other businesses whose investigations are done offline and for a fee.*

I could generate a better list by spending an hour or two with various Internet search engines. (In fact, I have, for this book's Web site.) If people ordered this "Internet guide" expecting anything secret, exciting, or new, they were sorely disappointed.

The spammer offered a "money-back guarantee," but anyone who wrote the mail-drop address to demand a refund would be disappointed. The spammer closed up shop and moved the scam to a post office box in the same city a few months later.

This story has an interesting sequel: A second spammer started selling the same list, using pretty much the same hype, a couple of months after the first one hit the Web. I had to chuckle, wondering whether the first rip-off artist would be suing the second.

Another favorite was an offer that promised to tell AOL members how to get online any time of day or night, with no busy signal. I didn't order this one, but I can tell you how to do it, at no charge. Get an account with an ISP, log on, and fire up your AOL software. Go into AOL's Setup, switch the Network setting to TCP/IP Connection, and log on normally.

*Still another entry in the category of otherwise free or useless information is the free email-service spam. Getting free email service is simple: Sign up for Juno—**http://www.juno.com**—or one of the other advertiser-supported services. (Or you might go to work for an online service or ISP.)*

ORDER FROM A SPAMMER?

As you have probably realized by now, responding to a spammer's ad with an inquiry or order is probably a waste of time and money. You'll doubtlessly feel stupid, too, for being taken. Still, if you are tempted to respond to spam, apply the following questions, as appropriate:

- If the product is so good, why isn't it being sold in stores?

- If the moneymaking prospects are so good, why does the spammer have to sell it to me? A system this good should make him enough money that he doesn't have to sell.

- If I wanted the merchandise being offered, why would I order it from someone who has no track record, and no business location?

- How do you know the seller will be around to honor any guarantees?

A final word: If you respond to a make-money-fast ad, don't quit your day job.

Staying Off Spammers' Lists

Can you do anything to avoid email spam? Yes. Avoiding spammers' email address lists is easy—but unless you have a brand-new email account, you are probably already on one or more lists. The list brokers—and sometimes individual spammers—use a variety of tools and techniques to grab email addresses wherever they may appear online. If you do any of the following, you will end up on one or more lists:

- Post on an online service's or Internet bulletin board.

- Post in a USENET Newsgroup.

- Spend time in chat rooms on an online service.

- Have a listing in an online service's member directory.

That's not very encouraging, as nearly everyone participates in at least one of these activities. Members of most major online services are vulnerable to specialized software that rapidly compiles lists of user IDs. Various programs can search through membership directories, forum message bases and other bulletin boards, and chat rooms on America Online, CompuServe, DELPHI, Genie, and Prodigy and grab the IDs of anyone who uses these areas. The lists are then used to send spam email, and they are sold to still more spammers.

Once you get on a spammer's list, you are pretty much doomed to continue getting spammed. Many spammers mail the same scam offers repeatedly—I guess they figure you'll order if you get hit enough in the face with their pitch. Other spammers try different cons on the same list. Worse, once spammers finally realize that they're not going to get rich offering scams, cheap junk, or whatever else via email, they often turn into list brokers—that is, to recover the money they've spent on lists and making this Internet scheme work, they take another shot at becoming Internet millionaires by selling and reselling their email address lists. (It's worth noting here again that the list brokers and others selling to spammers are the only people who really make money by spamming.)

The simple solution is to use the tactics I showed you in earlier chapters to keep your information private. Specifically, don't post in public, stay out of chat rooms, and don't have a member-directory entry.

WHAT IF I WANT TO BE PUBLIC?

What if you want to post in Newsgroups and other public venues, or maintain a public profile on one of the online services? Is there no hope of keeping your email box relatively free of electronic junk mail?

You might, if you are a heavy email user, set up two accounts or IDs on the service(s) you use. Use one account for posting on public boards or visiting chat rooms. The email you receive here will be filled with spam; simply ignore or delete all messages. Use the other account for email only; the only people who have that email address will be those from whom you want to receive email.

If this isn't practical, the next move is to complain to the spammer's Internet service provider.

GETTING REMOVED FROM A SPAMMER'S LIST

Many spammers offer to remove you from their lists. All you have to do is send a message to a given address or include a specific word or phrase in the subject header or message body.

This sounds good, but it works less than half the time. The spammer may ignore the request, or the "remove" address may be nonexistent. More often than not, the offer is simply a way for the spammer to dodge angry responses. If you think you've been removed from the list, you won't bother to flame the spammer or complain to his or her ISP. Still, go ahead and send your remove request—but complain to the spammer's ISP, too.

A similar dodge that spammers use to avoid flames and complaints to the ISP is to put a statement at the beginning of a spam message stating that this is a one-time mailing and that you won't receive any more messages if you don't respond to this one. You should complain, however; otherwise, the spammer is free to spam again, often using the same list.

How Do I Complain, And To Whom?

Your first instinct upon receiving spam might be to send off a blistering reply. But the best response may be no response. All you will likely get back are more sales pitches from an *autoresponder*, a program that sends prepared messages to any address from which it receives email. You might also get nasty messages or threats from the spammer.

Don't be tempted to try dirty tricks, such as mailbombing or getting autoresponders to talk to one another, as a solution to your spammer problems. These actions can get you in trouble. Harassment is illegal, even if it is against someone who harassed you.

The strongest—and most effective—action you can take in most cases is complaining to the spammer's ISP. This tactic stops most spammers because, with few exceptions, ISP sysops don't like spam emanating from their systems any more than you like receiving it. (The exceptions are the few ISPs that actually encourage spammers.)

An ISP's reaction is usually swift, as most ISPs have set terms of service or rules that prohibit email or USENET spamming. Depending on the ISP's policies, a spammer might receive a warning or lose his or her account. This—along with hundreds or thousands of complaining messages—is often enough to discourage most spammers.

The typical spammer enters the Internet unaware of the strong feelings against spamming and will abate upon learning that not only is the Internet not a ripe market, but the recipients of spam are quite angry and proactive about it.

Your complaint to the ISP should consist of a forwarded copy of the spam message (including all headers) along with a brief note explaining that the attached spam appears to have come from that ISP and that you would like such mailings to stop. Don't flame or accuse; until someone like you tells them, the ISP managers are unaware of the spam.

The offending message and your complaint should be forwarded to the address "postmaster" at the spammer's ISP. Thus, if you receive a spam from bobbyspam@scumbag.net, you would address your complaint to postmaster@scumbag.net.

Larger ISPs and online services have special addresses for handling spam, among them AOL (abuse@aol.com), Netcom (abuse@netcom.com), and InterRamp (abuse@interramp.com). Visit the ISP's home page to see if it has a special address for spam complaints.

This address may not always get a response, however. If the spammer has his or her own domain name (as explained later), any mail to postmaster@scumbag.net will go directly to the spammer. Watch out for an unlikely address, such as stealmoney.com or cashtome.com—or an address that is obviously tied into the spammer's line, such as Moneyman@CashMale.com; the odds are that the domain name (.com or .net) is faked or will simply go right back to the spammer.

Because of this, be sure to check through all the headers to determine the source of the message, as explained in the next section.

Deciphering Message Headers

Spammers often fake their message headers—particularly the "From:" line. If they are running a scam that requires you to contact them by phone or fax, or send money to a post office box, they will fake as many of the headers as possible, including the "Reply To:" and other lines. This can get confusing, but if you take your time, you can determine the real source of most faked email messages.

Two major elements are involved in tracking down an ISP: the domain name and the IP address. The domain name identifies the provider. Examples are netcom.com, compuserve.com, aol.com, and iag.net (all of which are responsive to complaints about spam, by the way). The IP address is a series of four numbers separated by periods, like this: 222.22.222.2. It is a numeric version of the domain name. (Note that an ISP may have more than one IP address.)

Now, take a look at the following example:

```
Sende  r: freeca  sh@scumbags.com
Received: from nowaves.com (mail.nowaves.com [222.222.22.2]) by
hil-img-4.compuserve.com (8.6.10/5.950515) id BCC09029; Sat, 31
Aug 1996 02:16:33
       -0400
Received: from upstream (77-x.nowaves.com [222.222.23.23]) by
77x.nowaves.com
       (8.6.13/8.6.12) with SMTP id WAA29981; Sat, 31 Aug 1996
22:41:17 -0700
Message-Id: <199708310111.WAA29981@nowaves.com>
Comments: Authenticated sender is
From: "Your Friend"
Organization: Making You Rich
To: suckerlist@scumbags.com
Date: Sat, 31 Aug 1997 00:17:57 -600
MIME-Version: 1.0
Content-type: text/plain; charset=US-ASCII
Content-transfer-encoding: 7BIT
Subject: Extra Income For Everyone!!!
Reply-to: bigmoney@youfool.com
Priority: normal
X-mailer: Pegasus Mail for Win32 (v2.31)

Hello. Years of research indicate that you want to buy into
a dream and be ripped off. So:

Send money--cash only--to: P.O. Box 666666, Noway, OH 99999,
and I will send you instructions on how to send email
begging cash, how to fake your Ids, and more. Enough suckers
will reply that you will be rich, and can spend all your time
cruising the net!

P.S. If you don't want to get any more dippy messages like
this one, hit reply and type remove in the subject line.
```

At first glance, this might seem to be from freecash@scumbags.com. But wait— the "Reply-to:" field says bigmoney@youfool.com. To which of these unlikely addresses should you send your opinion of this message?

Neither; both are bogus addresses. You can check this by using the Web Interface to whois, located at **http://rs.internic.net/cgi-bin/whois**. The whois utility provides information about a domain name—the name, address, and telephone number of the company that owns it, names and email addresses of key management personnel, and domain names it uses, along with their IP addresses (those groups of four numbers separated by dots).

In our example, you would enter either "scumbags.com" or "youfool.com", and whois would have no information for these domain names—because they don't exist. Figure 7.2 shows a fictional lookup of scumbags.com.

(For a "live" example, enter your ISP's domain name. You will see all available information displayed.)

Okay, so the spammer has faked his "From:" and "Reply-to:" addresses. You can neither reply nor complain to his or her ISP—or can you? While you may not be able to send anything directly to the spammer, you can divine the name of the ISP.

How? Check the "Received from:" headers. Internet messages are relayed from one computer to another, and the "Received from:" headers provide a backward trail to

Figure 7.2   The Web interface to whois.

the spammer's host system. The first header tells us that this message was sent to an address at CompuServe (compuserve.com), and that CompuServe received it from a computer at nowaves.com.

The next header shows that nowaves.com passed the message on from another computer at nowaves.com. The trail ends on the next line, beginning with "Message-Id:". In this line is a unique series of numbers and letters, beginning with the date the message was sent (19970831) and ending with an alphanumeric message identifier and the source of the message: nowaves.com.

Note that spammers sometimes fake these headers, inserting the domain names or IP addresses of large, well-known ISPs or online services. This is to throw you off, in the hope that you will complain to one of those hosts. (Here, again, is a reason not to flame the ISP, which might also be a victim of spoofing. If you flame the ISP, the people there may be less willing to help you track down the real source.)

Even if the spammer managed to fake the "Received from:" headers, he or she probably did not fake the message ID number. Just in case, though, get the numeric IP address for nowaves.com (it follows the message ID number in our example). You can do this with another utility—IP Address to Host Name and Vice Versa—at **http://cello.cs.uiuc.edu/cgi-bin/slamm/ip2name**.

When you enter the domain name, this utility will give you the four-number IP address. Ideally, it will match the IP numbers in the "Received from:" headers. If not, that's okay; the spammer has faked those numbers, but you got a good name. You can take the name back to the Web Interface to whois and get the name of a contact person to whom you can send a copy of the spam and your complaint.

You can also compare the numeric IP address with other IP addressees in the "Received from:" headers. If you find a match, this ISP is likely the source of the spam.

On the other hand, you might not have to do any of that. If you're lucky, you will see a line like the next one in our example:

```
Comments: Authenticated sender is [spamfool@nowaves.com]
```

or:

```
X-sender: spamfool@nowaves.com
```

The chances are good that the sender named in either of these lines—spamfool@nowaves.com—is the source of your message. Most mailers will go ahead and insert one or the other of these lines, even if the sender is faking most of the rest of the headers.

Sometimes, however, these lines are missing, stripped, or blank; or they might include the IP's numeric address rather than its name. You can get the domain name by typing in the IP address at the IP Address to Host Name interface. At this point, you'll want to forward the message to the ISP's contact, as listed in the whois interface, or the system postmaster.

On rare occasions, you will receive a message in which all the headers seem to be faked. With persistence, though, you can track down the source. Run every IP address and domain name through the whois and IP Address to Host Name interfaces, and see if two of them match. If you seem to have a source, but aren't sure—forward the message to the ISP's postmaster or contact with a query as to whether the message came from their system.

You can also take unidentified domain names you find in the headers to a more elegant version of the whois interface: a Gopher search of the InterNIC database at **href="gopher://rs.internic.net/7waissrc%3A/rs/whois.src**. Using this search, I have backtracked bogus domain names to their source on several occasions. (In each instance, the spammer had purchased the domain names from an ISP, and the spammer controlled the names completely. The whois database, however, showed who hosted those domain names—and that's where I directed my complaints.)

Just to be sure, though, you might run the earliest numeric IP address in the headers through a Traceroute gateway, such as the Internet Tools Gateway at **http://www.magibox.net/~unabest/finger/index.html**.

Tale Of A (Would-Be) Master Spammer

One of the most entertaining spammers to come down the information pike in a long time was a fellow I'll call Trevor. If grades were being handed out for spamming, he would have gotten an E for effort—but an F for execution.

Trevor's spam was simple: He offered a way to spam without being mailbombed—guaranteed. He was so confident of his techniques that he invited recipients to mailbomb him.

He shouldn't have done that. He was blown off the Internet.

*He was easy to look up. In less than 10 minutes, I found two email addresses for him, plus his home address and telephone number. I sent him a terse note: "You got it all wrong! Try again—but leave me off the list." But I wasn't the only one. Word of Trevor's challenge spread quickly, especially among folks who frequented the anti-spam Newsgroup, **news.admin.net-abuse**. Thousands obliged Trevor by mailbombing him, and everyone thought he was gone for good.*

Surprisingly, Trevor returned two months later. Apparently, he had spent the hiatus perfecting his technique. From the supposed security of a new ISP, he once again roared forth to challenge the Internet with his "bulletproof" spamming techniques.

Once again, he was greeted with thousands of angry email messages. That was in mid-1996. No one has heard from Trevor since.

Going Over Their Heads

When a spammer has his or her own domain, as mentioned earlier, you are not going to get results by complaining to the postmaster there. A quick check of the whois information for a domain will often tell you if a spammer owns the domain, as will a visit to the URL in question. If it doesn't look like a legitimate ISP, or if the name of the ISP's administrative contact in the whois information is the spammer's name, odds are it's the spammer's domain.

In this case, as well as in cases where a "rogue ISP" (one who permits spamming) is involved, you need to go over their heads and complain to the company that provides the spammer or rogue ISP with service. To find out who that is, run the ISP's name through the Traceroute interface and see what services or domains are listed before the ISP in question. As shown in Figure 7.3, the service providers, and *their* providers, are listed in reverse order.

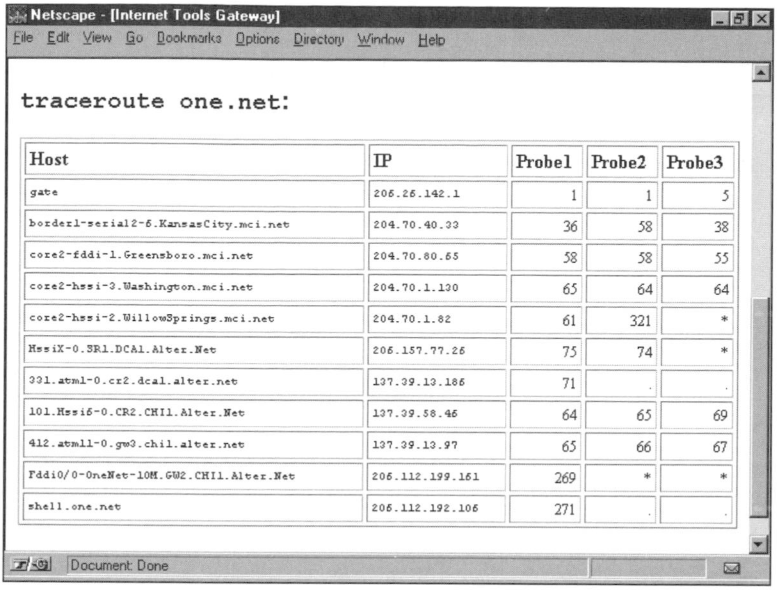

Host	IP	Probe1	Probe2	Probe3
gate	206.26.142.1	1	1	5
border1-serial2-6.KansasCity.mci.net	204.70.40.33	36	58	38
core2-fddi-1.Greensboro.mci.net	204.70.80.65	58	58	55
core2-hssi-3.Washington.mci.net	204.70.1.130	65	64	64
core2-hssi-2.WillowSprings.mci.net	204.70.1.82	61	321	*
HssiX-0.SR1.DCA1.Alter.Net	206.157.77.26	75	74	*
331.atm1-0.cr2.dca1.alter.net	137.39.13.186	71	.	.
101.Hssi6-0.CR2.CHI1.Alter.Net	137.39.58.46	64	65	69
412.atm11-0.gw3.chi1.alter.net	137.39.13.97	65	66	67
Fddi0/0-OneNet-10M.GW2.CHI1.Alter.Net	206.112.199.161	269	*	*
shell.one.net	206.112.192.106	271	.	.

Figure 7.3 Traceroute shows the path of service providers that a message from a specific ISP takes.

Take the names of the two service providers preceding the troublesome ISP and run them through the whois interface to get the name and address to which you should send your complaints.

Other Aids To Stopping Spam

Here are some other ways to slow down or stop spam.

Complain To The Spammer's Customers

You can complain not only to the spammer and the spammer's ISP, but also to the spammer's "clients." If a spammer is sending out classified ads in the form of a "free newsletter," complain to the people who paid for the ads—at least, those who include email addresses with their ads.

Many such advertisers don't know that the newsletter is being bulk-mailed to a random list. Spammers running this game often tell their clients that they are mailing to a list of "subscribers" (almost nobody asks to be on such a list) or to a "targeted" group (the email lists are almost always random). If you complain to each advertiser who has an email address, you'll find a surprising number of them are as unhappy as you are. This, of course, knocks out the support for the spammer.

Be careful, though; spammers sometimes load up a collection of classified ads with their own ads and sprinkle in a few copied and fake ads. Almost no email addresses but the spammer's will be legit, and complaining to the spammer, of course, gets you nowhere. So watch out for ad collections with an inordinate number of ads with email addresses that go to the same domain.

Use An Email Filter

If your ISP or online service offers an email filter (as AOL does) or email filtering software, use it to block domains or specific addresses sending spam.

More technically oriented email users can use programs or add-ons to filter out email and USENET messages based on the sender's name, ISP, or the subject line. With these tools, you can avoid most spam.

One such tool, available for those who have access to procmail, can be found at Paul Milligan's Web site (**http://www.mindspring.com/~pjm/myproc.html**). He has a ready-to-use script that you can plug into your email system on your ISP. He also provides a fun trick that those who have Web pages can use to frustrate *spambots* (programs that crawl around the Web, copying email addresses from Web sites). That delightful item is at **http://www.mindspring.com/~pjm/webtrick.html**.

These tend to be beyond the scope of many Internet users' activities, but those interested can get more information at The Filtering Mail FAQ, located at **http://www.jazzie.com/ii/faqs/archive/mail/filtering-faq/**.

Complain To Your ISP

Given enough user complaints, ISPs might begin to block the worst sites. Complain to your own ISP every time you get repeated spam from a specific site and request that mail from the site be blocked. You can also request that your ISP develop and implement software that lets its customers block by ID, domain, or subject.

True Names And Other High-Pressure Tactics

I once got on a really inept spammer's mailing list. He sent me not one, but two email messages every day for more than a week, exhorting me to mail his autoresponder for information on something he wanted desperately to sell me. The mailings would not stop, no matter how or how many times I asked. (I suspect that he wasn't getting any buyers and figured that people would finally buy just to get rid of him.)

The mailings promised to continue relentlessly, and I couldn't track down the ISP from which he was sending the spam in order to complain. Using Internet "people finder" resources, however, I was able to determine his identity, one valid email address—and a lot more. To that email address I sent three words, "Stop mailing me," followed by his real name, address, work and home telephone numbers, and his parents' name and address. No threats—just those three words followed by his personal information. I immediately received an angry reply stating that I had been removed from his list. I haven't heard from him in the three years since.

I do not suggest that you pull this on every spammer; you might find yourself mailbombed by some. But it is interesting how this spammer sat up and took notice once his identity was compromised.

Keeping Your Email Address Out Of Public Postings

While you cannot change your ID in most online service and Web-site BBSes, you can exclude your ID from USENET postings by using a phony email address in your headers when posting. Certain email systems provided by ISPs allow you to change the email address that is inserted into message headers. Thus, you can change your name/email address to something like "nospam@here.com."

Other email programs also allow you to do this, as do Web browsers. The methods vary, depending on the email program or browser you're using. I will show here how to change your ID with Netscape and Microsoft Internet Explorer:

- *Netscape*—Select Mail and News Preferences...on the Options menu. Then press the Identity tab. Delete your name from the Your Name field. In the fields labeled Your Email and Reply-to Address, enter a bogus address.

- *Microsoft Internet Explorer*—Open Internet Mail by selecting Read Mail on the Go menu. Then select Options...on Internet Mail's Mail menu. Press the tab labeled Server and delete your name from the Name: field. Then enter a bogus address in the Email Address: field.

Your real email address will not be included in the headers of your USENET postings. (Write down the information you delete or alter in your browser or email program's setup; you will have to replace it before you can send or receive email.)

If you want people who read your postings to have your email address, you can place it in the posting itself—but not in clear form, because the programs that pull email addresses from USENET Newsgroups get them from postings as well as headers. Write it in this format, and spammers' programs won't grab your address: "yourname AT server.com." Thus, if your email address was bitsko@realweb.net, you would write it as "bitsko AT realweb.net." Humans can parse the information; address-gathering programs cannot.

Another approach is to use an anonymous remailer, as discussed in Chapter 11.

Keeping Your Postings Out Of Deja News USENET Archives

Remember: To keep your USENET postings out of Deja News and other archives, add this line to your headers, or as the very first line in your postings: x-no-archive: yes.

Get Your Email Address Out Of The Public Eye

Ideally, you have already removed your finger listing, if you have one, and deleted or omitted posting an online profile. This, along with hiding your address in public postings, or using an address dedicated to public postings, cuts down your exposure considerably. One big area remains, however, that you need to cover: Web email directories.

These are services that both solicit Internet users to add themselves to their directories and quietly compile even more additions from various legal sources. Fortunately, you have the option of requesting that your name and email address be removed from such directories (along with your telephone number and address, where relevant). Here's a list of the major online directories, with URLs:

- American Directory Assistance—People Search **http://www.lookupusa.com/ lookupusa/adp/peopsrch.htm**

- Bigfoot—**http://bigfoot.com**

- ESP Mail Search Program (U.K.)—**http://www.esp.co.uk**

- FOUR11.COM—**http://www.four11.com**

- Internet Address Finder—**http://www.iaf.net**

- Netfind—**http://www.nova.edu/Inter-Links/netfind.html**

- People Finder—**http://www.peoplesite.com/indexnf.html**

- Switchboard—**http://www.switchboard.com**

- SearchAmerica, Inc—**http://www.searchamerica.com**

- WED World Email Directory—**http://www.worldemail.com**

- Who's Who Online—**http://www.whoswho-online.com/**

- WhoWhere? Email Addresses—**http://www.whowhere.com**

- Yahoo People Search (U.S. White Pages)—**http://www.yahoo.com/ search/people/**

What else can you do? Well, you doubtless know better than to encourage spammers by asking for more information or buying into a scam. Beyond that, tell your friends and associates about the techniques described here.

Spammers' Last Stand: Chat Rooms

One other area where spammers may hit you—and over which you don't have a lot of control—are online-service and IRC chat rooms. While some online services do a fair job of policing chat rooms, they can't be everywhere at once. The same is true of moderated IRC channels; the op can't be everywhere at once. So, spammers often barge into chat rooms and broadcast their insipid messages to everyone present, or they use a whisper command to send private spam messages to participants. Either way, it ruins the chat.

When this happens, use the command required to block private sends as well as public lines in the chat room. Also make a note of the user ID of the person sending the spam, so you can report him or her to the online service management or IRC op. Ideally, the spammer will be blocked from doing this again. (Use the who command to get the miscreant's email address.)

The other spam-related problem in chat rooms is, of course, the visibility of your email address. Spammers can use their address-gathering programs to get your address from chat rooms in addition to other venues. The only solution to this problem, aside from staying out of chat rooms, is to dedicate one ID to chat rooms (or to chat rooms and public postings, if necessary). Using this ID, you can either block all email or ignore mail sent to it.

SPAMMING AND THE LAW

At present, spamming *per se* isn't illegal, although it seems to violate the U.S. "junk fax law." In fact, several recipients of spam have vowed to pursue having violators charged, under the theory that wording in the law applies to email. Civil lawsuits, involving spammers who cause a "denial of service" by preventing other email from arriving in a timely manner, are in the works, as well.

AOL, CompuServe, Prodigy, and others have won court battles against some of the more obnoxious spammers, gaining injunctions against spammers who fake their systems as the source of spam and getting legal permission to block certain spammers' incoming junk email.

Many spammers try to hide behind "freedom of speech" in defending their money-grubbing activities. But they actually operate *against* freedom of speech: Spammers force us to hear them—at their convenience and as frequently as they wish—at our loss. Freedom of speech has nothing to do with those issues. Nor does freedom of speech grant or even lightly infer a right to disrupt conversations.

Eventually, we will have a law against this—and hopefully one with teeth. Until then, the cheap cons who convince spammers that angering people is the way to make a fortune will continue to bring new spammers online. They're out to get your money, folks, and they won't take "no" for an answer. They'll continue their mindless bombardments of email boxes, Newsgroups, and chat rooms with their demands until they are forced to stop.

Let's hope it's soon.

FOR MORE INFORMATION

The following sites and documents provide more useful information about online cons and spam:

- Frequently Asked Questions About Spam—**http://www.vix.com/spam/faq.html**

- The Net Abuse FAQ, maintained by J.D. Falk—**http://www.cybernothing.org/faqs/net-abuse-faq.html**

- The BIZ Newsgroup FAQ—**ftp://ftp.xenitec.on.ca/pub/news/faqs/biz.faq**

- USENET Newsgroup on Net abuse and spam—**news.admin.net-abuse.announce**

- Mark Eckenwiler on applying the U.S. junk fax law to spam—**http://www.panix.com/~eck/junkmail.html**

- Blacklist of Internet Advertisers—**http://math-www.uni-paderborn.de/~axel/BL/**

- List of domains blocked by AOL due to spam—**http://www.idot.aol.com/preferredmail/**

- Dan Gillmor on Spam as Extortion—**http://www.sjmercury.com/business/gillmor/dg072196.htm**

- Howard Rheingold: The Tragedy of the Electronic Commons (The story of some of the earliest large-scale spammers to hit the Internet—and they hit it hard)—**http://www.well.com/user/hlr/tomorrow/tomorrowcommons.html**

- Advertising on USENET: How To Do It, How Not To Do It—**http://www.cs.ruu.nl/wais/html/na-dir/usenet/advertising/how-to/part1.html**

- Internet Spam Boycott—**http://www.vix.com/spam/**

- Fight Unsolicited E-Mail and Mailing List Vendors! (a nice collection of links to anti-spam Web pages)—**http://knet.flemingc.on.ca/~surly/junkmail.html**

Anti-Spam Software

Finally, if you want to take a more proactive stand against spam, you may want to look at some free anti-spam software for windows called *Spam Hater*. I have not tested this, but it claims to help locate the source of spam and provides you with several editable responses to spam. For more information, visit **http://www.hitchhikers.net/hotsoftware.shtml#Spammers**. (In addition to working with Netscape, Internet Explorer, and all the most popular email programs, it also works with AOL software.)

The Invincible Spammer

As I was completing this chapter, a rather interesting piece of mail showed up in one of my email boxes. The mailer, sending from a rogue ISP, opened with a hearty, "HA HA HA HA" and went on to advise me that I was on a "...published list of people who hate commercial mail...." After a bit of name-calling, this master netrepreneur went on to say that he intended to "publish the list everywhere" to stop complaints about spam. He wrapped up by gloating that his current ISP would let him send whatever he wanted to send.

The next day I received two spams supposedly "signed" by two well-known anti-spam proponents. The headers revealed the spam to be from the same guy as the previous day's threats. These were sent to the same list of recipients as his previous message.

This was followed a week later by six duplicate messages, with headers faked to make the messages appear to come from a certain ISP. A rambling, rather cryptic message went on about how a spammer on the system could not be controlled (at least, that seemed to be the point; the message was all but incoherent). This message, too, appeared to be from the threatening, but now "invulnerable" spammer.

I will be curious to see what this person broadcasts next. I assume that, at some point, he will get around to sending fake spams from everyone on his "published list of spam haters." I fully expect the email address to which the above harassment was delivered to be mailbombed. I've been mailbombed before, and I can't protect against that at this particular ISP. But I suspect that, if this spammer does scale up to mailbombing or other, more intense harassment, some of those on his list will become more proactive than the spammer ever thought possible.

This example gives you some idea of what sort of people spammers are—not to mention their level of "success." In any event, this spammer blames his failure on people who don't like spam. This makes him another spammer who just doesn't get it: Forcing solicitations into people's email boxes does not force them to buy. In most instances, it sets them against ever buying anything that the spammer has anything to do with.

Let's turn our attention now to tracking down those who might be harassing you for whatever reason. Whether your problem is a frustrated spammer or an online stalker, Internet resources can be used to defend yourself by learning about your adversary. You can learn all about those resources in Chapter 8.

Chapter 8

People Information Resources On The Internet

Chapter 8

People Information Resources On The Internet

Chapter 8

At times you may want to identify, locate, or otherwise track down someone on the Internet. Why? Self-defense. As many others have discovered, harassing email and other bothersome online activities often stop once you let the people behind it know that you have their real-world identity. With useful information, such as alternate email addresses, real names, and home addresses, you have all sorts of defensive and proactive options.

Often, when you set out to find someone, all you have is an email address, or maybe a name. No matter how little you start with, you can learn quite a bit about someone if you are patient and use the right tools and techniques.

This chapter covers those tools and techniques. You can use them to track down almost anyone (but not everyone) online. This isn't limited to tracing online connections. I'll also show you how to search out certain information—such as a person's general location, home address, telephone number, and more—given the appropriate data.

I'm not talking about finding credit histories, auto registrations, criminal records, and the like—none of those are available on the Internet. (Such information *is* available, but you have to pay for it. For those who are really serious about searching for information, I've included some sources for comprehensive background information and investigations at the end of this chapter.)

The tools we'll focus on here are online directories, archives, and databases— although you may not think of some of them as such. The majority of these resources are free, but a few charge a fee. As for the techniques, some involve interpolation, inference, or intuition. Others are more straightforward. I'll cover those techniques throughout the chapter.

People Information Online: An Overview

People may not realize how much information about them is available online. As you may recall from this book's introduction, I was able to accumulate a surprising amount of information about an editor with a half-hour's online research. This was a man who rarely used his email account and had no other online connections, so you can imagine how much information is available about someone who is really active online—like me, for instance (see Chapter 2 for a catalog of what you can learn about me online).

You can even find information about people who have never been online. One of my brothers, for example, has never been online and doesn't even own a computer. But, though he is rigorous about keeping his life private, I found one of his addresses and his telephone number online, along with the municipality where he had most recently worked. I knew all of this, of course. The point is, that sort of information is available to *anyone*.

I once met a woman online who claimed to be divorced and a successful self-employed professional. Some of what she told me didn't quite ring true, however. We had exchanged mailing addresses, so I ran hers through an online database. I learned that she was apparently married—at least living with a man who had the same last name. One of two phone numbers at her address was in his name (a second number was in her name). Curious, I searched elsewhere and learned that she lived not in a luxury condo as she had said, but in a trailer park. (Perhaps worse, she later told me that she was not divorced, but living with her husband, she said, because she could not afford a divorce.)

All of this information came from online sources that anyone can access. I didn't use any credit bureau or law-enforcement databases (I don't have such access). Nor did I get into any institutional or organizational resources. Everything came from several free sources on the Internet, AOL's member directory, and two surcharged services on CompuServe.

What Does It Cost?

What's more, the information came cheap. I ran these searches back when per-minute billing was alive and well. Yet the grand total for gathering information on the editor, my brother, and the woman with the confusing background came to just $9.25. With flat-rate pricing for unlimited use of the Internet, I would have paid only $3.25. (That charge was for records retrieved from two specialized databases.)

Most of the time, you won't have to pay to learn someone's real name, some alternate email addresses, or even a home address, phone number, and other personal information.

Where Do I Find It?

Where do you find this information? You already know a few of the sources, which I told you about in Chapter 4—places where you should avoid posting personal information, or remove if it is already there. These include online-service member directories and profiles, home-page directories, ISP finger listings, ph and other directories available at .edu domains, Web-page guest books, classified ads, and public postings.

That's only the beginning. Several Internet email directories are online, as well as online "white pages" with addresses and telephone numbers. Internet "yellow pages" let you search for information on businesses. Complementing these are general and specialized Internet search engines and other, more specialized resources.

By category, the major online sources of information about people are:

- ISP and online service member directories, personal profiles, and home-page directories.

- ISP finger listings, and ph and other directory listings at .edu domains.

- ISP information tools.

- Web-site guest books and classified ads.

- Public postings, in USENET Newsgroups and online-service or Web-site BBSes.

- Internet email directories.

- Online white pages and business directories.

- Internet search engines.

- Specialized search engines.

- Surcharged databases.

- Commercial tracing services.

WHY IS ALL THIS INFORMATION AVAILABLE?

That's quite a list, and everything on it is available to you. Most information is free or minimal cost. Why is it there at little or no cost? For several reasons:

- First, and perhaps foremost, the Internet and online services are all about information—sharing, finding, collating, and creating it.

- Second, once information is on the Internet, it is easy to copy and spread around. It's also difficult to remove; a given bit of information ends up being spread around so much that finding all instances of it is usually impossible. (This sometimes leads to old or erroneous information from Internet sources.)

- Finally, almost everyone tends to try out everything when they first get online. New and enthusiastic online-service and Internet users tend to post online profiles, gab about all sorts of personal matters in public postings, sign Web-site guest books, post classified ads, and so on. All this takes place before the users realize that almost everything they have ever posted is up for grabs.

Cumulatively, the typical Internet user makes a lot of personal information available. This information ends up being archived and shared in the most unlikely ways. Various services archive public postings, for example, and the online email directories compile their listings from a surprisingly wide variety of sources—including public postings, guest books, classified ads, and many others. (Listings are also voluntarily supplied.) Spreading information is the nature of the Internet.

Yet another reason for the wealth of personal information online—at least where Web sites that offer email, phone, and address directories are concerned—is more pragmatic. Some vendors with mailing lists, CD-ROMs full of phone and demographic data, and related products use Web sites to demonstrate and market their products. Still others sell services related to email (such as lifetime email addresses) and accept advertising.

These vendors obtain the information from a variety of sources. One major source is the content of white pages sold in electronic format by telephone companies around the country. Lists compiled by marketing companies is another. Other major sources include companies that compile local "city directories," subscription lists, and membership organizations' lists.

You can likely find information out there about almost anyone you need to track down. Whether they volunteered the information themselves, or it was taken and shared without their knowledge, is immaterial. What's important is that you can find it.

Member Directories And Profiles

ISP or online-service directories are the first places to look for information about a person, if you have his or her email address. The first part of the address (before the "@") gives you the user ID, and the second part (after the "@") tells you where to look. Thus, if you need information on someone who has sent you harassing email with the return address mbitsko@jerks.net, your target is probably someone who is a customer of jerks.net and uses the ID mbitsko.

Don't Jump The Gun

While a bothersome email message or posting may appear to be from a specific email address, don't count on it. Anyone who wants to can change the return email address that shows up in the From line of an email message or USENET posting. (This can't *always* be done with mail from an online service, however, unless the sender knows a couple of tricks.) All that's required is to change a couple of settings in a browser or email program.

Given this, you can't automatically assume that a message came from where it appears to have come. To be sure, take a stroll through the message headers and isolate the ultimate source of the message—that is, the ISP or online service where it originated. For information on how to determine a message's originating ISP, see the section headed "Deciphering Message Headers" in Chapter 7. If the originating ISP matches the ISP in the From address, the message probably came from the email address in question. This at least gives you a place to send a complaint—the ISP's postmaster. (Remember to be polite; the postmaster isn't the one harassing you.)

Once you identify a message as coming from a specific user ID, you can do some basic lookups on the email address. If the address is at an ISP, you might begin by visiting the ISP's home page. There, look for a user directory and/or a home-page directory. Some ISPs offer one or the other, some offer both, and some neither.

If the sender uses an online service, you will have to log on to that service to look for a member directory entry or a profile. (Membership directories usually contain a name, user ID, and maybe the city and state where the person lives. Online profiles contain as much information as the user wants to include; they are searchable by content.) If you don't have an account with the service, perhaps a friend or colleague does.

HOME-PAGE DIRECTORIES

You do not have to log on to the online service in question to check home-page directory entries, though. AOL, CompuServe, and other online services offer directories of members' Web pages. These are usually easy to find from a service's home page. Here is a list of URLs for Web-page directories hosted by several major online services:

- AOL—**http://home.aol.com/index.html**

- CompuServe—**http://ourworld.compuserve.com**

- DELPHI—**http://people.delphi.com/**

- Prodigy—**http://pages.prodigy.com**

(You might try appending a user ID from one of the previous online services as a shortcut to that user's home page. For example, to see whether CompuServe user "spamhead" has a home page, enter **http://ourworld.compuserve.com/spamhead**.)

You can also look up home pages on the Web in general using the Ahoy (a front end for MetaCrawler, WhoWhere?, and other search engines). Ahoy's URL is **http://ahoy.cs.washington.edu:6060/**.

Customer Confidentiality

You may feel that the best way to identify people who are harassing or threatening you is to ask the Webmaster or administrator of their ISP. However, you will find that few, if any, ISP or online service staffers are willing to give you the names or other information about any of their customers. Doing so might lay the service and the staffer open to a possible lawsuit or criminal charge.

Customer confidentiality is a trust placed with ISPs and online services, much as is the case with telephone companies. So, no matter what the malefactor's deed, his or her name is not likely to be released to anyone except law enforcement or other authorities.

Finger, Ph, And Other Directory Listings

If the sender's email comes from a standard ISP, you will, of course, want to use finger to check for information on the offending party. (Finger will not work with online services.) If your ISP is Unix-based, or you use an email program or browser that handles finger requests (such as Eudora or Netcom), you can finger the user that way. But using a Web finger interface is usually simpler. Several are listed here:

- **http://www.magibox.net/~unabest/finger/index.html**

- **http://httptest.bsdi.com/finger/gateway**

- **http://www.mit.edu:8001/finger?**

- **http://cs.indiana.edu/finger/gateway**

- **http://www.public.iastate.edu/cgi-bin/finger?**

If the ISP has its finger program enabled, and if the user hasn't removed his or her information, you will see something like the listing shown in Figure 8.1.

An interesting note on finger: In addition to other information, it may show you if a user is currently logged on.

If you want to identify someone who has sent email to you from a college or university's Web site, you can use finger (often disabled) in favor of the system directory, or the system's ph server. (*Ph,* which is short for phonebook, serves as the main faculty, staff, and student directory at most schools.) Usually, all you have to do is enter a first or last name or a user ID. The ph server displays information on the individual(s) who match the name or ID you enter. The type or quantity of information varies, but it will at the very least consist of a first and last name.

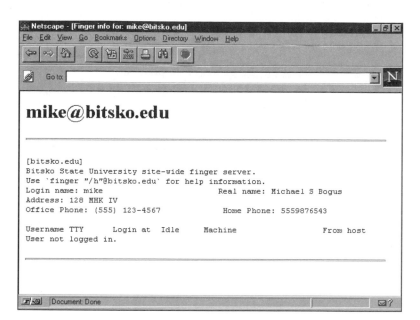

Figure 8.1   A finger listing provides information about a user on a specific system.

While there are several Web interfaces to ph servers, each is able to search the ph entries of dozens of schools; the easier route is usually just to visit the institution's Web site and access ph listings there.

Reverse Lookups With Ph And Finger

In the right circumstances, you can use ph or finger to find an email address and other information using only a person's name. Many college and university Web sites include not only faculty and students, but also general staff and alumni in their ph servers or other directories and databases. If, for example, you're seeking information on an old college boyfriend and you know only his name, you can probably learn his email address by entering his last name as a search keyword in such a database.

Similarly, some finger programs at ISPs are set up to search by a character string, such as a name, as well as by a user ID. You can enter a first or last name with the finger command, instead of a user ID. The system then shows finger information—including user IDs—on everyone with that name. Enter "Mike," and you would see information on Mike Adams,

Mike Jones, Mike Smith, and so forth. Enter "Smith," and you would see information on Bill Smith, Ginny Smith, Mike Smith, and everyone else with the last name Smith. (Systems set up like this are in the minority, but it is worth a try.)

ISP Information Tools (Whois And More)

Knowing who is responsible for the administration and technical operation of an ISP, or who supplies service to an ISP, is sometimes useful. You can find this information using two utilities with Web interfaces: whois and traceroute. If you have only a site's numeric IP address, you can use yet another utility to translate it to the name of the ISP that uses it: IP to Hostname.

WHOIS

Whois shows the name and address of the company operating the ISP in question, along with the names of administrative and technical contacts and their email addresses. Other information may or may not be shown. Figure 8.2 is a sample whois listing.

Whois interfaces are available at these URLs:

- **http://rs.internic.net/cgi-bin/whois**

- **http://www.magibox.net/~unabest/finger/index.html**

- **http://www.hgp.med.umich.edu/cgi-bin/whois**

- **gopher://rs.internic.net/7waissrc%3A/rs/whois.src**

Whois is particularly useful when you are dealing with a "rogue site" that sponsors spammers or harassment, or when the sender of bothersome email has his or her own domain. Complaining one step up can often resolve the conflict.

*The gopher site, **gopher://rs.internic.net/7waissrc%3A/rs/whois.src**, can be used to do a sort of "reverse lookup." You can enter an individual's name; if that person is associated with a domain, the information will be*

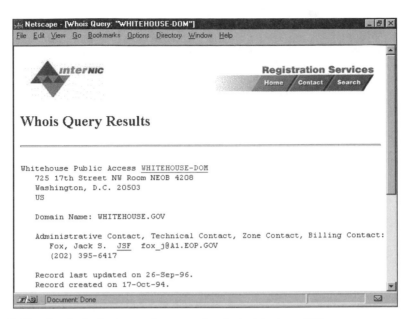

Figure 8.2 A whois listing tells you who is behind an ISP.

displayed. You may have to browse several listings, though; it's the nature of the search tool.

Finding Out Where They're Located

Whois is often a good way to find out the city or general region where someone who sent you email is located. This works only if the sender uses a regional or local ISP. Users of CompuServe, Netcom, AOL, Microsoft Network, or another online service or national ISP could be dialing in from anywhere.

You can also use Stephen Lamm's Host Name to Longitude/Latitude (**http://cello.cs.uiuc.edu/cgi-bin/slamm/ip2ll**) to see an ISP's latitude and longitude. The utility interfaces to a couple of map servers, so you can see the location on a map, if you wish.

TRACEROUTE

Traceroute reveals the path data takes from its originating site, in reverse order through its service providers and to the Web "backbone," from which it is routed to you. ISPs have service providers, too. They are links to carriers, such as Sprint, MCI, and UU.NET, which are the major carriers of Internet traffic. They are, in effect, ISPs for other ISPs, in addition to providing Internet access for thousands of individual customers. Below these major carriers are still other ISPs that provide service for individual customers and still more ISPs, and on down the line. Some ISPs or private domains have two or three levels of providers above them.

That's a simplified picture of a complex arrangement. Traceroute is an Internet utility that can sort out who provides service to whom. Traceroute is simple to use: Enter an ISP name or a site's numeric IP address (such as 222.28.43.12), and you'll see a list of ISPs through which traffic from the original ISP is routed, as shown in Figure 8.3.

The ISPs above the one you enter are the ultimate service providers for the address you entered. In our example, mail from One Net goes through Alter Net (UU.NET) on its way to the MCI Internet backbone. Alter Net is One Net's service provider. Traceroute gateways can be found at:

- **http://www.magibox.net/~unabest/finger/index.html**

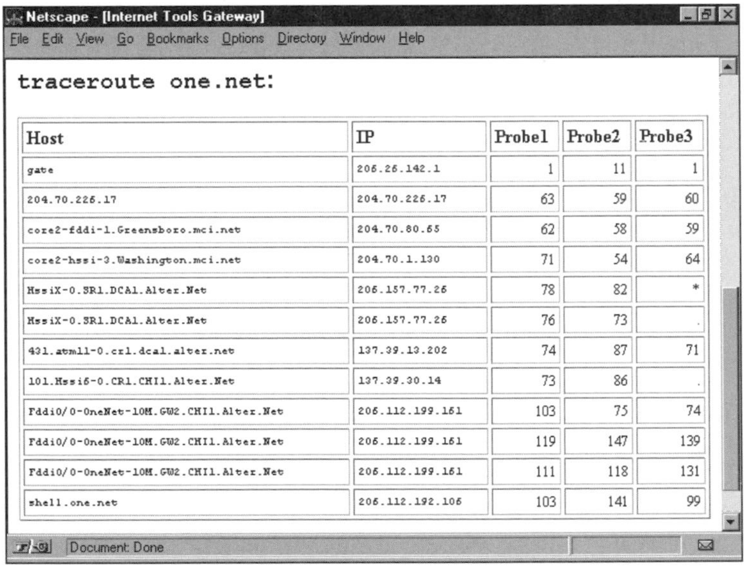

Netscape - [Internet Tools Gateway]
File Edit View Go Bookmarks Options Directory Window Help

traceroute one.net:

Host	IP	Probe1	Probe2	Probe3
gate	205.26.142.1	1	11	1
204.70.225.17	204.70.225.17	63	59	60
core2-fddi-1.Greensboro.mci.net	204.70.80.65	62	58	59
core2-hssi-3.Washington.mci.net	204.70.1.130	71	54	64
HssiX-0.SR1.DCA1.Alter.Net	205.157.77.25	78	82	*
HssiX-0.SR1.DCA1.Alter.Net	205.157.77.25	76	73	
431.atml1-0.crl.dcal.alter.net	137.39.13.202	74	87	71
101.Hssi6-0.CR1.CHI1.Alter.Net	137.39.30.14	73	86	
Fddi0/0-OneNet-10M.GW2.CHI1.Alter.Net	205.112.199.161	103	75	74
Fddi0/0-OneNet-10M.GW2.CHI1.Alter.Net	205.112.199.161	119	147	139
Fddi0/0-OneNet-10M.GW2.CHI1.Alter.Net	205.112.199.161	111	118	131
shell.one.net	205.112.192.105	103	141	99

Document: Done

Figure 8.3   Traceroute shows the path taken by email.

- http://www.llv.com/~lasvegas/traceroute.cgi

- http://www.medicine.wisc.edu/cgi-bin/traceroute

Rogue Sites And Private Domains

You may need to know who provides service to an ISP in the following two circumstances:

- The first involves what is known as a *rogue site*, a term usually applied to ISPs that allow spammers to harass Internet users freely with mindless messages.

- The second is when someone has his or her own domain (such as myplace.com).

In either case, you can't appeal to the postmaster of the site from which you are receiving, say, dozens of unsolicited email messages every day. The postmaster either doesn't care or is the one causing the problem.

One recourse is to complain to the problem site's service provider. First, you have to establish just who is providing service to the site giving you a problem. Traceroute is one way to find out. Be careful when you are reading the traceroute report, though; sometimes, the next two levels above a site are the same operation. If the name of the next site above the problem site is similar, or traceroute shows only a numeric IP address, look one or two sites higher. To confirm everything, ask someone at the higher site to make sure that it is the site supplying service to the problem site.

NSLOOKUP

If you need to know an ISP's numeric address or who provides service to the ISP's site, a utility called nslookup (short for name-server lookup) can provide that information, and often more. Here are two Web front ends for nslookup:

- http://ldhp715.immt.pwr.wroc.pl/util/nslookup.html

- http://www.uia.ac.be/ds/nslookup.html

Full Disclosure

A final hint regarding ISP information services: If someone you're looking for turns up online with his or her own registered domain (say, **www.mickey-bitsko.net**) you have a good chance of getting an address and phone number for your target. An InterNIC ISP listing usually carries full contact information for the people responsible for the domain. Go to the InterNIC whois front end, enter the domain name in the form, and the information you want will be displayed. The administrative contact is most likely to be the person you want.

IP Address To Hostname And Vice Versa

Occasionally, you may need to find out who is using a numeric IP address (most likely when someone has attempted to disguise the origin of an email by messing around with message headers). A utility called IP Address to Hostname and Vice Versa translates a numeric address, such as 165.247.88.201, into an IP name (in the example, **coriolis.com**). The utility is located at **http://cello.cs.uiuc.edu/cgi-bin/slamm/ip2name**.

A traceroute can sometimes be used to track down an ISP for which you have only a numeric address. Simply request a trace using the numeric IP address rather than a site's name.

Web-Site Guest Books And Classified Ads

Web-site guest books are a means for visitors to say hello and leave comments. Most visitors include their name, email address, and/or their Web-page address if they have one. Guest books are usually set up so that all comments and names are displayed to all visitors.

Searching for someone by visiting hundreds or thousands of Web sites' guest books is not practical. Fortunately, you can search many thousands of guest books simultaneously. Search engines, such as AltaVista and Webcrawler, catalog guest-book pages along with all the other pages at sites they cover. So, if you enter a name or email address as a search keyword, a search engine may well return some Web-site guest-book pages among its hits.

Another good place to search out someone is classified-ad pages. Classified ads are posted on the Web by just about anyone who has something to sell. So, if the person you seek has ever offered a product or service for sale, chances are his or her name will turn up on a page of classifieds. As is the case with Web-site guest books, classified-ad pages are cataloged by search engines. You can sometimes find information in an ad that you won't find posted elsewhere, such as an address or phone number. (You'll find more information on Web search engines later in this chapter.)

Online-service classified-ad areas are not very good sources. You must be on the service in question to search them, and they tend to be removed after a few weeks. Also, online-service classified ads are not usually searchable by the name of the person who posted the ad.

Public Postings

As you know, a careful searcher can assemble quite a bit of knowledge from public postings. (See the story of John Kaufman in Chapter 3.) So can you. You might also use hints and clues found in postings as pointers toward still more information.

Postings in USENET Newsgroups are the easiest to search. No matter how you access the Internet, you can read current messages by Newsgroup or search them using any of several general search engines. Past postings can be searched with Deja News (which is discussed later in this chapter).

Since Web-site BBSes are composed of Web-site pages, they are cataloged by search engines. Search-engine searches, therefore, can return postings from Web-site BBSes.

Searching For Clues In Public Places

Many email spammers, among others, post messages whose content is the same as or similar to their email messages. They often do this using a different account from the one they use to send email. So, you can sometimes find an alternate email address for someone by searching for their postings in Newsgroups. (Deja News will be your best tool for this.)

Spammers usually use some of the same lines in every posting or mailing they do, or at least include the same contact information for their scams. Thus, if you search on a key phrase, a phone number, or an address, you may find the same spam you received via email in a Newsgroup, posted from a different email address. (Quite often, spammers start on USENET before graduating to email.)

You can use the same strategy to track down anyone who might use the same line in public postings and private email (someone with a personal vendetta or campaign), or who exhibits any idiosyncrasies in phrasing or spelling. Some people even repeat typing errors.

Don't neglect the Web in this kind of search. Your target may well have Web pages carrying the same information that can identify him or her. (The best tools for finding Web pages are search engines. As with a USENET search, enter phrases or words likely to be unique to the target person's messages.)

Online-service postings are, of course, not accessible from the Web. Only members of the online service in question can read them. If you aren't on the service, perhaps an acquaintance can search postings for you. The structure of online services is such that you cannot search all BBSes at once; you have to go to the area that hosts a given BBS. This could mean searching scores of areas on a given service.

BBS messages on online services usually scroll away or are deleted after a certain period of time. The length of time messages last (weeks or months) is usually determined by the message traffic; the busier a BBS, the less time messages are available before they are deleted. (Deleted messages are sometimes archived and made available for download, but don't count on this.)

Internet Email Directories

The Internet has no member directory, as such. However, the Web hosts several email directories, some connected to postal address and telephone directory services. Together, they list the email addresses of nearly 20 million Internet users. The addresses include those of online-service users, as well as those who use conventional ISPs.

I'll show you the major email directories here. You won't find a lot of how-to instructions, because the directories are relatively simple to use.

Before we begin, it is worth noting that all email directories have this in common: None are 100-percent accurate. This is largely because addresses are not verified regularly. (I expect this is because it would be such an expensive undertaking—far more complex than, say, your local telephone company updating its white-pages directory every year.) So, as Internet users change ISPs and email addresses, bad addresses accumulate. Then, too, pranksters enter bogus email addresses (such as the "Rush Limbaugh" addresses you'll see in the example screens over the next few pages).

Still, the majority of the email addresses in the directories are valid. Sources for addresses include postings in USENET Newsgroups, mailing lists bought or "borrowed" from listservs and list brokers, and listings provided by Internet users who want to be "findable."

You will find that some directories charge for advanced searching. I can't say whether such services are worth the charge, as I can typically find what I want using first one directory and then another, until what I'm searching for comes up.

INFOSPACE EMAIL DIRECTORY

This directory claims to be the largest and most accurate database of Internet addresses. This may well be true; at least Infospace works toward keeping addresses up to date. (I found only one "bad" email address for me—even though they missed eight good ones. But, then again, I don't make all my addresses available.)

Located at **http://email.infospace.com/info/index.htm**, the Infospace email directory offers a straightforward search form, as you can see in Figure 8.4.

When Infospace displays a match, it provides links to any additional information about that person. It also has an automatic link to the Infospace telephone directory, which looks up address and phone information for the person you're seeking.

Infospace also offers a free lifetime email address for a small charge.

Broaden Your Search

Most email directories' search forms let you enter several search criteria: first and last name, city and state of residence, and so on. While providing as much information as you can may seem a good idea, it's not. A directory may not have all the information you do about a person, and thus can end up excluding exactly the listing you are trying to find.

For example, if you include the city and state for your search subject, and that person's listing doesn't include that information, the directory

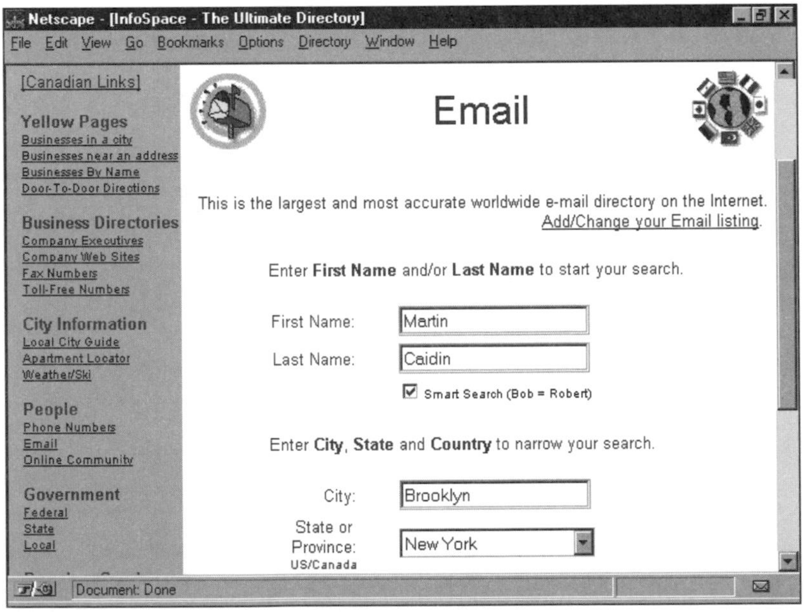

Figure 8.4   The Infospace Email Directory is one of the more accurate Internet address directories.

won't find it for you—even if the person has an unusual last name. So, start all searches using only the subject's name; if you get too many matches, you can narrow the search by other criteria.

FOUR11 DIRECTORY SERVICES

With more than 10 million listings, "The Internet White Pages" is among the largest of Internet email directories. Operated by Four11 Directory Services, it is often called simply "Four11." Located at **http://www.four11.com**, it is also among the most popular and easiest to use email directories. Four11 lets you search for people based on their last name and other criteria. It uses a simple form for entering the information you know about someone. As shown in Figure 8.5, this can include first name, last name, ISP, city, state or province, and country.

After you enter the desired search words, Four11 lists all matches to your query. Figure 8.6 shows a sample list of matches.

Click on a match, and Four11 displays a page with email addresses for that person, along with other information, if available, such as city, state, and country; alternate

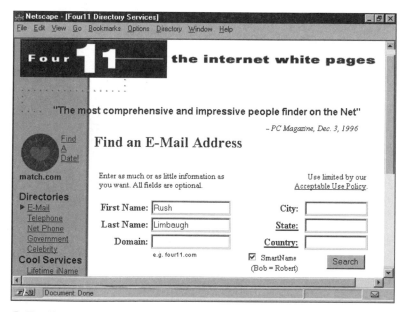

Figure 8.5 Four11 Directory Services offers an easy way to search for email addresses by name.

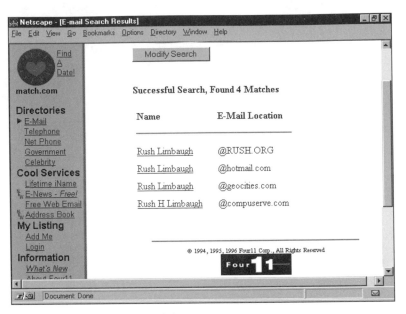

Figure 8.6   A hit list from Four11.

email addresses; Web-site URLs; and perhaps organizations with which he or she is affiliated. (Spammers are easy to spot in this directory; they almost always include some bogus yet grandiose company name, such as Eternal Wealth for Nothing, Ltd., as their organization.)

The page listed for each email match carries a link to a telephone and address lookup for that person. This nicely ties together Four11's major services—email and phone/address lookup. It also has databases containing listings from six major Net phone directories, a government directory, and a celebrity directory.

Four11's listings come from a variety of "publicly accessible" sources, which Four11 doesn't detail. (This may be to avoid arousing the ire of people who don't like their names, addresses, or phone numbers listed *anywhere*.) Internet users themselves are a major source of listings. Those who wish can enter their listings at no charge; roughly 20 percent of Four11's listings come from users.

Four11 also offers a lifetime email address service. You establish an address (with your choice of several domains), and all mail sent to that address is forwarded to an email address of your choice. As promoted by Four11, this service allows you to change ISPs (and, thus, your real email address) without having to give a new address to all of your correspondents. It's also a way to have an email address that doesn't give away much information about you.

INTERNET ADDRESS FINDER

Internet Address Finder (**http://www.iaf.net**) is another popular email directory, and one with a feature that few others offer: reverse lookups. As you can see in Figure 8.7, Internet Address Finder (IAF) lets you search by name or email address.

I often use IAF's reverse lookup feature rather than finger. This is because the IAF listing sometimes includes supplementary information. Of course, the address in question must be in the IAF database, which currently contains some 6 million email addresses. As with Four11, IAF gets its listings from Internet users who supply their own listings, as well as a variety of other sources.

Also like Four11, IAF offers a lifetime email address, through a company called iName. (Visit **http://iaf.iname.com** for complete information.) Finally, Internet

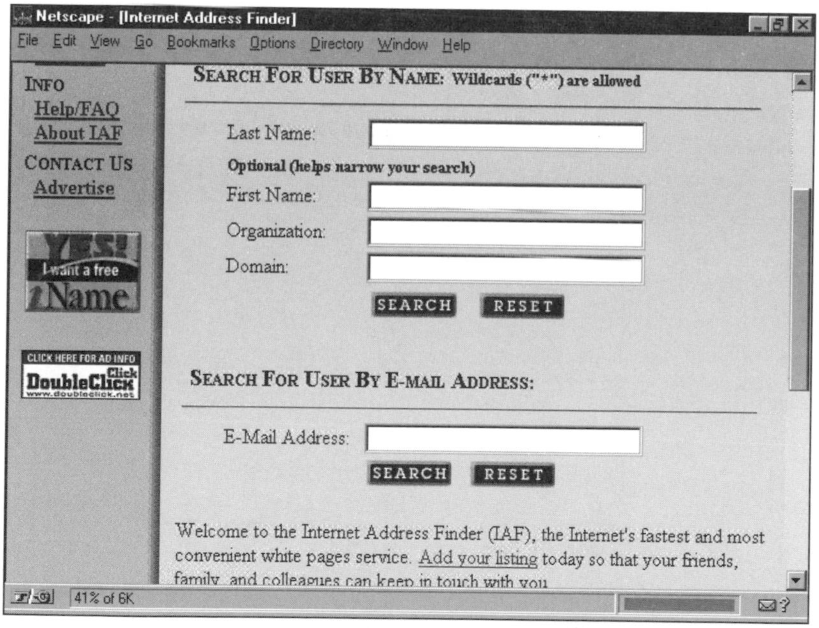

Figure 8.7   Internet Address Finder lets you search for an email address by name, or run an email address through to find out who owns it.

Address Finder is available in six languages: English, Dutch, French, German, Italian, and Portuguese.

Always Look Twice

Don't stop looking when you find a name to fit an email address. Run the name through several more email directories. Chances are you will find other email addresses. Use finger, IAF, and/or online directories to look those addresses up.

Most people who have been online for a while have had several email addresses. Some lose their service or move on to a better ISP, while others have multiple addresses for a reason. Spammers and others who like to make nuisances of themselves often have one address for sending out bothersome email or public postings, and another for "legitimate" business.

You will find that some people attach fake names to some email addresses, but use their real names with other addresses.

Searching multiple directories may seem like overdoing it, but it's not. Each new email address you look up may come with additional useful information—such as the person's employment, phone number, or just about anything else attached to the address in an Internet mail directory, finger file, or online profile.

Bigfoot

Bigfoot (**http://bigfoot.com**) is among the newer email directories, and as easy to use as the others. As you can see in Figure 8.8, Bigfoot provides a simple name-search database.

Bigfoot functions as both an email and address/phone number directory, which is the trend for online people-finders. Most email directories either offer phone and postal address information or have a reciprocal link to a telephone/address finder.

Like most other email directories, Bigfoot offers a lifetime email forwarding address.

Figure 8.8   Bigfoot is a straightforward email directory; enter a name, and
Bigfoot displays a list of email addresses that match it.

NETFIND

Netfind, which offers a more free-form approach to searching, is particularly useful when you have a name and at least a rough idea of your target's geographic location. Rather than searching with keywords by field, Netfind has you enter a name, along with one or two other keywords in one field. It then searches its database for records that match all the keywords. If you wanted to find an email address for Mickey Bitsko, for example, and you know he works for the environmental lab at Miami University in Ohio, you might enter: **bitsko miami Ohio** or **bitsko Ohio environmental**. You can also enter a user ID in place of the name. (Either way, you can use only one identifier—first name, last name, or user ID.)

Located at **http://www.nova.edu/Inter-Links/netfind.html**, Netfind is one of the faster Internet address directories.

INFOSEEK EMAIL SEARCH

Infoseek, one of the better-known search engines, lets you toggle search criteria between the Web, USENET Newsgroups, and several other search objectives, including email addresses. It's a fairly fast bare-bones search tool that works with the Four11 database. It cross-references the phone directory used by Four11, as well. I prefer this over Four11 because the screens load faster. The search is probably not any faster than Four11; it only seems that way. To check it out, go to **http://guide.infoseek.com/Home?pg=Home.html&sv=N1.**

ALL-IN-ONE SEARCH PAGE

If you want to speed up search logistics, check out the All-in-One Search Page (**http://www.albany.net/allinone/all1user.html**). This tool serves as a front end to the search tools and directories shown in Figure 8.9, plus several more.

Other people directories available through the All-in-One front end include Four11, IAF, Netfind, The Seeker, World Email Directory, WhoWhere? People Search, and several postal address and telephone lookup services.

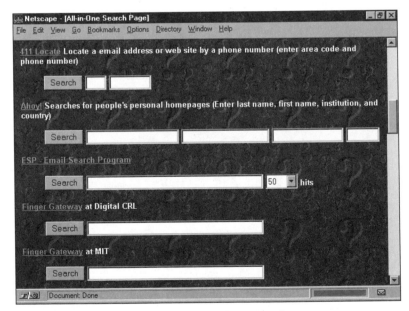

Figure 8.9 The All-in-One Search Page provides fast access to a number of the more popular email directories.

OTHER INTERNET EMAIL DIRECTORIES

Here's a quick list of other useful email directories:

- The E-Mail Address Book—**http://www.emailbook.com/**

- ESP (Email Search Program)—**http://www.esp.co.uk**

- The Internet Sleuth lets you search your choice of 6 major search engines simultaneously—**http://www.isleuth.com/**

- Lycos, otherwise known as a Web search site, has its own email lookup page, called EmailFind—**http://www.lycos.com/emailfind.html**

- People Finder—**http://www.peoplesite.com/indexnf.html**

- USENET Addresses is a list of email addresses of people who have posted in USENET Newsgroups—**http://usenet-addresses.mit.edu**

- WED (World Email Directory)—**http://www.worldemail.com**

- Who's Who on the Internet, a Web-age registration site—**http://www.infospace.com/submit.html**

- Who's Who Online is just what the title says. The majority of people listed provide their own entries—**http://www.whoswho-online.com**

- WhoWhere? Email Addresses—**http://www.whowhcre.com**

- Yahoo is one of the more popular search sites on the Web—**http://www.yahoo.com/search/people/email.html**

- InterNIC White Pages Directory Services, located at **http://ds.internic.net/tools/wp_text.html**, is a frequently updated collection of people-finder links, with form front ends for several popular online directories

Online White Pages

Once you have a name, online white pages can help you locate that person. They are mostly free, but I don't see this lasting long. Already, a couple such directories charge on a per-lookup basis, and I expect more to go that way.

Most of these services are online companions of products that are sold on CD-ROM or by other means. As such, they tend to have good information. With one exception (Phone*File on CompuServe), using them is pretty much the same. We'll check out a sampling of these services here.

A reminder: These directories list people who are not on the Internet, as well as those who are. (There are probably more listings for the former than the latter.)

AMERICAN DIRECTORY ASSISTANCE

This is one of the larger address/phone-number databases. It's also just about the easiest to use. As is obvious in Figure 8.10, you have to worry about very few criteria. Enter a last name, then a first name, city, and/or state to narrow things down.

If necessary, you can enter a partial name, followed by a wildcard. For example, you would enter **bilderb*** to search for bilderback, bilderbeck, and bilderbach.

Located at **http://www.lookupusa.com/lookupusa/adp/peopsrch.htm**, American Directory Assistance is a free service of American Business Information Inc., a company that sells CD-ROM address collections, business profiles and credit ratings, and targeted mailing lists.

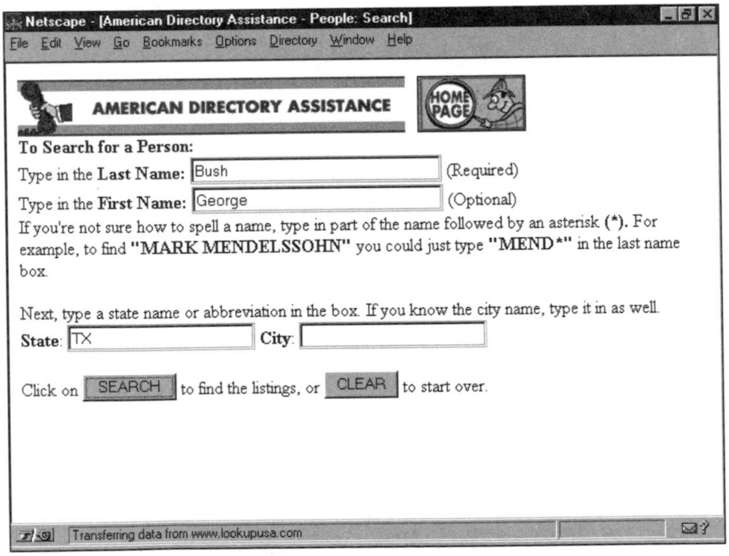

Figure 8.10   American Directory Assistance provides a simple search form.

SWITCHBOARD

The appropriately named Switchboard is another service provided by a company that sells mailing lists and related compilations offline. It features more than 100 million residential listings. The Switchboard interface is simple and direct, as shown in Figure 8.11.

An interesting feature is the Affiliations field at the bottom. Here you can select any of dozens of organizations (from AARP to YWCA) that your search target might be affiliated with. This can be a help if you're looking for someone with a common name and need to narrow your search.

You can reach Switchboard's people search off the company's main menu at **http://www.switchboard.com**, or you can go directly to the search page shown in Figure 8.11 with this URL **http://www.switchboard.com/bin/cgiqa.dll?CHKKNOCK=1&MEM=1&**. (A few Switchboard listings include email addresses.)

PRO CD (AMERICA ONLINE WHITE PAGES)

This service, available to all AOL members at no extra cost, lets you look up people by name in specified regions, with optional specifications for city and state.

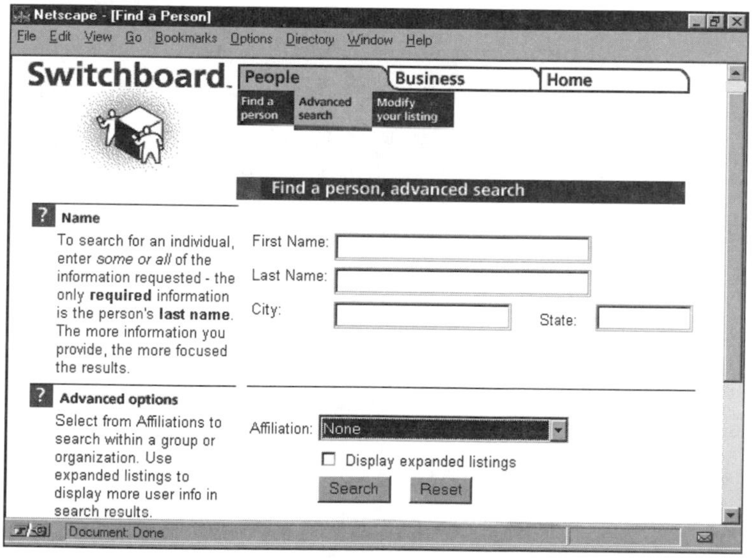

Figure 8.11   Switchboard's search form, with optional affiliation specification.

Information returned is name, address, and telephone number. The search form is shown in Figure 8.12.

The publisher sells regional white pages on CD; you can order them in the AOL White Pages area. Use the keyword **White Pages** or **Pro CD** to get there. (Pro CD also has a Web site at **http://www.procd.com/pi/td/td.htm.**)

PHONE*FILE (COMPUSERVE)

Phone*File is a name/address/telephone-number database service hosted by CompuServe and available only to CompuServe members. I have used this service quite extensively since the late 1980s. It provides access to around 100 million households in the U.S. and offers flexible searching. The Phone*File menu shown in Figure 8.13 will give you some idea of just how flexible Phone*File is.

You can search by last name, combined with state, city, metropolitan area, ZIP code, or address. You can also enter a street address to find out who lives there. Each successful search provides one or more records, each of which has the following information:

- First and last names of resident (the person whose name the phone is in).

- Street address.

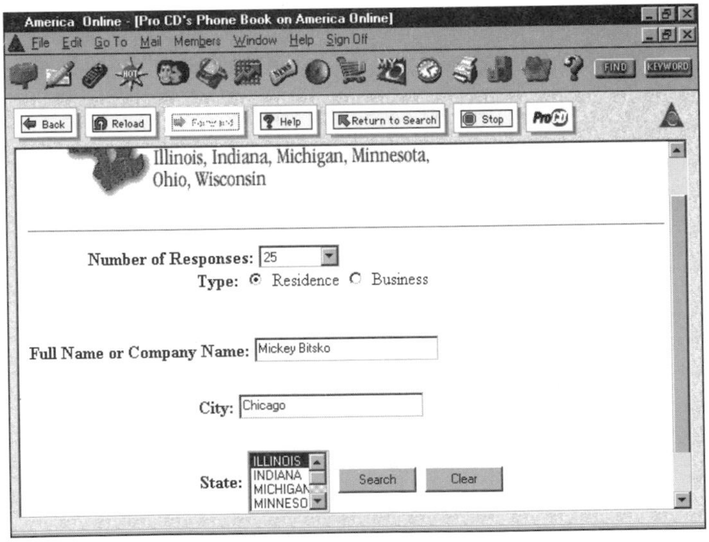

Figure 8.12   The Pro CD white pages on AOL are easy to search.

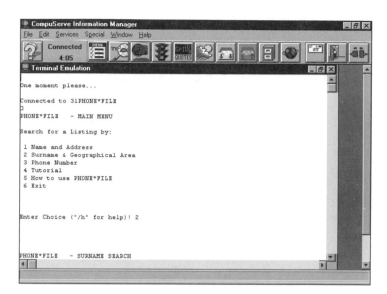

Figure 8.13   Phone*File offers flexible searching.

- Telephone number.

- Name of spouse.

- Number of years there (this is actually the number of years the person has had the phone number shown).

Again, you can search using as little or as much information as you have. In addition, Phone*File lets you search by telephone number (quite handy for those who have Caller ID and are receiving harassing telephone calls). Few unlisted telephone numbers are included in the database, which means some records come with only a name and address.

The database appears to be updated every six months for most regions, although some regions are being updated later. (I found one of my brothers' addresses more than a year after he had moved from that address.)

Phone*File carries a surcharge of $15 per hour (25 cents per minute). The price isn't bad, considering that you can do two or three lookups in three minutes or less.

Use GO PHONEFILE to get to Phone*File on CompuServe.

Search America

SearchAmerica (**http://www.searchamerica.com/**) is a commercial service that charges less than a dollar for each successful search page retrieved. (A page can include up to 10 listings, priced at 35 cents as of mid-1997.) The company makes available extensive commercial databases totaling "220 million Surnames, Businesses, and Telephone Numbers."

SearchAmerica claims its links cover 95 percent of the households and businesses in the U.S. Through the service, you have access to various databases, including those of a number of regional telephone companies.

To sign up for SearchAmerica, you must supply a credit card. The company sells prepaid searches in $10 increments.

Other Address And Telephone Directories

Here are some other useful white-pages sites to consider:

- Lycos, a site well known to many Web searchers, has a phone-number database. Check it out at **http://www.lycos.com/pplfndr.html**.

- PeopleFinder, sponsored by Database America, lets you look up people by name or telephone number. Use this URL at **http://www.databaseamerica.com/html/ gpfind.htm**.

- Yahoo, another popular Internet search engine, offers Yahoo People Search (U.S. White Pages), at **http://www.yahoo.com/search/people**; and Yahoo White Pages: Individuals at **http://www.yahoo.com/Reference/White_Pages/Individuals**.

- The Infospace is located at **http://email.infospace.com/info/index.htm**.

- For a set of links to telephone directories worldwide on the Web, visit the Telephone Directories on the Web page at **http://www.contractjobs.com/tel/**. This page has links to listings of telephone and related directories in several dozen countries. (An email-directories list is available here, too, listed as being in the "country" of Cyberspace.)

Online Yellow Pages

You know the name of a business connected with an email address, or the name of someone who has a business of a certain type in a certain area, or maybe you just need a list of businesses of a certain type. A number of online yellow pages directories may come in handy.

Most of these are organized by type of business and geographic area, but some let you input a business name or telephone number.

- The AT&T 800 Directory (**http://www.tollfree.att.net/dir800/**) lets you find 800 numbers and who owns them.

- American Yellow Pages (**http://www.lookupusa.com/lookupusa/ayp/ aypsrch.htm**) offers more than 14 million yellow-pages listings, covering most U.S. cities.

- BELLSOUTH Net Yellow Pages (**http://yellowpages.bellsouth.com/**) offers links to more than a dozen yellow page directories.

- BigBook is operated by a purveyor of mailing lists and various business services, located at **http://www.bigbook.com**.

- Biz*File is a business counterpart of Phone*File (q.v.). This directory, available only on CompuServe, lets you look up a business by category, address, phone number, and more. Use GO BIZFILE to get to Biz*File on CompuServe.

- EUROPAGES is a searchable directory of European businesses. Check it out at **http://www.europages.com/home-en.html**.

- First Worldwide International Yellow Pages (**http://www.worldyellowpages.com/ yellowpg.html**) offers links to yellow-pages directories all over the world.

- GTE Super Pages (**http://yp.gte.net/**) is one of the better searchable business directories. (Lycos and other Web sites link to this site.)

- Infospace Yellow Pages located at **http://www.infospace.com/info/ 2index_yp.htm**.

- The National Address Browser (**http://www.semaphorecorp.com/default.html**) is a free service of Semaphore Corporation. (This is a quick way to get "Zip+4" ZIP codes.)

- The Seeker is located at **http://www.the-seeker.com/**. Here you can search for people on the basis of why you want to find them (relatives, lost friends, reunions, generally seeking, and so on). While this lists mostly people who *want* to be found online, you may find it useful.

- World Wide Yellow Pages contains paid business listings (**http://www.yellow.com/**).

- The Yahoo Yellow Pages link can be found on the main Yahoo page at **http://www.yahoo.com**.

 Several of the white-pages providers in the preceding section also have business listings.

Internet Search Engines

The Web has no real index or table of contents, but it does have search engines. These are as close to card catalogs or indices as you will find on the Web. They use sophisticated software to catalog tens of millions of Web pages worldwide. Frequently updated, the catalogs are placed at your disposal in searchable format by search engines.

Search engines are useful in tracking down people who are active on the Internet. If someone has posted on a Web-page BBS, placed an ad at a Web-site classified service, or signed a Web-site guest book, you can probably find these virtual "tracks." If your target has a Web site, the odds of finding that person are even better.

We'll survey a few general search engines here. But first, a bit of background on search engine operation.

How Search Engines Work

Search engines exist as Web sites. Visit one, and you will find a form where you can enter a query, as shown in Figure 8.14 (this is AltaVista, located at **http://www.altavista.digital.com/**).

The search engine uses your query to assemble a list of Web pages that meet the criteria specified by your query. (Several of the results of a search, or *hits*, can be seen in Figure 8.14.)

Keywords And Search Terms

Don't let the term *query* mislead you. You can't just type a question into a search engine's form and get an answer. You have to tell the search engine to find what you want using *keywords* or *phrases* (also known as *search terms*).

A keyword is a word that is associated with what you want to find. Just as you enter a last name when you want to find someone in your name and address database, so you enter a major associated word when searching for information on a certain topic. For example, a keyword for finding information on Muslim life in the 19th-century Russian Empire would be *Muslim*. If you enter that in a search engine's query form, you will get a listing with something on the order of 40,000 Web pages.

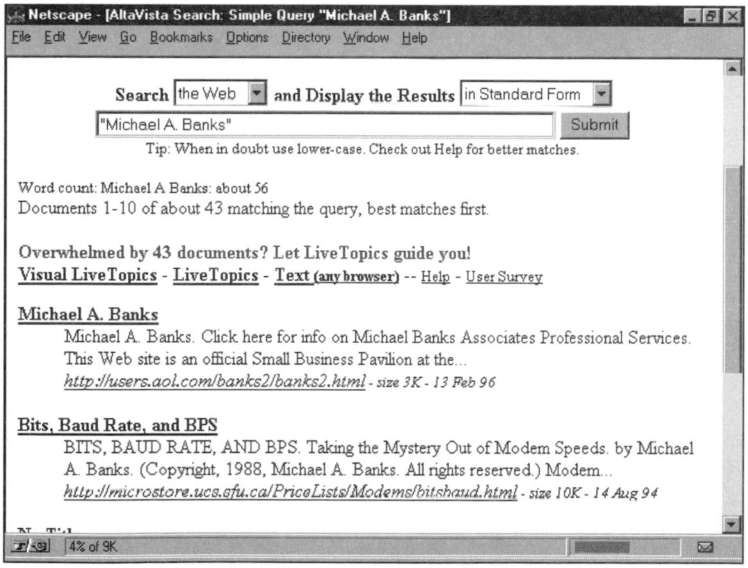

Figure 8.14   AltaVista, one of the more powerful search engines on the Web.

Search engines look for information you request based on the contents of Web pages. Thus, if you query a search engine with a keyword, you are asking it to show you all Web pages that contain the word you've specified. A word like *Muslim* would get all sorts of Web pages—current events, news, religious essays, personal resumes, and so on.

Knowing that search engines look at the entire content of every Web page they catalog, you have a better idea of how to narrow your search. All you have to do to limit the number of hits is to get specific by adding a couple of keywords—in this case, maybe *Russian* and *19th*. This tells the search engine that you want to see *only* Web pages that contain the words *Muslim*, *Russian*, and *19th*. This will return few enough Web pages that you can go through a listing manually and find what you want.

Search Phrases

With many search engines, you can use phrases as search terms. (You may find this disappointing; not everyone thinks in the same way, and the phrase that you think should be in any document about a given topic actually may be in none.) For example, if you enter "Muslim life in the 19th-Century Russian Empire," you will see a list of all Web pages that contain that literal phrase—all of those words, in that specific order.

(For the curious: There really is a Web site devoted to this somewhat obscure topic. The URL is **http://www.uoknor.edu/cybermuslim/russia/rus_home.html**.)

Putting A Search Engine To Work

Every search engine operates a little differently. They vary in how you enter multiple keywords, literal phrases, and so on. For example, AltaVista requires that you enter multiple keywords linked by AND operators, like this: **+Muslim +Russian +19th.**

That set of keywords tells AltaVista that you want to see all Web pages that contain *Muslim* AND *Russian* AND *19th*. This is also known as an AND search. Without the + signs, AltaVista would interpret the request as, "Show me all Web pages that contain *any* of these words"—that is, *Muslim* OR *Russian* OR *19th*. This approach—called an OR search—would give you a few hundred thousand Web pages. Other search engines may require that you enter multiple keywords separated only by spaces.

Search Controls

A few search engines have buttons or selections to specify an AND or OR search with multiple keywords. One such search engine, known as Hotbot, is shown in Figure 8.15.

Hit Lists

A search results in a *hit list* of Web pages, which is actually a temporary custom menu in hypertext format. You select an item (URL) by clicking on it. If the description or context accompanying the URLs on the hit list is not detailed enough, most search engines offer you a choice of how items in a list are displayed—with or without terse or verbose explanations.

A few search engines offer advanced versions of the AND/OR searches, employing *boolean logic*. With them, you can specify operators, such as AND, OR, and even NOR, to include documents that have a given phrase, but not a given word in addition.

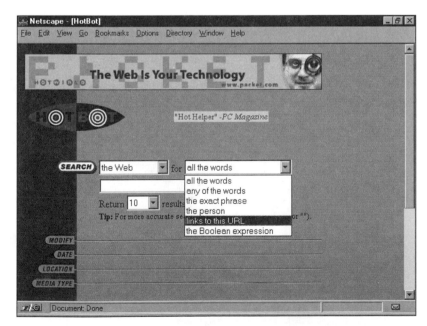

Figure 8.15   Hotbot—a search engine with search controls.

Scored Results

Some search engines, such as Lycos, do not do AND searches and will interpret a multiple key word entry as an OR search. Search engines that operate in this manner, however, usually give you a *scored* list of results, as shown in Figure 8.16. This means Web pages that contain all three words are listed first, those with two of the three words second, and so on.

Major Search Engines

Several hundred search engines are on the Web. Many are redundant, offering the same data as others. The following list shows the most popular and effective general search tools on the Web:

- AltaVista—**http://altavista.digital.com**

- Excite—**http://www.exite.com/**

- Hotbot—**http://www.hotbot.com/**

- InfoSeek—**http://www.infoseek.com/**

- Lycos—**http://www.lycos.com**

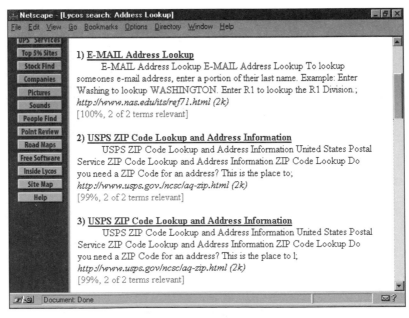

Figure 8.16   A scored listing of search results from Lycos.

- Magellan—**http://www.mckinley.com/**

- C:Net's Search.Com—**http://www.search.com**

- Webcrawler—**http://wc1.webcrawler.com/**

- Yahoo—**http://www.yahoo.com**

Some search engines, such as Yahoo, catalog Web sites and pages in what is sometimes called a *hierarchical index.* (Others, such as Lycos, use this and content for cataloging.) A hierarchical index consists of entries arranged in various groups, or hierarchies, often based on human decisions. The content of pages thus cataloged is searchable, but by index terms or groups, rather than actual content. This means hit lists won't necessarily contain the precise search term you used.

WEB SEARCH STRATEGIES

As noted, search engines catalog the *content* of every Web page they visit (except for those search sites whose contents are organized into related groups—effectively indexed by individuals). Thus, you can use them to find people in a variety of ways. Email addresses, run through a general search engine, often turn up personal or business Web pages, which have still more useful information. Email addresses can also show up in Web-page guest books, BBSes, classifieds, and USENET postings. Remember, too, that phrases, odd word usage and spelling, and even repeated typing errors can be used to track down your subject.

Be Literal

If you have only an email address, you can search using the entire address, or simply the user ID at the beginning of the address. If you have a name, search using that as a literal search term. (*Literal* means telling the search engine that you want to find all the words in the order you are presenting them, complete with capitalization, if possible.)

If you are searching for someone based on a frequently used phrase, or personal spelling or typing habits, you must enter the phrase or other term as a literal. I find AltaVista to be one of the best search engines for this purpose, as it searches for literal matches for anything enclosed in quotes. This includes odd capitalization, "liKe This."

Narrow The Search

If your search returns too many hits, narrow it by adding a likely word—perhaps the abbreviation for the state where the person you're seeking is located, or maybe an unusual word that the target uses in email or postings.

Finding Hidden Information

When you visit pages on a hit list, don't give up if you don't see what you're looking for right away. Use your browser's search function (select Find... on the Edit menu) to search the contents of the page for your search term, in case you missed it.

Also, view the page's source code. (With Netscape, select Document Source on the View menu; with Microsoft Internet Explorer, select Source on the View menu.) Search engines sometimes catalog words in the source code that don't show up when you view the page conventionally. Also, investigate any likely links on the page; some search engines will catalog a page because it links to a page that has the search term you're seeking.

Searching USENET Newsgroups

As I've noted elsewhere, anyone who is active on the Web is likely to post in a USENET Newsgroup. Spammers often begin with Newsgroups, and change accounts when they switch to sending junk email. Many argumentative individuals, people with a cause, and even Web psychos—the same sorts of people you might find harassing you someday—post in Newsgroups. Given this, Newsgroups can be a real gold mine of information when you're trying to track someone down.

Searching USENET Newsgroups may at first seem to be a hopeless proposition. For openers, there are some 20,000 Newsgroups. (For a current listing of Newsgroups, visit **http://www.yahoo.com/news/usenet**.) Within most groups, hundreds of new messages are posted daily, while old ones go away. The sheer volume of text to be scanned certainly precludes any sort of manual search.

Fortunately, you don't have to deal with a manual search. As noted previously, several Web search engines can be directed to search USENET Newsgroups. They are:

- AltaVista—**http://altavista.digital.com**

- Excite—**http://www.exite.com/**

- Hotbot—**http://www.hotbot.com/**

- InfoSeek—**http://www.infoseek.com/**

These are invaluable when you want to examine current (or past) discussions on a given topic. Use them the same way as when you are searching the Web; the only difference is that you are redirecting the search to Newsgroups.

The general search engines search only current Newsgroup postings.

DEJA NEWS

The absolute best search tool for Newsgroups is Deja News, located at **http://www.dejanews.com/forms/dnq.html**. Shown in Figure 8.17, Deja News is a database of all Newsgroup postings from the early 1990s through today.

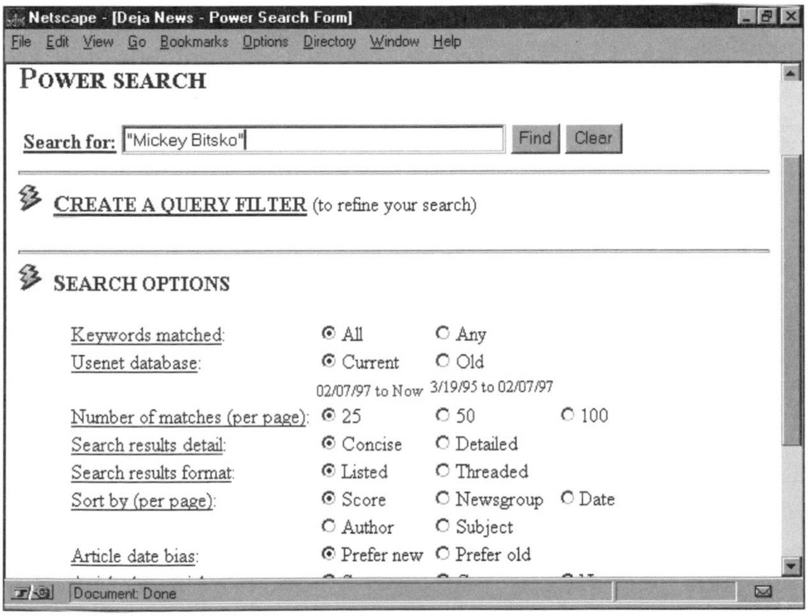

Figure 8.17   Deja News, a database and search tool for USENET
Newsgroups.

The Deja News has an advantage because it has more Newsgroup content than any other archive or index.

Deja News will eventually have in its database pretty much everything ever posted in USENET Newsgroups since their inception in 1979. As far as searching for people is concerned, five years' worth of postings is more than enough. If your search subject posted something in a Newsgroup, it was almost certainly done within the preceding five years.

Using Deja News

As you can see in Figure 8.17, Deja News is straightforward. You enter your query in the field provided. If you enter two or more words, Deja News will find all postings that contain *all* of those words, in the order you placed them, or not. If you want a literal search, seeking the words you entered as a phrase, enclose the words in quotes.

Control buttons let you enhance the search. You can specify how Deja News finds and displays messages that match your criteria using these options:

- Find either any or all keywords (along with context operators, quotes, and boolean operators).

- Find either current or old messages.

- How many hits are displayed per screen page.

- The detail of description provided with hits on the hit list.

- Whether or not to display messages as threads.

- How hits are sorted when displayed (by date, Newsgroup, or three other options).

- Whether new or old messages are displayed first.

The USENET Addresses Database

The USENET Addresses Database (**http://usenet-addresses.mit.edu/**) is an unofficial "directory" of people who have posted in Newsgroups. With this tool, you can search by a specific phrase, first name, last name, nickname, pseudonym, or organization. Searching is simplified by a form into which you can enter any or all of the previous information.

The database searches archives of Newsgroup message "from" headers, and presents a list of possible hits. Select one of them, and you are shown a screen from which you can email the person, or use finger to check for more information about the ID shown. This is a useful adjunct and backup to searching with Deja News.

The Internet Sleuth

This search engine front end will search USENET postings with up to four search engines (including AltaVista and Deja News) simultaneously. The Internet Sleuth's URL is **http://www.isleuth.com/**.

SIFT (Stanford Information Research Tool)

This relatively new search engine specializes in searching 16,000 USENET Newsgroups and more than 1,000 mailing lists. Archives consist of the past month's postings and mailings. To try SIFT, visit **http://www.reference.com/**.

Newsgroup Search Strategies

I have found that Newsgroup postings are good for ferreting out alternate email addresses used by someone I'm tracking down. This is particularly true with spammers, who typically use and lose several email addresses in a short period of time. (Some supply alternate email addresses in their postings.) Getting an alternate email address is, of course, valuable, because you can use it to find still more information about your search target.

But email addresses aren't the only bit of information you'll be seeking. Anything that might indicate where the person lives or works, other interests, or anything else can be useful—it often leads to still more information. (Remember that your ultimate goal is to find as much information about someone who is harassing, threatening, or otherwise bothering you, as a means of self-defense.)

Look For The Person, Not The Address

Your main search strategy should be to search for anything likely to have been posted by the same *person*—not necessarily using the same email address as you have on hand. So, you want to look for the sorts of unique phrases or usage I've mentioned before. (Almost everyone has some distinct elements in their messaging. For example, I tend to overuse certain phrases and one unusual word, and often type "the" as "teh." Look for similar repeated usage or errors in your target's messages.) If the person you are seeking writes frequently on a specific subject, you might want to use search terms that are closely related to that subject.

Keep Your Search Narrow And Specific

The best way to approach searching for people in USENET postings is the opposite of what I recommended for searching the Web. You should begin with a precise search term. If you don't get results, broaden the search by making your entry less precise.

For example, if you begin with a lengthy phrase, cut it gradually until you get some hits. A quick scan of those will tell you whether you are on the right track.

Double-Check Your Findings

When you do get a hit that seems to be what you are looking for, don't immediately grab the email address out of the header or names from the posting. First, make sure that what you are reading isn't something that has been quoted in a reply (some people quote the entire message to which they're replying—annoying, and it can throw you off). If you are reading a quote, the address in the message header is that of someone replying to a message posted by the person you're seeking.

Getting Professional Help

What if you have exhausted all the resources discussed, and have nothing more than a person's name, email address, and general idea of where they are located? You may recall my discussion at the beginning of Chapter 4, about the sorts of information that is compiled about you. Information such as your work, criminal, military, medical, and credit histories—not to mention your home address and telephone number.

As you might correctly surmise, that information is also available about someone who may be harassing, stalking, or otherwise bothering you. Unfortunately, you cannot access all that information. Privacy and other laws, business practices, and the cost of maintaining access to such information excludes most people.

ENTER THE INTERNET

While the Internet is not the one-stop source of information on everything about anyone that many hope it to be, you can use its resources to go after more in-depth personal information in another way. If you are willing to pay, you can get a surprising amount of information on someone through commercial investigative services.

Sometimes called private detectives or investigators, such services promise to find out anything about anyone that is in public records—and sometimes things that aren't in public records. Through subscriptions to specialized and expensive reporting services, special online "skip-tracing" and general information services, and other sources, they can obtain:

- Credit reports.

- Home address and telephone number.

- Current employment information and employment history.

- Information on past or current civil actions against or initiated by an individual.

- Property and other assets (bank accounts, investments, etc.) owned by an individual.

Again, this sort of information isn't available to just anyone, nor is it free. But, depending just what you need to know and, sometimes, how difficult it is to get the information, investigative services might cost less than you think. Most of the information just listed can be obtained for less than $50. All you need to get started is a name and, usually, a general location.

Several of these services are available via Web sites, for those who have credit cards. You can also "shop" for private investigators if you need service in another state, or even order searches for certain information online, with the results to be delivered to you via email. Either way, you don't have to call around to find an investigator who can do what you want.

INVESTIGATIVE SERVICES' SITES

Among the more active of such services online is a company called Informus, at whose Web site (**http://www.informus.com/avlsrch.html**) you can order some searches, and obtain information about others. Informus offers are a "free sample" of their information and search capabilities at **http://www.informus.com/ ssnlkup.html**. Other Internet resources for those in need of professional investigators include the following.

David Guss maintains a site with links to a number of "Investigative Resources on the Web." Among the many interesting pages at his site is a list of links to private investigators (**http://www.inil.com/users/dguss/gator14.htm**).

A similar set of links can be found at The Private Investigator's Home Page (**http:// www.pihome.com/pihome/index.cgi**).

Another searchable directory is maintained by the National Association of Investigative Specialists (NAIS), which offers a plethora of services (including a online sign-up that allows you to access fee-based databases from your computer over the Internet). The NAIS Member Directory is located at **http://www.pimall.com/ nais/dir.menu.html**.

With the information here, you should be able to find anyone who is "findable" online—and learn just about anything there is to learn about them. Happy searching!

Now, for a look at Web sites that support online safety and privacy in Chapter 9.

Chapter 9

Safety And Privacy Web Sites

Chapter 9

Web Sites Devoted To Online Privacy

Web Sites Devoted To Online Safety

Safety How-To And Education

Consumer And Internet Users' Organizations

"Watchdog" Sites

Miscellaneous Sites Of Interest

Safety And Privacy Web Sites

Chapter 9

You and I are not alone in our concerns about the Internet. A number of organizations, companies, and individuals use Web sites to promote privacy and safety online. Some sites provide information, and some offer a means of sharing information about Internet problems—or reporting online incidents and hazards.

Among the latter are sites sponsored by several quasi-official organizations that have taken on the job of helping to police the Internet. Their efforts are interesting, to say the least—and quite often have a positive effect on online malfeasance. They also serve as clearinghouses for information about scams, problem Web sites, and many other Internet crime and safety issues.

Unless stated otherwise, all sites discussed in this chapter are free. Official government sites are designated as such.

Web Sites Devoted To Online Privacy

The issue of privacy garners more online publicity than any other—including spam, stalking, frauds, scams, spoofing, and harassment. Obviously, online privacy is of more than passing interest to the Internet population.

This has quite a bit to do with federal and state attempts to regulate Web and USENET content, as well as behavior on the Internet in general. Most discussions of Internet legislation have to do with the somewhat bruised concept of freedom of speech. The driving force behind most arguments seems to be a fear that states or the federal government will put too much control on the Net, and thus stifle free speech.

Privacy sites concern themselves with much more than freedom of speech, however. The following sampling of sites is representative of privacy and related concerns on the Web. Note that most also concern themselves with email and general data encryption.

CODEX SURVEILLANCE & PRIVACY PAGE

This site (**http://www.thecodex.com**) is loaded with information on privacy, online and off. Sponsored by "Spy King," it covers techniques, products, and services for surveillance and privacy in the information age. Exploring this site may make you more conscious of security and privacy than you wish to be.

ELECTRONIC PRIVACY INFORMATION CENTER (EPIC)

EPIC is a public interest research center that focuses on civil liberty, privacy, First Amendment, and constitutional issues. Its site (**http://www.epic.org/**) often carries breaking news on issues that affect online privacy, as well as extensive background on related issues.

The International Electronic Rights Server

The International Electronic Rights Server (**http://www.privacy.org/**) is host to the Internet Privacy Coalition (IPC) and Privacy International.

Internet Privacy Law

This site (**http://www.mother.com/~ono/tjw.htm**) carries an excellent analysis of legal issues associated with online privacy and anonymity.

The Junkbusters Alert On Web Privacy

This page (**http://www.junkbusters.com/cgi-bin/privacy**) provides a lucid explanation of how you can be identified and tracked on the Web. (The site has a wealth of useful information to offer. You will read more about Junkbusters in later pages in this book.)

Junkbuster Privacy Resource Links

Junkbusters, an anti-junk communications site (**http://www.junkbusters.com/ht/en/links.html**), offers many links to safety and privacy resources.

The PRIVACY Forum

The PRIVACY Forum (**http://www.vortex.com/privacy.htm**) consists of a Web site and a mailing list, both devoted to privacy issues associated with online communications and information and database collecting and sharing. It is supported in part by the Association for Computing Machinery (ACM), internetMCI, and Cisco Systems.

Figure 9.1 gives you some idea of the ACM PRIVACY Forum's content.

To subscribe to the PRIVACY Forum, send email to: **privacy-request@vortex.com**. The message should contain the statement "subscribe privacy <your full name>" on one line ("your full name" should be literally your name, in full).

The Privacy Page

The Privacy Page (**http://www.unimaas.nl/~privacy/index.htm**) is a Dutch site devoted to privacy law. Although the emphasis is on Holland, you'll find a number

Figure 9.1   The ACM PRIVACY Forum.

of links to similar sites in other countries. A visit here is helpful if you want to get a global overview of privacy on the Web.

PRIVACY RIGHTS CLEARINGHOUSE (PRC)

PRC (http://www.privacyrights.org/) has useful coverage of privacy rights issues online and off, including guidance on dealing with threats to your privacy.

THE STALKER'S HOME PAGE

The Stalker's Home Page (http://www.glr.com/stalk.html) is hosted by Glen L. Roberts, privacy advocate and host of the "Net Connection" radio show. It carries interesting articles on Web safety. The site also offers safety and privacy products for sale.

OTHER SITES OF INTEREST

The preceding sites are, as noted, merely a sampling of what's available. For those who wish to delve deeper into privacy, check Yahoo's list of privacy sites at http://www.yahoo.com/Government/Law/Privacy/. (The list is updated frequently.)

You may also find these sites of interest:

• Anonymity and Privacy on the Internet—http://www.stack.nl/~galactus/remailers/

• Andre Bacard's Privacy Site—http://www.well.com/user/abacard/

- Center for Democracy and Technology (CDT) demonstration and explanation of how a Web page can snoop on you—**http://www.13x.com/cgi-bin/cdt/snoop.pl**

- Computer Professionals for Social Responsibility (CSPR) Privacy and Civil Liberties page—**http://snyside.sunnyside.com/dox/program/privacy/privacy.html**

- The Electronic Frontier Foundation—**http://www.eff.org**

- Internet Privacy Coalition—**http://www.privacy.org/ipc/**

- FACTnet International—**http://www.factnet.org/**

- Cyber Stalkers—**http://www.cyberstalkers.org**

PRIVACY DISCUSSIONS IN NEWSGROUPS

Those who are interested in additional information on privacy may want to check out these USENET Newsgroups:

- **alt.politics.datahighway**

- **alt.privacy**

- **alt.privacy.anon-Server**

- **alt.security.pgp**

- **comp.risks**

- **comp.society.privacy**

- **sci.crypto**

Web Sites Devoted To Online Safety

As awareness and knowledge of online crime increase, so do the number of resources devoted to helping educate Internet users, resolve conflicts, and protect against harassment and other sorts of abuse. This section is a sampling of such resources, in the form of Web sites. Some are maintained by individuals, while others are the work of established organizations, such as the Better Business Bureau, or of new organizations created to promote online safety.

SAFETY HOW-TO AND EDUCATION

These sites are tutorials and/or references on various aspects of online safety. You'll find background information, tips on prevention, and help with responding to online threats and problems at these sites.

The Computer Virus Myths Home Page

While not direct threats, hoaxes can be costly, and at times they obscure real threats. The Computer Virus Myths home page (**http://www.kumite.com:80/myths/**) should be a frequent stop for anyone who wants to stay on top of viruses. As you can see in Figure 9.2, this site covers its subject completely.

This page carries the most up-to-date news of hoaxes and myths about viruses and other topics. It's entertaining, too.

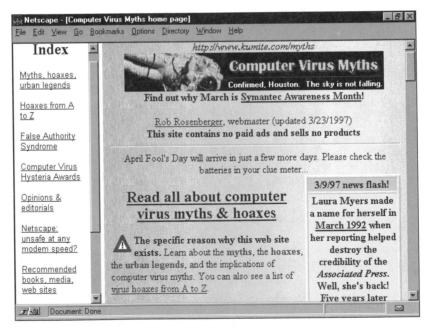

Figure 9.2   The Computer Virus Myths home page.

Data Security FAQ

The Data Security FAQ (**http://www.qualix.com/sysman/info/securityfaq.html**) is a good starting point for learning about the more technical aspects of safety issues. Among the subjects addressed by this FAQ are encryption (including public-key encryption), authentication, and digital signatures.

DigiCrime, Inc.

DigiCrime, Inc. (**http://www.digicrime.com/**) is a marvelous parody of computer crime tools and services. With a motto like "Make a crime out of bytes," what would you expect? But not only is this site entertaining, it is very educational.

Figure 9.3 gives you an idea of what the DigiCrime site is all about.

Looking Up People And Addresses

This category includes three useful reference and tutorial sites:

- Masha Boitchouk's "Guide to Finding Email Addresses" (**http://sunsite.unc.edu/ ~masha/**) provides some of the more useful resources for searching out an email address.

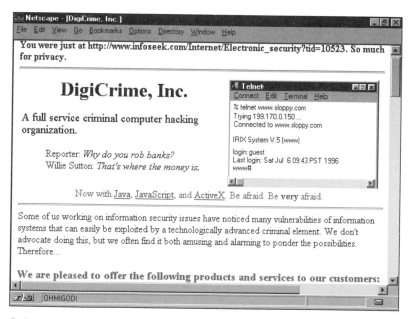

Figure 9.3   DigiCrime, a parody site with a message.

- Probe Internet (**http://pihome.com/pirc/incoming/piin.html**) is a "free experiment in investigative education." Richard F. Mauzy, an experienced investigative researcher, has set up a guide to finding people online that is based on Internet resources. As you can see in Figure 9.4, the approach is that of a tutorial.

- Mauzy provides a wealth of resources and step-by-step tutorials for using them, along with extensive background information. I recommend this one very highly.

- David Alex Lamb's "FAQ: How to Find People's E-mail Addresses" (**http://www.qucis.queensu.ca/FAQs/email/finding.html**) is a convenient general guide to finding an email address. Lamb explains addressing conventions and a lot more. This will give you a good understanding of Internet and online-service mail and addressing structures, as well as some basic approaches to determining email addresses.

National Computer Security Association (NCSA)

NCSA (**http://www.ncsa.com**) provides security alerts, the latest information on computer viruses, and more.

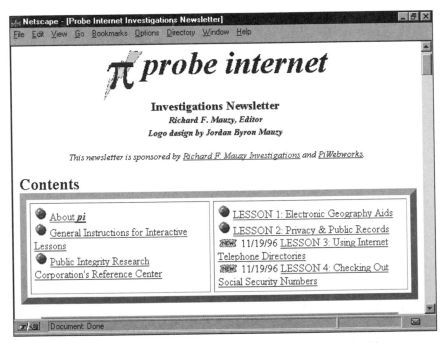

Figure 9.4   The Probe Internet site provides a tutorial on looking up people on the Internet.

Symantec Anti-Virus Research Center (SARC)

At its SARC (**http://www.symantec.com/avcenter**), Symantec offers information on current viruses, with how-to information on detecting and eliminating them.

CONSUMER AND INTERNET USERS' ORGANIZATIONS

In this section, I list established organizations that have come online, as well as new organizations formed in response to the need for Internet safety education and support.

The Better Business Bureau (BBB)

Many will argue that the presence of the BBB has been sorely needed on the Web from the beginning. Well, it is online with the BBBOnLine Web site. Point your Web browser to **http://www.bbbonline.org/**, and you'll see the welcome screen shown in Figure 9.5.

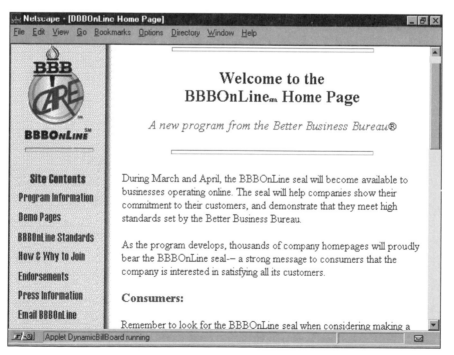

Figure 9.5   The BBBOnLine Web site.

In addition to providing consumer information and consumer arbitration, BBBOnLine is asking commercial sites to join in offering services that meet the BBB's high standards. Businesses that join will display the BBBOnLine symbol seen at the upper left of the screen in Figure 9.5, and link to BBBOnLine. Founding sponsors include Ameritech, AT&T, GTE, Hewlett-Packard, the Eastman Kodak Company, Netscape, Sony Electronics, USWEST Media Group, and Visa International.

Cybergrrl Webstation

This site takes a proactive approach to making the Internet safe and fun. Billed as "The Premier Place for Women and Girls Online," the Cybergrrl Webstation (http://www.cybergrrl.com) offers material of interest to women, as shown in Figure 9.6.

This is a recommended starting point for women, new to the Web or not. Frequently updated news and feature content, as well as a newsletter, realtime chat, and an entertaining serial ("The Adventures of Cybergrrl") make for an entertaining approach to enjoying the Web.

Figure 9.6   The Cybergrrl Webstation.

Netcheck Commerce Bureau

The Netcheck Commerce Bureau (**http://www.netcheck.com**) was established to promote ethical business practices online and to increase buyer confidence in purchasing products and services on the Internet. As shown in Figure 9.7, the organization provides consumer as well as business services.

This organization also investigates potential frauds and consumer problems. Like the BBBOnLine, Netcheck encourages companies that are online to join and pledge compliance with its ethical standards.

Women Halting Online Abuse (W.H.O.A.)

This organization (**http://whoa.femail.com/index.html**) addresses Internet issues exclusively from a woman's viewpoint. It places much emphasis on educating people about online harassment and encouraging ISPs and online services to create problem-free environments.

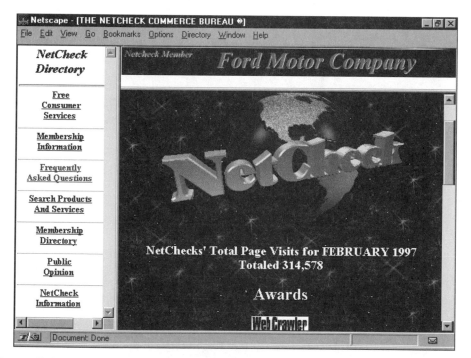

Figure 9.7   Netcheck Commerce Bureau.

"WATCHDOG" SITES

These sites provide information about scams, frauds, harassment, and other illegal or unethical Web activities. Some also accept complaints and reports, and may investigate, take action, or refer complaints to other agencies for action.

CyberAngels

Devoted to fighting crime on the Internet, CyberAngels (**http://www.cyberangels.org**) is an all-volunteer Internet safety organization. It was founded in 1995 by senior members of the International Alliance of Guardian Angels, the well-known crime-prevention organization. Colin Gabriel Hatcher serves as director.

CyberAngels is international in scope, with more than 1,000 active members in 32 countries. Shown in Figure 9.8, CyberAngels provides education, support, and advice for online victims, among several other services.

The CyberAngels site provides links to cyberstalking and anti-harassment resources, safe-surfing links, news reports of Internet-related crimes, and a wealth of education and information resources.

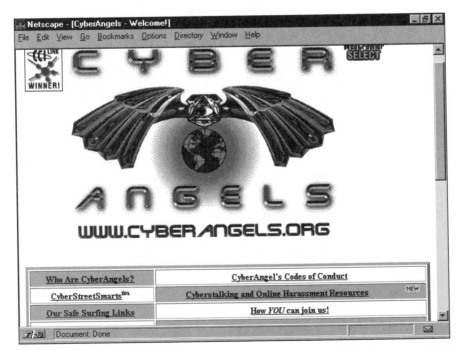

Figure 9.8   CyberAngels, an international online crime-fighting organization.

Internet ScamBusters

Internet ScamBusters (**http://www.scambusters.org**) is a Web site (see Figure 9.9) and a free electronic newsletter devoted to protecting businesses from online scams.

This site usually has the latest information on online scams, and the newsletter is a must for those who want or need to stay current on Internet scams.

Internet Commerce Commission (ICC)

The Internet Commerce Commission (**http://www.icc-911.com**) is a private consumer protection agency that deals directly with Web-related fraud. The ICC's primary goal is to insure all Web users have a safe and enjoyable environment in which to conduct any legal activity they wish. The ICC is open to all Web users.

ScamWatch

ScamWatch (**http://www.scamwatch.com**) consists of a group of Web developers and citizens, headed by Peter Hampton, who maintain a watch on consumer and other types of fraud on the Internet. The organization provides a Web site where anyone can receive assistance with fraud and scam issues. Visitors can also post

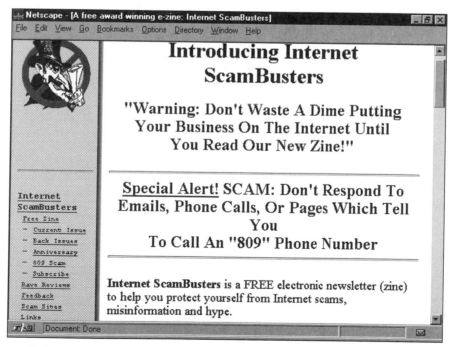

Figure 9.9 Internet ScamBusters.

information about suspected scams for others to read. (In the interest of equal time, ScamWatch allows accused "scammers" to post their viewpoints.)

ScamWatch investigates and verifies scams and frauds, then turns them over to the appropriate agencies. The organization also posts site reviews and ratings, as well as alerts and other information on Internet scams, as shown in Figure 9.10.

Vice Squad

The Vice Squad site (**http://207.15.223.224/vicesquad.htm**) is a clearinghouse for information on online crime and fraud. You can report incidents here, as well as pick up information on current problems.

Web Police

Allied with ScamWatch, Web Police (**http://www.web-police.org**) takes reports on Web crimes and incidents, investigates them, and turns them over to the appropriate agencies. The organization's site offers news bulletins, a public forum, a chat room, and other services.

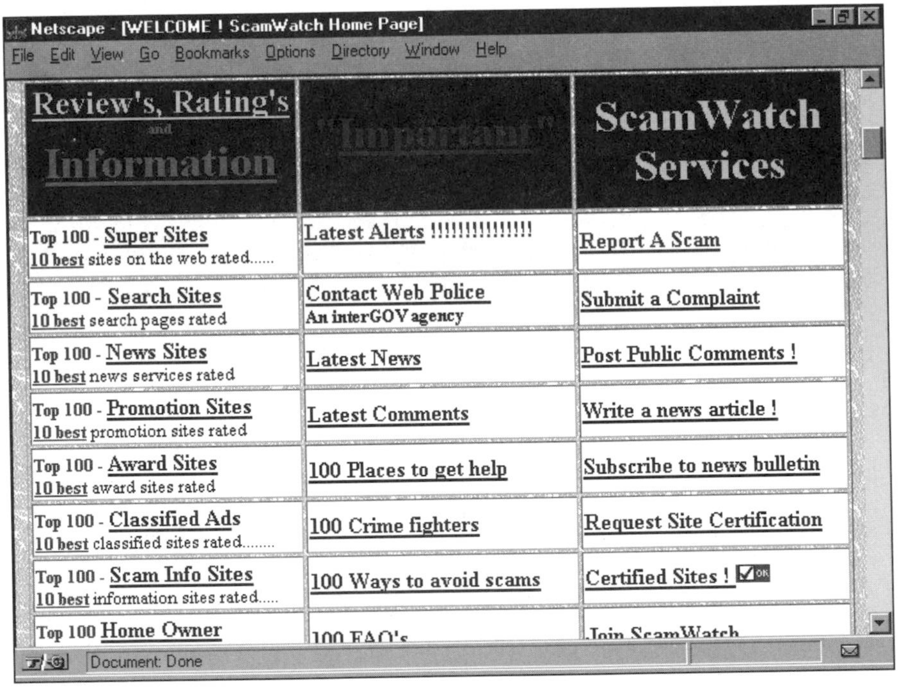

Figure 9.10 ScamWatch menu.

As indicated by the menu shown in Figure 9.11, Web Police covers quite a bit of territory. The organization also offers an informative newsletter, issued as frequently as Web events dictate.

Miscellaneous Sites Of Interest

The following sites offer information and other resources having to do with privacy, fraud, or online safety in general.

AIMC Consumer Corner

The AIMC Consumer Corner (**http://aimc.com/aimc/consumer.html**) provides bulletins and general information of interest to consumers. Much of the information has to do with frauds and scams that are encountered online as well as offline. The site also offers dozens of useful links. (AIMC stands for American Individual Magazine and Coffeehouse, the sponsor of the Consumer Corner site.)

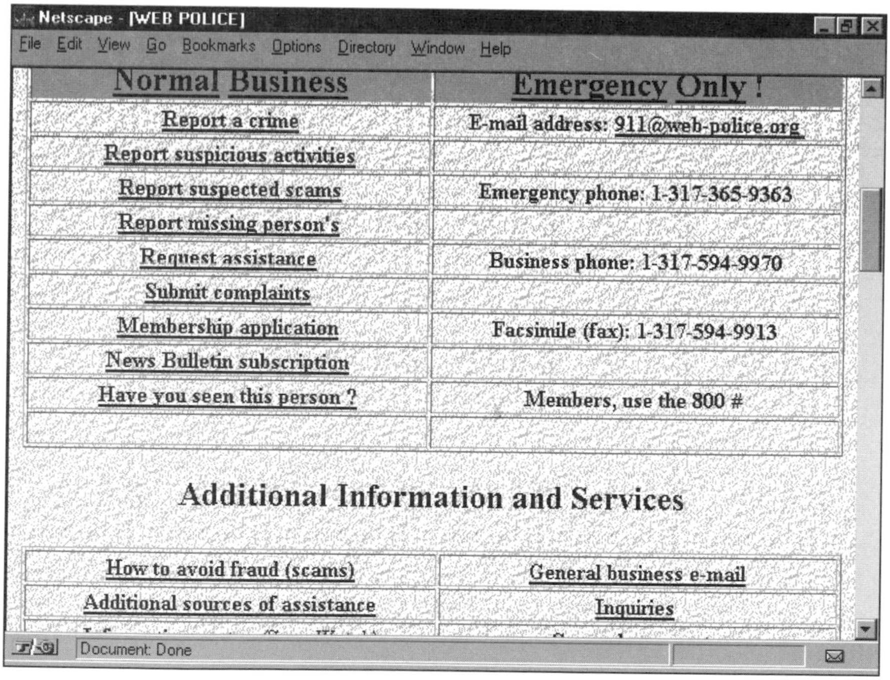

Figure 9.11   Web Police menu.

Computer Incident Advisory Capability (CIAC)

CIAC (ht.//ciac.llnl.gov/ciac/) provides computer security services to employees and contractors of the United States Department of Energy.

The Computer Law Observer

The Computer Law Observer (http://www.lawcircle.com/observer) is a free monthly email newsletter. Written by William S. Galkin, Esq., the newsletter covers cutting-edge legal issues related to computers, the Internet, and technology in general. Visit the Web site for complete information on the newsletter, to subscribe, and to view back issues.

Consumer Fraud Alert Network

Sponsored by MicroSmarts, the Consumer Fraud Alert Network (http://www.pic.net/microsmarts/fraud.htm or http://www.world-wide.com/Homebiz/fraud.htm) provides information on current frauds and cons, online and off. The site accepts reports on online frauds and scams from Internet users, and provides what may be the largest quantity of information on these topics anywhere online. The home page carries bulletins and "Scam Alert" notices of special interest.

Consumer World

Consumer World (http://www.consumerworld.org) provides access to more than 1,500 of the Web's consumer links, many of which are crime or fraud oriented.

The Ecash Home Page

This site (http://www.digicash.com/ecash/ecash-home.html) operated by DigiCash, provides interesting information and links for those who wish to investigate secure cash transactions (as consumers or merchants).

Federal Trade Commission (FTC)

The FTC (http://www.ftc.gov) is the government's watchdog organization for fraudulent business practices in the United States. As discussed in Chapter 7, the

FTC carries valuable information related to consumer (and business) frauds and scams, with particular attention to those perpetrated via the Internet. Detailed descriptions of how various cons and scams operate—and why they take in so many victims—are among the highlights of this site.

National Fraud Information Center (NFIC)

Also discussed in Chapter 7, the NFIC's Web site (http://www.fraud.org/) is a central clearinghouse for information on fraud, online or off. The site encourages people to report fraud, and it has a wealth of information on specific frauds and fraud in general.

National Security Agency (NSA)

The NSA (http://www.nsa.gov:8080/) is charged with specialized technical functions in connection with protecting U.S. communications and gathering intelligence. As such, it has a particular interest in information systems (computer) security. This page provides some interesting background on the NSA's work.

Online Fraud Newsletter

Published by Mark Edward Taylor (mtaylor@onlinefraud.com), this low-cost newsletter provides a lot of information about specific frauds being perpetrated online. The newsletter also carries information on fraud perpetrators who are being prosecuted, and the outcome of such cases.

Security & Exchange Commission

The SEC is the government agency responsible for administering federal securities laws. A special page at its site (http://www.sec.gov/consumer/cyberfr.htm) provides excellent background on investment fraud and abuse on the Internet.

World Wide Web Security FAQ

This FAQ (http://www-genome.wi.mit.edu/WWW/faqs/www-security-faq.html) deals largely with security issues involved in running a Web site, but it also includes some information from the Web browser's perspective.

This chapter by no means covers all the online privacy and safety resources available, but the listings here include some of the best that the Web has to offer.

Now that you've seen how the Web can help protect your privacy and safety, we'll look at software that does the same, in Chapter 10.

Chapter 10

Safe Surfing With Software

Chapter 10

Safe Surfing Software Overview

Online Service And ISP Tools

Browser Security And Web Access Control

Email Filtering And Encryption For Email And Files

Cookie Cutters And Spam-Haters

Safe Surfing With Software

Safe Surfing Software Overview

As I stated early in this book, the Internet is about as close to total anarchy as any social gathering short of a riot can be. Controlling what's available online is virtually impossible. Some moderated USENET Newsgroups do a fair job of controlling content—but the control extends only to keeping the content in line with a given Newsgroup's topic area. (Thus, a sexually oriented Newsgroup will carry just about anything and everything having to do with sex—but nothing else. Whether that content is objectionable or offensive to some people is irrelevant.)

Online-service BBSes and databases tend to be more controlled, generally excluding anything that might be offensive or inappropriate. The same is true of other content areas on online services. *Offensive* and *inappropriate* are subjective judgments, however, especially in certain areas, such as those that involve sexuality or lifestyles.

Controlling what goes on in chat rooms is impossible. However, some online services try to keep an eye out for trouble in their chat rooms, and the "ops" in many Web chat rooms do a good job of enforcing their loose rules.

As for email, you have literally no control over what someone sends you. The ideal defense here is to keep your email address out of the hands of people you don't know. As you learned in earlier chapters, however, that can be an impossible task.

Then there's the Web. Except in extreme cases, nothing is censored, controlled, rejected, or excluded on the World Wide Web. Sites carrying pornographic material abound, as do sites with violent, racial, and other potentially objectionable themes.

You can ignore any Newsgroups, BBSes, chat rooms, and Web sites you don't like. But that is too limiting for some, and still leaves the problem of email. If you have a child online, the problem is compounded. You don't know what that child will encounter—accidentally or intentionally—when he or she gets online. You know that some content a child is likely to find or seek out on the Web involves subjects you don't want them to see or have to deal with, at least not before a certain age.

What it all comes down to is that the online world seems pretty much out of control. You have to take the bad along with the good—or do you?

Taking Control

Even though the Internet at large is pretty much out of anyone's control, you can determine how much and what type of Internet content comes to you. In addition to the techniques discussed throughout this book, a number of programs and Web sites can put you in charge of the Internet.

Want to take control of your email? With the right software, you can delete most spam messages without ever seeing them. Specialized software can also analyze the source of seemingly anonymous or "spoofed" messages, and do other interesting things with bothersome messages.

If you need to keep someone who uses your computer out of Web sites and Newsgroups with certain types of content, or out of chat rooms—the source of more than a few problems—software can help you with those tasks, too. This goes not only for children, but also for employees who may be browsing sites of personal interest on company time. Such programs can log the sites someone has visited. Some limit the amount of time a user can spend browsing.

Online services build in access controls and search features that allow you to lock users out of certain areas on the service, as well as the Internet. If these feature aren't available, you can use special add-on software discussed in this chapter.

Note that in many cases, software designed to restrict access to the Internet can also be put to work keeping away content, such as spam and harassing email, that you don't want.

What you'll see in the following pages will give you some idea of how you can control the Internet. In many instances, what you see offered by one online service, ISP, or software package is not offered by others. You may not be able to find every feature you need in one service or program, but let's hope this changes in the near future.

Online Service And ISP Tools (Parental Controls, Mail Filtering, And More)

Responding to customer demand, most online services and some ISPs provide tools to limit access to their content and/or the Internet. Several also provide a means of blocking bothersome email, whether from spammers or the psycho haunting your favorite forum. Some have had such tools in place for several years.

Conventional ISP's

Conventional ISPs have been slow to provide or create tools that their customers can use to control or otherwise limit access to Internet content. Some more technically oriented users can take a number of steps to block access to the Web and Newsgroups, and filter email. But these people are a definite minority.

A few ISPs provide email filters on the system level. These are relatively complex scripts and programs that are usually run in the user's directory on the ISP. More and more ISPs are beginning to offer blocking software, such as Cyber Patrol, which is described later in this chapter.

In addition, a few ISPs are rating their own content using one of several rating systems discussed later in this chapter. A few offer filtering systems, again based on a popular rating system.

America Online (AOL)

AOL's access control and security begin with on-staff guides, who are available 24 hours a day for trouble reports. They often visit chat rooms to monitor for abusive or illegal activities. Where email is concerned, the AOL staff is always ready to help with problems having to do with offensive or harassing mail, as well as spam.

In addikqon, AOL offers the most advanced access-control features of any of the online services. The parental-controls system lets you control access to just about every AOL feature, as well as many Internet sites and activities. This is done by setting access levels or custom access limitations on names using your AOL master account.

Password Security For AOL Users

As you may know, AOL software lets you store your password on your computer, so you don't have to type it in when you want to sign on. This is convenient, but it also means that anyone who has access to your computer can log on to AOL and pretend to be you. This person could even set up his or her own account by creating a screen name from your master account. This can cause you lots of problems, and may cost you money and your account. (Remember what happened to the woman in Chapter 2 who stored her AOL password on her computer?)

So, memorize your password and disable the automatic password feature. This is done in the Preferences area of My AOL.

Parental Controls

AOL's Parental Controls can block or restrict the use of chat rooms, instant messages (IMs), email, binary file downloads, and Newsgroups through AOL. Web access is controllable, too.

Accessed with the keyword **Parental Controls**, the system provides several options, as shown in Figure 10.1.

You can restrict access by selecting preset levels—Child, Teen, and General. Or, you can use custom controls to limit access to various AOL or Web elements, as explained below. (These custom controls can also modify default settings for Child, Teen, and General access levels.)

Chat restrictions include blocking access to all chat rooms, private chat rooms, or open conferences, as well as IMs on AOL.

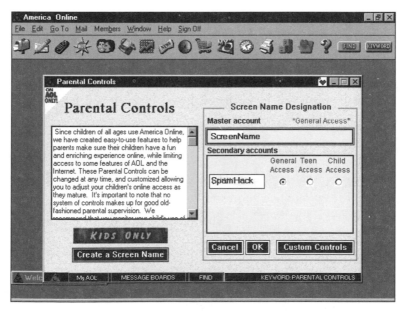

Figure 10.1   America Online's Parental Controls provide a flexible means of controlling access to AOL and Internet content.

Downloading restrictions can include FTP sites, as well as AOL software down-loads and email attachments.

Newsgroup options include blocking access to all Newsgroups or specific Newsgroups, or blocking Newsgroups whose names contain specific words (.alt or .sex, for example). You can also block users from adding Newsgroups by name.

Many Newsgroups—particularly those dealing with sex—provide downloadable graphics in MIME-encoded format. If you block downloads, the user cannot download such images for offline viewing.

Email restrictions are quite flexible (and are explained in the next section).

Options for Web restrictions include blocking all Web access or permitting access to sites approved by age group—6- to 12-year-olds or 12- to 16-year-olds. (Site designation is based on standards established by Microsystems, whose Cyber Patrol software and proxy service are available for those using conventional ISPs, as explained later in this chapter.) If you use Netscape, rather than AOL's built-in Web browser (which is a special version of Microsoft Internet Explorer), there are special procedures for implementing Web restrictions.

Filtering Email With Mail Controls And Preferred Mail

AOL's Mail Controls are a model for other services. Available on the Parental Controls menu, or with the keyword **Mail Controls**, the system provides three major options, as shown in Figure 10.2.

You can block all email to a screen name, allow mail from only selected addresses, or block mail from specified addresses. These options can be useful for your own AOL account—especially if you find yourself getting objectionable email or repeated spams from the same addresses.

You should consider carefully how you approach the matter of blocking email. Usually, blocking mail from specified addresses might seem the best route to take—until you find your email box still overflowing with spam. Both spammers and those bent on other types of harassment can easily change the From and other headers of their messages to overcome email blocking. Therefore, setting up the

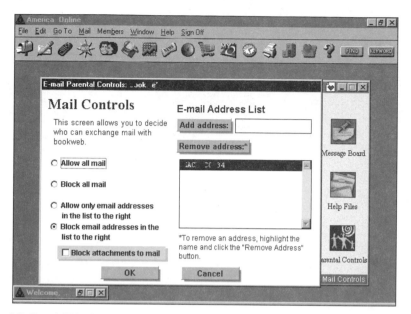

Figure 10.2   AOL's Mail Controls let you block all mail, block selected addresses, or permit mail from only selected addresses.

mail-blocking system to allow mail only from specified users is usually more expedient. Even if you have 50 correspondents, adding them all doesn't take long using cut-and-paste for the addressing.

If, however, you want to be able to receive email from people you don't know (save for spammers, of course), you will have to go the route of blocking only specific addresses. This might leave you open to quite a bit of spam, except for AOL's Preferred Mail service. Accessed with the keyword **PreferredMail**, this service blocks well-known spam sources, some of which you can see in Figure 10.3.

Any AOL member is free to receive all the spam he or she wants—contrary to reports circulated by individuals who sell mailing lists and spam mailing services. An overwhelming majority of AOL members elect *not* to receive spam—as might be expected. Preferred Mail also takes care of the one element lacking in AOL's mail controls—the ability of individual AOL users to block entire domains—but AOL in large part takes care of that by blocking spam sites.

AOL encourages members to help put a stop to junk email by forwarding copies of spam to a special AOL address. When enough complaints are lodged against a site

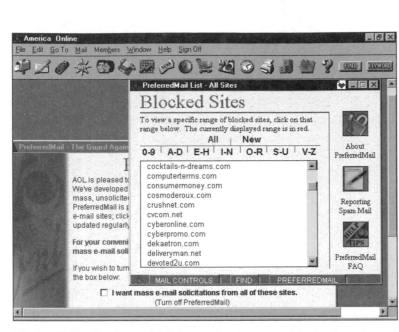

Figure 10.3   AOL's Preferred Mail service lets you block sites found to be sources of spam.

that is spamming, it is blocked. (At present, AOL and DELPHI are the only online services providing spam-site blocking in response to user requests. Others may join in, in the near future, as may many conventional ISPs.)

My AOL

You can also customize and control AOL with the My AOL area (accessed, appropriately enough, with the keyword **My AOL**) and the Preferences area (keyword **Preferences**). Menus for both are shown in Figure 10.4.

In addition to providing menu access to the Parental Controls and Mail Control systems, these services let you establish your preferences for how you use AOL in several ways. You can specify how AOL looks and acts in various aspects, set up Web security levels, and more.

CompuServe

CompuServe provides commands that let you ignore certain other people in a chat room and hide your identity in a chat if you wish. Beyond this, CompuServe offers a useful set of controls in its Parental Control Center, with support provided by a

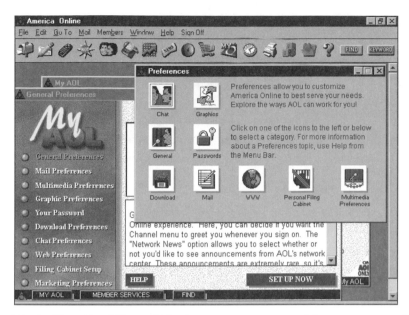

Figure 10.4   The My AOL and Preferences areas enable you to specify choices in most aspects of AOL operation.

free Parental Control Forum. CompuServe breaks down access control into two areas: one for CompuServe content, the other for Internet access. (As of this writing, CompuServe was still sadly lacking in mail controls of any type, although they have been promised for CompuServe front-end programs.)

CompuServe Control Center

The CompuServe Control Center (**GO CONTROLS**) offers password control of CompuServe content access and a gateway to Internet access control. Shown in Figure 10.5, the Control Center provides access to related areas of interest, as well as information about controls.

You can control access provided by CompuServe to Newsgroups, FTP sites, and Telnet. (This is separate from Web-related activities, and Newsgroup, FTP, and Telnet access via your Web browser. CompuServe offers access to those areas of the Internet separately or via your browser.) It also lets you block selected CompuServe products and services that contain adult-oriented content. CompuServe works with Cyber Patrol in establishing which CompuServe products and services are so rated.

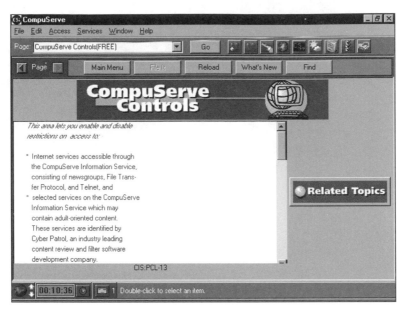

Figure 10.5   CompuServe's Control Center is your gateway to controlling
access to CompuServe and Internet content.

Parental Control Forum

The Parental Control Forum (**GO PARCON**), shown in Figure 10.6, offers the
same features as other CompuServe forums.

Here you will find a message board, software downloads, and other features and
content of interest to those who want to limit access to the online world's less
savory elements.

Internet Control Center

The Internet Control Center (**GO PCL-10**) is the other half of CompuServe's
Control Center. Here, you can control access to Internet sites that may be objec-
tionable. The Internet Control Center uses the same user interface as the Parental
Control Center, as you can see in Figure 10.7.

As a part of its Internet control services, CompuServe provides for a free download
of Cyber Patrol software (discussed later in this chapter).

Overall, CompuServe's access controls are fine. The service needs email
controls, however.

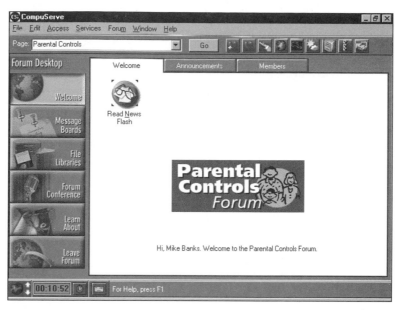

Figure 10.6   CompuServe's Parental Control Forum supports the Parental
Control Center.

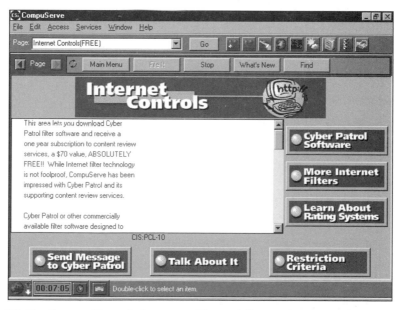

Figure 10.7   CompuServe's Internet Control Forum lets you determine how
much and what type of Internet content can be accessed via
CompuServe's Web browser.

DELPHI

DELPHI, second only to CompuServe in longevity among online services, suffers from few of the problems plaguing other online services. DELPHI's forums and other special-interest areas are self-policing, in that forum staffers keep an eye on realtime conference and bulletin-board activity. DELPHI staffers do not do any surreptitious monitoring.

Several DELPHI features let you limit other users' access to you in DELPHI conferences (chat rooms) and forum BBSes. Chat commands enable you to block specified members and/or stop private sends from other users. In forum BBSes, powerful search commands can be used to ignore and not display messages from specified members. (DELPHI's BBS software is the most powerful and efficient offered by *any* online service.)

The DELPHI postmaster takes care of excessive spamming by either blocking sites that send large quantities of mail or working with the postmasters of other ISPs where blocking is not possible. This is based on member complaints about spam. Other email enhancements are being implemented as you read this.

GENIE

The GEnie online service offers few control features *per se,* as of this writing. Chat-room commands can be used to insure privacy on the service, but Internet controls are pretty much nonexistent. You'll have to use add-on programs to limit Internet access if GEnie is your provider.

MICROSOFT NETWORK (MSN)

MSN's major security and control features are found in its browser, Microsoft Internet Explorer.

PRODIGY

The online-service side of Prodigy offers parental control features and blocking tools for some of its content. In addition, Prodigy bulletin boards are policed extensively by staff members, and Prodigy has moved in the past to block sites sending excessive commercial email to its members.

Prodigy also offers a Parental Controls area, as shown in Figure 10.8.

The Parental Controls area lets parents turn off email, chat, and bulletin boards, as well as the Web browser on Prodigy Classic. The account owner, whose ID ends in an *A*, is the only person who can do this.

Prodigy Internet uses the ratings features offered by Microsoft Internet Explorer, its built-in browser. The service also provides free copies of Cyber Patrol to its members.

Browser Security And Web Access Control

Web browsers offer few security features. With Netscape, you can set passwords to control when or if your personal and site certificates are used. (A *personal certificate* is a sort of digital signature that can be transmitted to a Web site to let it know you

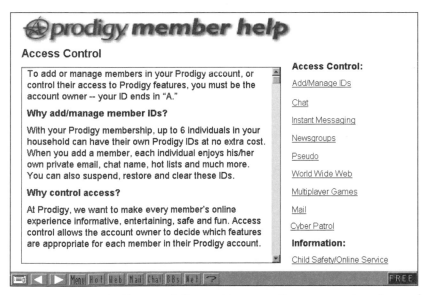

Figure 10.8   Prodigy's Parental Controls area offers several options.

are really you. A *site certificate* lets you know that the site with which you're exchanging data is authentic.) Netscape can also be set up to remember your password and issue it for you when you go to get mail. This is not a good idea, however; leaving that feature enabled could mean that anyone who has access to your computer can read, delete, reply to, and otherwise mess up your email.

Netscape also has settings to enable or disable Java applets and to establish secure server notification parameters—that is, whether you are notified when you are entering or leaving a secure site, and when you are transmitting data to an unsecure site.

Most access-control features for Netscape have to be added externally. If others use your system, you may want to consider password-protecting Netscape—or your entire system—with any of several programs that can do this. (Windows 95 users: don't rely on the Windows 95 password, which is easily circumvented by pressing the Esc key.)

Microsoft Internet Explorer offers a few more security and access features than Netscape. In addition to personal and site certificates, Internet Explorer makes available a password-protected ratings system, shown in Figure 10.9.

As you can see, the Content Advisor lets you set the level of language, nudity, sex, and violence permitted in available sites. The Content Advisor by default uses ratings established by the Recreational Software Advisory Council. You can see complete descriptions of the ratings at **http://www.rsac.org/ratingsv01.html**. (Also see the section on Content Rating Systems and Proxies later in this chapter.)

Internet Explorer also lets you set up personal and site certificates, enable or disable Java and ActiveX content, and set security notification levels.

Other popular browsers offer similar security and control features, but most browsers cannot be trusted for total access control.

A Browser For Children

One Web browser that does provide good access control is KidWeb, a product of ConnectSoft (**http://www.connectsoft.com**). KidWeb is a just-for-kids browser that features animated characters and graphic controls, as shown in Figure 10.10.

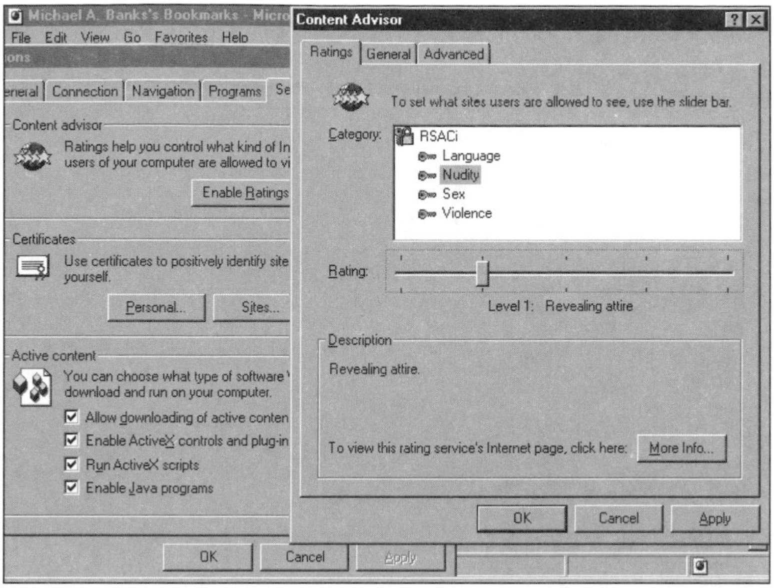

Figure 10.9   Microsoft Internet Explorer's ratings and Content Advisor let you lock out some objectionable Internet sites.

Figure 10.10   KidWeb lets parents set up a list of approved Web sites for browsing.

KidWeb's main feature, from a parent's viewpoint, is blocking. The browser blocks any sites not on a list of pre-approved sites. It offers multiple access levels and keeps a log of a child's online activities. It also has quite a bit of built-in content.

KidWeb works with any ISP. It adds music and a child-friendly design to provide an appropriate gateway to the Internet. I would recommend this for children under 12, especially for those who haven't used the Web before, because it provides a smooth transition from learning programs and games to the Internet. KidWeb is available for Windows users only.

Content Rating Systems And Proxies

Some services rate the content on online services and Web sites and pages. Ratings dictate whether a site or service might be appropriate for adult audiences, or younger audiences, based on the level of sex, violence, nudity, obscene language, drug or alcohol abuse, and/or other factors. The presence of certain types of graphic images are sometimes taken into account. You won't have much direct contact with rating systems, but you should know that they are responsible for what's blocked and what's rated at what level on online services and the Web.

There is currently no set standard for online-service and Internet content ratings, although existing rating systems pretty much follow the proposed Platform for Internet Content Selection (PICS). I expect that PICS will eventually be embedded in browsers, but not as one set of ratings. Rather, users and services will be able to customize it. (For more information on PICS, visit this Web page: **http:// www.w3.org/pub/WWW/PICS/.**)

Among the better-known rating services are NetShepherd, RASCi, Safe For Kids, and SafeSurf. You will see these referred to in literature for safe-surfing and blocking software products, as well as by online services that use one standard or another to label or rate content. Some rating services are designed to be used with specific software, while others are freely accessible. Depending on the service, Web sites may rate themselves based on the service's criteria, or they may be rated by the service in question. The rating process may be manual, and/or make use of Web-crawling programs that examine sites for certain keywords.

Proxy Servers

A proxy server acts as an agent or surrogate, communicating with outside sources—as when your system is behind a security system, such as a firewall, which allows no external content in. It can bring in what it picks up from outside sources, perhaps filtering it for certain content before passing it on to you. (The Anonymizer, mentioned in Chapter 4, and again in Chapter 11, is an example of a slightly different sort of proxy, whose main application is to shield you from being identified by sites from which you get information.)

You can use specialized proxy servers to obtain Web-site and -page content. As with browsers, a proxy server can be preset to access or pass along only certain qualifying sites and pages. You will sometimes see these referred to and even used by Web filtering or blocking software. (At present, no proxy servers comply with the PICS standard.)

If you want to check out how a proxy server works, visit Microsystems' Cyber Patrol proxy server at **http://www.microsys.com/proxy/proxserv.htm**. It's an interesting "live" demonstration.

Blocking And Monitoring Software For Children And Adults

Blocking software is the most popular and usually the first line of defense against exposing children to inappropriate Web content. Many businesses also use it to lock employees out of browsing for fun during work hours.

Acting as a Web browser "supervisor," a blocking program prevents access to sites considered inappropriate for the person using the browser. The decision as to what is inappropriate is usually based on listings compiled by one of the rating services.

The person who sets up the blocking software can add his or her own selections to block. A blocking program may also offer varying degrees of blocking, much like the Content Advisor used by Microsoft Internet Explorer, discussed earlier in this chapter.

Some companies accept recommendations from users for sites to be blocked or unblocked. Several offer online updates to their lists of blocked sites for free or by subscription—a useful service, since several thousand new sites can show up on the Web in a few months' time. (Most blocking programs feature Web sites with explanations of their blocking criteria, and some provide lists of blocked sites.)

In addition to blocking access to Web sites, blocking programs may impose time limits on Web browsing or allow browsing only during set periods. Some blocking programs provide a log of users' activities (including attempts at accessing blocked sites). All are designed to be set up by one person who has password access, perhaps with lower-level access to a second trusted person. At least one—Cyber Patrol—cannot be overridden by deletion; deleting the program disables Internet access.

Blocking programs can be quite literal. At least one will not let you access a site or page carrying the surname or title *Sexton*, because the word *sex* is contained in that name. Their helpfulness, however, more than overcomes the occasional confusion over meaning.

Monitoring programs track and record activities on the computer or the Web. Some blocking and filtering programs have monitoring functions built in.

Note that most blocking, filtering, and monitoring programs run in the background, usually undetectable until a user tries to access a blocked site.

We'll take a look at the more popular blocking, filtering, and monitoring programs here.

BESS

Bess, subtitled "the Internet Retriever for kids, families, and schools," is designed to protect children (and others) from sexually explicit and adult-oriented sites. At the same time, the program promotes and enhances exploring educational and entertainment sites.

Strictly speaking, Bess is not a blocking program. Rather, it is a national ISP that provides a proxy server, through which users can access only approved sites. Sites with adult content, Web chat rooms, and many Newsgroups are blocked outright.

Available for Windows and Macintosh, Bess is a subscription service. Users are provided with special software and dial the Bess server directly as their Internet gateway. The service offers access to several thousand education and entertainment sites.

Figure 10.11 shows the Bess home page, where you can see how Internet content is organized.

Teenagers and adults who do not want to use the Bess menus can access a simplified home page.

Interestingly, Bess controls email, too. All mail (incoming and outgoing) is checked, then returned to the sender if it contains inappropriate language.

For more information, visit Bess at **http://www.bess.com**.

Figure 10.11   Bess is a proxy server that allows users to access approved sites by category.

CYBER PATROL

Cyber Patrol is among the more successful Web filtering programs. It is used by America Online, A&T WorldNet, Bell Atlantic, British Telecom, and CompuServe, among other online services and ISPs, and it is bundled with some PCs. Users can set it up to control access to the Internet and Newsgroups based on a variety of criteria, including references to drug or alcohol abuse, sexually explicit material, nudity, violence, and racial or ethnic slurs.

Parents can set up Cyber Patrol to grant access only to Cyber Patrol's list of approved sites (some 40,000) and block the rest of the Web. Figure 10.12 shows the Cyber Patrol setup screen, where a parent can select operating and access criteria.

A particularly interesting feature of the program is an option that blocks children from typing in or viewing objectionable words or phrases, based in part on a default list of profanity. Users can delete words from this list or add to it—which means parents can set up Cyber Patrol so children can't communicate certain facts online, such as their last name, phone number, or address.

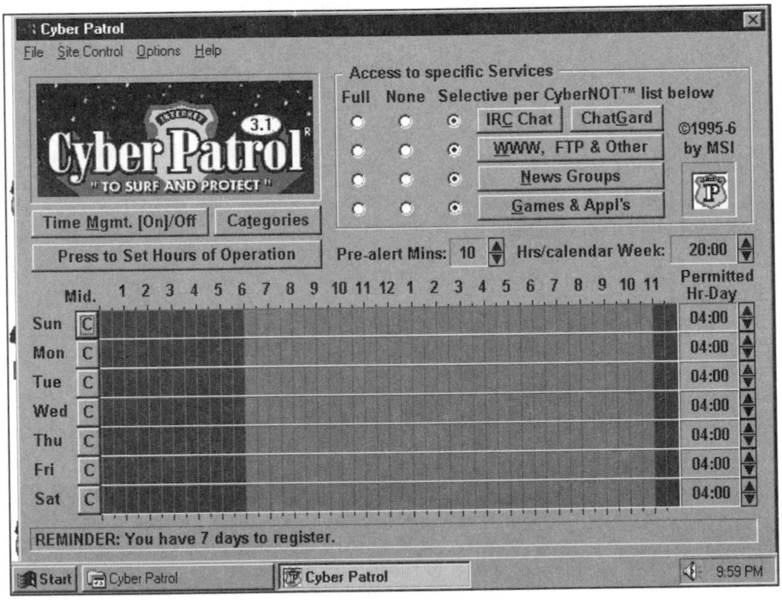

Figure 10.12   Cyber Patrol allows parents to block sites and set browsing time limits.

Cyber Patrol also has a time control feature that lets adults determine when and for how long children can use specified programs on the computer. This feature can, of course, be used to restrict Internet access to certain days and times, too.

Available for Macintosh and Windows, Cyber Patrol can be set up for as many as nine users. It also has a corporate filtering feature for business users, and a Cyber Patrol proxy feature. A special subscription service provides online updates to Cyber Patrol's site lists.

For more information, and to download a free trial version, visit http://www.cyberpatrol.com.

CYBERsitter

CYBERsitter is an interesting filtering/blocking program that runs in the background at all times and claims to be virtually impossible for a child to detect or defeat. It works on several fronts. By default, it not only blocks access to adult-oriented Web sites, Newsgroups, and images, but also logs any attempts to access same. (This can be changed simply to put an alert in a log file, or block without alerting.) Email—both incoming and outgoing—is filtered to remove offensive language, as are any attachments. The same filtering takes place for Web pages, Newsgroup messages, and downloaded files. The program can maintain a complete history of all online activity, including attempts to access blocked material. Setup is flexible, as you can see from the CYBERsitter setup screen in Figure 10.13.

Web sites and Newsgroups that are blocked include any with adult, sexual, bigotry, racist, drug-related, or similar content. Adult-oriented chat sites are also blocked. Blocking and filtering are based on lists provided with the program, but parents can add their own words to the lists. When filtering, CYBERsitter examines words and phrases in context, which should eliminate much of the ambiguity of blocking.

In addition to working with the Internet, CYBERsitter provides password protection for programs or data files on the host computer. Online updates to its filter file are free. The program is available for Windows and Windows 95 users, and will operate with any conventional ISP, plus CompuServe version 3.0 or higher.

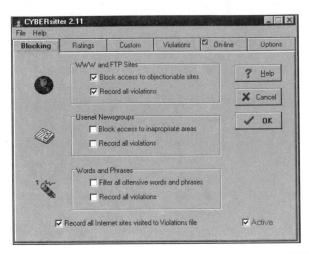

Figure 10.13   CYBERsitter allows you to set up a variety of blocks, filters, and other operating parameters.

For more information about CYBERsitter, or to download a free trial version of the program, visit **http://www.solidoak.com/**.

INTERNET WATCHDOG

Internet WatchDog is a program that allows a parent, teacher, or employer to monitor and record all activity on the user's computer. It is presented as an aid for increasing employee productivity, as well as an aid to parents in monitoring children's Internet activity.

Among many other options, Internet WatchDog can capture screen shots of current computer activity at specified intervals.

Internet WatchDog is available for Windows or Macintosh. For more information, visit **http://www.charlesriver.com/titles/watchdog.html**.

KINDERGUARD

KinderGuard combines the SafeSurf (**http://www.safesurf.com**) rating system with parameters set by a parent or administrator to filter material that is inappropriate for children or employees. The program handles material from Web, Gopher, and FTP sites, as well as Newsgroups and mailing lists.

To rate Internet sources, KinderGuard uses an in-house editorial review, a Web crawler that searches pages at sites, and customer feedback. The program uses the same rating codes as video game manufacturers (EC—Early Childhood, KA—Kids to Adults, T—Teens, MA—Mature Audiences, and AO—Adults Only). Various rating levels can be set for multiple users.

When you encounter a Web page that you want to rate and add to the list of blocked sites, you can do so with a few mouse-clicks.

For more information about KinderGuard, visit **http://www.intergo.com/wow/kguard.htm**.

Net Nanny

Net Nanny is a program designed to manage Internet and PC access. You can use it to monitor, screen, or block access to anything that is on or running into, out of, or through your computer, online or off.

The program comes with a list of blocked sites and other blocking parameters, which can be updated at no charge at the Net Nanny Web site. Users can add screening specifications.

Net Nanny operates on the Internet, dialup BBSes, AOL, CompuServe, and Prodigy, as well as locally on the host PC. (It operates within the content of online services, as well as the Internet at large.) Online, the program monitors and filters access to the Web, Newsgroups, Web chat rooms, FTP sites, downloads, and email. Locally, you can use it to block access to specific programs or data files and to reject loading data or programs from unauthorized floppy disks and CD-ROMs.

Online blocking includes scanning at the word and phrase levels. You can use two-way blocking to keep someone from sending telephone or credit-card numbers, passwords, or any other information you don't want going out.

Net Nanny is available for Windows or DOS. See **http://www.netnanny.com** for more information.

NetShepherd

NetShepherd is an Internet content rating service that filters the results of AltaVista searches. Its PICS-compliant ratings database can be used with Microsoft Internet Explorer or NetShepherd's own daxHOUND program, a content filtering tool.

For additional information on NetShepherd, visit **http://www.netshepherd.com/**. Information about daxHOUND (and a download) can be found at **http://www.netshepherd.com/products/daxHOUND2.0/daxhound.HTM**.

SurfWatch

SurfWatch is a filter that screens for unwanted material on the Internet. As with other filter and blocking programs, SurfWatch can be used with almost any Web browser. Various levels of access control are available, and the program cannot be easily disarmed by deleting it or by other means. (SurfWatch comes bundled with a time-control program called Time's Up!, discussed in the following section.)

SurfWatch screens Web sites, Newsgroups, FTP and Gopher sites, and Web chat rooms. Blocking is based on a list of sites generated by in-house research and customer reports. Online updates are available via subscription.

SurfWatch alone doesn't allow adults to modify the list of sites, nor does it attempt to block sites that are violent in nature or include material that is hateful or otherwise potentially inappropriate. A free add-on called SurfWatch Manager enables parents to edit the list of blocked sites. Full information on SurfWatch, along with its list of blocked sites, is available at **http://www.surfwatch.com**.

Time's Up!

Time's Up! is a time-monitoring program that can be used to control access to the Internet and any other programs running in Windows on the host computer.

Password controls allow separate limits to be established for several users. Each users' access can be customized for specific programs, days, and hours. Schedules can be set in advance, and a hot key lets users see how much time they've used for the day or for a specific program. Time can be paused, too.

Time's Up! provides reports on demand, by user, program, and day and time. You'll find complete information on Time's Up! at **http://www.timesup.com/**.

Email Filtering

In this section, we'll look at options for filtering email. As you are well aware if you've read earlier chapters, filtering email is often more than convenient. If someone is harassing, spamming, or mailbombing you, you probably won't want to continue seeing mail from the same person—especially if it is the same message over and over. With the right software, you can block unwanted messages, file them together, or have them deleted without ever seeing them.

You may have other reasons for filtering your email. You may wish to drop out of a mailing list temporarily or simply ignore mail from certain people—temporarily or permanently—for whatever reason. You may like to have your mail sorted for you, which is a task that certain email programs with filters do very well.

EMAIL PROGRAMS WITH FILTERS

Filtering messages—especially the ability to delete or return unwanted messages automatically—is a feature that all email programs should have, but don't. We'll look at three of the more popular email programs that offer such advanced filtering features, along with a special email program with filtering for children.

BeyondMail

BeyondMail is an Internet mail manager offered by Banyan Systems, known in the PC world for more than a few popular communications applications. BeyondMail is simpler to use, in terms of the relative number of features it offers, than either of its competitors (Eudora and Pegasus).

Designed to operate with dedicated ISPs only, BeyondMail offers a full suite of mail-management tools: an address book that handles mailing lists, a full-featured searchable filing system, customizable display elements, and spell checking, among other features.

Of special interest here are BeyondMail's filtering features. The program's filter, called the MailMinder in the Mail Clerk system, scans only the From and Subject fields, and doesn't allow wildcards in specifying text or strings to look for. Figure 10.14 shows the filter setup.

The system's simplicity is echoed in most of BeyondMail's other elements, which is a plus if you're new to Internet mail. You can at the very least file objectionable messages in the same folder and delete them *en masse* without reading them. The program's BeyondRules system lets you create more complex MailMinders that can do such tasks as deleting junk mail before you see it. BeyondMail can also send automatic replies based on the message's subject line or sender.

If you're a Windows user who is still feeling your way around the Internet, or if you have a relatively small email load, BeyondMail may be a good choice for learning about email capabilities and filters. You can learn more about BeyondMail at **http://www.coordinate.com/bmail/**.

EMail for Kids

EMail for Kids is, as the name implies, a program designed for kids. With this program, parents can regulate the content of email messages, address-book entries, and the amount of time spent online.

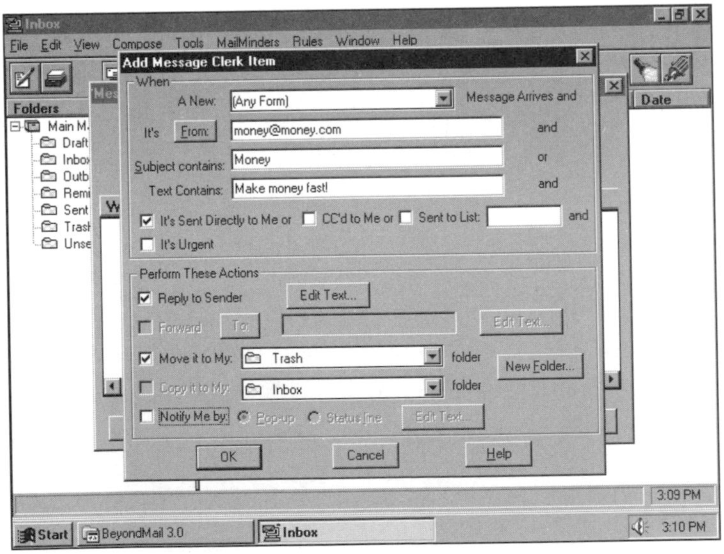

Figure 10.14   BeyondMail's filter setup, called MailMinder.

Among the program's more interesting features are "electronic stamps," which limit the quantity of outgoing mail. (Spammers should be required to use this program.) You can also restrict such information as home address and telephone number with outgoing email filters.

Many of the program activities are like games, with cartoon settings and animation to spice things up. Figure 10.15 gives you an idea of the approach the graphics take.

EMail for Kids also helps children write messages, with prewritten notes for several occasions. The program is available for Windows only. For more information, visit ConnectSoft's Web site at **http://www.connectsoft.com**.

Eudora Pro

Intended to work with dedicated ISPs (but *not* with online services, such as CompuServe or AOL in their current states), Eudora was designed from the ground up as an Internet email management tool. The commercial version, Eudora Pro, offers full email capabilities, with a lot of bells and whistles, including customized spell checking, a full-featured address book, and a complete filing system.

Figure 10.15 EMail for Kids features a lively graphic interface.

The powerful filing system features a sophisticated filtering system. You can tell the filter to search for phrases, words, or strings of characters in *any* message element—including To:, From:, Subject:, the carbon copy list, the Reply-To: field, the message itself, and/or any and all headers. You can use multiple filters and store filter sets for later use. Figure 10.16 gives you an idea of Eudora's filter flexibility.

Additionally, the filters can be set up to look for strings or words beginning or ending with a precise set of characters, thanks to the use of wildcards. You can use Eudora's boolean logic to exclude or include messages with given filter terms.

The filters also handle *message disposition*—placing messages that meet filter criteria into appropriate folders or deleting the messages. Eudora's filters operate on both outgoing and incoming messages. Finally, you can set up automatic replies to filtered messages.

You can download a limited version (Eudora Light) at Qualcomm's Web site (**http://www.qualcomm.com**), but I recommend that you use the full-featured commercial version, Eudora Pro. Both programs are for Windows only.

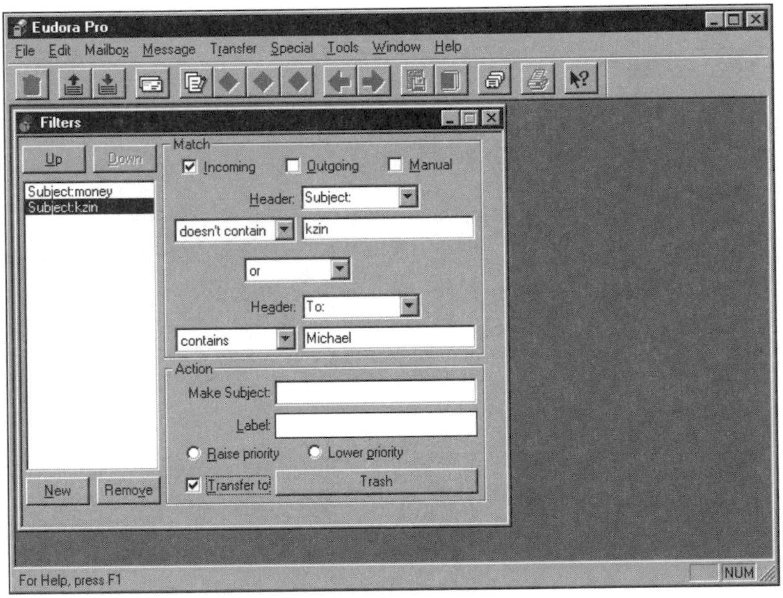

Figure 10.16 Eudora Pro's email filters can intercept messages based on almost any criteria.

Pegasus

Created, published, and supported by a group in New Zealand, Pegasus is a shareware program that accommodates email management on the Internet and on Novell networks. It has a number of interesting features—more features, in all, than any other email manager reviewed here. In certain aspects, Pegasus is an overachiever; it has features in some areas that few of us will use.

First, Pegasus has every email feature that exists: header definition/altering, a complex and powerful filing system, message filters (wildcards supported), a spell checker, mailing lists, message encryption, support for MIME and other encoding formats, a wide range of sort and search features for stored messages, folders within folders, customizable displays, and nearly every other feature offered by other Internet email managers.

Pegasus filters are powerful, using wildcards and multiple filter terms to search any message fields. Figure 10.17 shows Pegasus' available filter options.

The user interface is slightly more intimidating than Eudora's, and this complexity shows up in setting up filter search terms, as well as in the menu and command structure. Most users, however, really like Pegasus; the interface can grow on you.

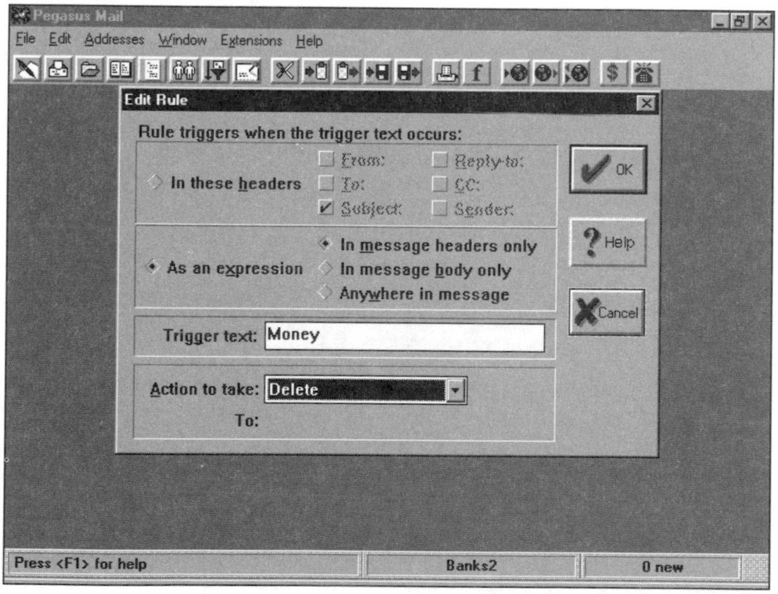

Figure 10.17   Pegasus provides powerful email filters.

You can download the complete Pegasus Windows or Macintosh package, along with several plug-ins, at the Pegasus Web site: **http://www.pegasus.usa.com/**.

TSW's eFilter: A Ready-To-Use Email Filter For ISP Users

TSW's eFilter is an email filtering tool with a definite anti-spam orientation. It works against spam by reading your mail while it's still on your ISP's server. If a message contains a typical spam phrase or keywords, such as "make money fast," eFilter deletes it. The program does keep a log if you want to keep tabs on how much spam you're getting, but that's as close as you'll get to spam once you start using eFilter.

Messages that pass the spam test are downloaded and opened with your email program. Any spam that does get through with odd wording can be prevented because you can set up eFilter to look for words you specify, as shown in Figure 10.18.

You can also have eFilter delete messages from specific email addresses (bobspam@spamspreader.com) and domains (spamspreader.com). The latter is a real plus.

Figure 10.18   TSW's eFilter checks messages for spam.

TSW's eFilter is a shareware program for Windows and can be used only with conventional ISPs. You can download it at **http://catalog.com/tsw/efilter/**. You can use it 10 times on a trial basis, after which you must pay a nominal fee to register the program. I recommend this for all those who want to cut the amount of spam in their email boxes.

ADVANCED FILTERING FOR ISP USERS

If you use a conventional ISP, a variety of scripts are available for keeping spam and other unwanted email from your inbox. Some are rather difficult to implement, while others are fairly simple.

Before you start looking at email filters, make sure your ISP grants you access to the directory in which your mail is kept (usually via your shell account). You should also find out whether you can run scripts and programs on the ISP's server. This is not usually a problem with Unix-based systems, but you should find out the ISP's policy first. (Read the online documentation at the ISP's Web site, or ask.)

The number of available scripts is large, so you should have no problem finding one to adapt to your needs. Personally, I like Paul Milligan's procmailrc email filters, available at his Web site. One, **http://www.mindspring.com/~pjm/ myproc.html**, kills all message autoresponders, mailer returns, and messages with certain curse words in the Subject: lines, along with selected domains. Plus, as Milligan says in his documentation, "It allows for exceptions, so friends that have the misfortune to be associated with spam domains can get through to me. Best of all, it bounces mailbombs, spams, and curses back to the sender and/or abusers." The filter also creates a log, in a file called .mailog, of every message that comes in and how it was disposed of.

Milligan's other filter, at **http://www.mindspring.com/~pjm/myproc2.html**, uses several simple priority levels to permit mail, set it aside, treat it as spam, or present it as not meeting any of those qualifications.

The following sites offer many more filters for procmail, ELM, PINE, et al., along with information on how to put them to work:

- Infinite Ink's Mail Filtering and Robots—**http://www.jazzie.com/ii/internet/ mailbots.html**

- Panix.com's implementation of site-wide email filters—**http://www.panix.com/ e-spam.html**

- Mail Filtering FAQ—**http://www.cis.ohio-state.edu/hypertext/faq/usenet/mail/ filtering-faq/faq.html**

- Mail Filtering FAQ (Unix)—**http://www.cs.ruu.nl/wais/html/na-dir/mail/ filtering-faq.html**

- The ELM Pages—**http://www.math.fu-berlin.de/~guckes/elm/**

- Lasu's Mail Filters—**http://www.cs.helsinki.fi/~wirzeniu/mailfilter.html**

- Lastly, the action-oriented will want to check out Adcomplain, a Unix script that automates sending complaints to spammers and their postmasters—**http:/ /agora.rdrop.com/users/billmc/adcomplain**

Who Or What Do I Filter?

If your email address starts getting out there and you would like to block spam before it comes, you'll need to know what addresses or sites you should block. A quick browse through the Newsgroup **news.admin.net-abuse** will give you a head start on blocking the more troublesome spammers.

For a quick list of addresses for sites that send large quantities of spam, check out AOL's Preferred Mail Blocked Site List at **http:// www.idot.aol.com/preferredmail/**. AOL posts this on the Internet as a welcome public service.

Encryption For Email And Files

The past couple of years have seen quite a lot of coverage in the mainstream media and computer press of the potential for email being intercepted and copied in transit. The truth is that your email *can* be copied and read in transit. The real question is if it *will* be intercepted. Present technology makes it rather difficult and time-consuming to trace the route taken by each packet containing part of an email message. (In fact, it is far simpler to kludge together a "bug" at the sending or receiving end; see Clifford Stoll's excellent book, *The Cuckoo's Egg*, for detailed information on how to do this.) So, unless you are known to be plotting some evil deed, no one is likely to go to the trouble of intercepting your email.

Your data is actually more at risk on your own computer. Still, you will feel safer knowing that your email can't be read by prying eyes along the way. Also, encrypting email messages is one way to verify that email was sent by you. I'll examine several encryption options for data on your system and email and files sent via the Internet—after a little background on the subject of computer data encryption.

Data Encryption

Internet users are concerned about the vulnerability of transmitted data. As you know, data is transmitted over the Internet by being relayed from one computer to another. Because of this, the possibility exists for data in transit to be viewed at any of the computers along the way. The likelihood of this happening is difficult to say.

You can deal with this potential vulnerability in several ways. The first and simplest is to avoid sending sensitive data over the Internet—including credit-card numbers. This makes sense to me, even though the apparent incidence of email "spying" is low.

Other approaches are to use browser and Internet data security features and, where email and other document transmissions are concerned, data encryption.

What Is Data Encryption?

Data encryption is not unlike data encoding (as when you send a MIME-encoded file attached to an email message). The intent is different, however. Rather than encoding data to enable it to be transmitted, data encryption encodes data so it is not recognizable. The idea, of course, is to prevent the data from being understood and used by those who don't have the means of decoding it. In other words, only those to whom you have provided a means of decoding the message can read it.

In practice, encryption is a process of *substitution.* An alternative value, or token, is substituted for designated elements of a message or other data. This is typically done on the character level. For example, the letter *r* might be replaced by *m*, and other characters similarly substituted for every character in the message. (This is similar to what happens when a binary file is encrypted using UUEncode or any other protocol; one group of characters is substituted for another group. The main difference, again, is that the goal is to make the data difficult to unscramble, except for those who have a means of *decrypting* it.)

In theory, encrypted data cannot be read without a guide or reference to all the substitutions that have been made. A simple, nonvarying pattern of character substitution is fairly easy to decode, however (for example, if *m* is always substituted for *r*, *z* is always *t*, and so on).

Most encryption schemes vary the pattern of substitution enough so that no recognizable pattern can be detected and used to decode the message. Under this sort of scheme, *r* might be represented by *m* the first time it appears, then by *o* or *n* or even *r* the next time, and yet another character after that.

Real encryption schemes for computer data are more complex than just described, but you can see the general idea. The encryption scheme not only renders the data in question indecipherable, but also endeavors to make the pattern of encryption vary enough so that it cannot be divined. Sometimes, an encryption scheme will use patterns within patterns—or even a lack of patterns. These are usually based on mathematical formulas.

Assuming an encryption scheme or pattern is too complex to be worked out, or "cracked," the only way you can read an encrypted message is with a *decryption program*, a guide to the encryption patterns used, or the original encryption program.

Data Decryption

Decryption is a process of reproducing data from an encoded message based on a known code, or *cipher*. The key to decrypting encrypted data is known, appropriately enough, as the *key*.

Simply described, a key is a reference or guide to decrypt encrypted data. In effect, it tells the user (or in the case of computer data, a decrypting program) which symbols represent which characters, and where and how.

Keys And Encryption Software

Encryption software usually performs decryption as well as encryption functions. This means that the receiver of encoded data must have the decryption key.

There are several approaches to encrypting and decrypting data. Some apply to one-way data transmission, such as when you send information from a Web site using a form on a Web page. Others apply strictly to email.

One-Way Data Encryption

Where one-way Internet data encryption is concerned, a program at the Web site encrypts data before it is transmitted. The recipient is the only person who has the key to deciphering the data. Thus, the recipient is in control of both encryption and decryption.

EMAIL MESSAGE AND FILE ENCRYPTION

Encryption of email is more "conventional" in that it requires the sender to encrypt a message, and the receiver to decrypt it.

You do not, of course, want to send a decryption key along with a message. You probably don't want to send the decryption key separately either, if there's a chance that it might be intercepted and used later to decrypt intercepted messages.

Public And Private Keys

Fortunately, we have a solution to this dilemma. A system of *public keys* and *private keys* was developed in the 1970s to allow encrypted messages to be sent without the need for the sender to provide the recipient with a code key. Thus, unlike older computer and non-computer encryption schemes, the sender does not have the decryption key.

The public/private key system uses a program (the public key) that encrypts data in a way that can be decrypted only by its counterpart (the private key). Anyone can use the public key, but only the holder of the private key (the message recipient) can decrypt a message created with the public key.

This works particularly well for someone who needs to receive encrypted email messages from many different people. But, overall, it works well in any situation where encryption is needed. In practice, all the sender needs is the recipient's public key. This enables the sender to use the program to encrypt a message in the required format. Once it is encrypted, no one but the recipient can decode it. This is because only the recipient has the private key.

Overall, using encrypted email files is analogous to sending a message in an envelope, as opposed to on a postcard. If this sounds like a good idea—something that anyone might use—you will probably find the following programs of interest.

PGP (Pretty Good Privacy)

The name may seem facetious, but the program is not. PGP is one of the best public-key/private-key encryption programs going. It is also the most widely used program of its type. This work of Phillip Zimmerman is distributed as freeware.

In addition to creating public keys, PGP, of course, unencrypts messages from those who have a public key—provided the creator of the public key is the recipient. PGP also provides message authentication with digital signatures created by the PGP program.

Public keys and signature files created with PGP are text files, and resemble the block of characters below:

```
—BEGIN PGP PUBLIC KEY BLOCK—-
Version: 2.6.2

foXwAAAQMjpgsAAAEDAMsiJK9Ah6VAXVfobv34chAeLeWxl
230LhBEskOAcO1nwbWugMgSs39/Oh7xLoU1G1ZvB7BRH8Z
hvEBtcG2Ht5wPgw4m8FE7QcU316eWd5IFNhbGVzIDxzYcrnO
```

```
hBEskBzehBEsk29V f3QJfoXou39Y29VfobvtPg===wPgwRTxV
—END PGP PUBLIC KEY BLOCK—-
```

With PGP, you can create your own public key and distribute it to friends, associates, and others. One way to distribute your public key is to include it after your "signature" at the end of each message. (You can do this most efficiently by adding it to your "sig file," which is a user-definable block of text that many email programs automatically place at the end of an outgoing message.)

Unifying Privacy

If all of your correspondents use PGP, you can use it to protect against unwanted junk email. If everyone who sends email to you uses PGP to encrypt messages, you can simply reject any email that comes through unscrambled.

You can also use public distribution centers to leave your PGP public key for others and obtain others' public keys. One such server is at **http://rs.internic.net/support/wwwpks/**.

To download PGP, go to **http://bozo.mit.edu:9999/pgp**. For more information on PGP's products, visit the PGP home page at **http://www.pgp.com/**.

PGP for PCs is a DOS application and works on files externally from the DOS command line—that is, you type commands while running the program in DOS, directing it to act on a file you wish to encrypt or decrypt.

If you prefer an easier interface than typing commands in DOS, several DOS and Windows front ends are available for PGP. A list of them, with links, can be found at **http://www.seattle-webworks.com/pgp/pgplinks.html**. (This page also contains links to front ends for using PGP with Eudora, Pegasus, and other email programs.)

Norton Your Eyes Only

Your Eyes Only is a public-key/private-key data-encryption system. If you encrypt a file, transmit it, and it's intercepted, your data is safe. No one can read the file without the public key.

The program operates on directories or individual files. It also has a feature that locks your computer from being accessed if you hit a hot key or leave it idle for a given length of time. You can also lock an entire PC, so only users who are authorized can access the hard disk, even if they try to boot from a floppy.

Check at the Symantec Web site (**http://www.symantec.com**) for complete information on Norton Your Eyes Only.

NORTON SECRET STUFF

A quick-and-easy means of encryption is Norton Secret Stuff (NSS). This small program turns any file you want into an encrypted, self-extracting archive. The archive can be extracted by running it—if you know the password created by the person who used the NSS program to encrypt it. You don't need a copy of Norton Secret Stuff, nor any other special software—just the .EXE file created during the encryption process.

Thus, if you have a text file that you want to send to someone, add it to the list—as shown in Figure 10.19—provide a password (3 to 50 characters) and a name for the .EXE file, and click on the Encrypt button.

Figure 10.19   Norton Secret Stuff is simple to use.

All the recipient has to do is run the resulting .EXE file in DOS or from the Windows Program Manager or taskbar, and provide the password when prompted. The original file is then extracted.

Any kind of file at all can be turned into an encrypted, self-extracting .EXE file. You can place as many as 2,000 files and directories in one encrypted archive. With NSS, even if the file you transmit is intercepted, it cannot be deciphered by someone else. (You will, of course, want to give the password to the recipient separate from the encrypted file.)

You can download Norton Secret Stuff at no charge at the Symantec Web site: **http://www.symantec.com.**

RSA Data Security

For more information about data security, security standards, and what various companies are doing about security on the Internet, visit RSA Data Security's Web site at **http://www.rsa.com/**. This organization is responsible for designing and implementing most of the security standards in use on the Internet. (RSA Data Security also makes available a personal online/offline data-security product called SecurPC.)

Cookie Cutters

Annoyed by the fact that Web sites can store and retrieve information about you in your browser's cookie file? You're not the only one. Version 4 of both Netscape and Microsoft Internet Explorer should be able to handle cookie content to an extent, but if you want a lot of control over the content in your browser's cookie file, you should look into programs that can help you. (Incidentally, the Internet Engineering Task Force has written a standard for tracking cookies. You can check it out at **http://ds.internic.net/rfc/rfc2109.txt**.)

At the forefront is the PGPcookie.cutter. A product of PGP (**http://www.pgp.com**), this tool for Windows users helps bring back anonymous browsing. Users can selectively block cookies that may spread too much information around and keep others that are valuable—such as passwords.

A different approach is offered by The Internet Junkbuster Proxy (**http://www.junkbuster.com**) and other anonymous surfing proxies. Such sites keep cookies from being read or placed on your system. (The Internet Junkbuster also filters out advertising banners.)

Just For Spam-Haters

Now for something different: a program that handles spam for you. Spam Hater is a free Windows program that helps track down and respond to spammers and their postmasters.

Shown in Figure 10.20, Spam Hater analyzes spam email and provides you with several options.

When you fire it up and direct it to a spam message, Spam Hater analyzes the message. Then, it extracts a list of addresses of postmasters, sets up a whois query to track the spammer, and prepares a reply for you to send. You can send your choice of legal threats, spammer insults, or a message of your own.

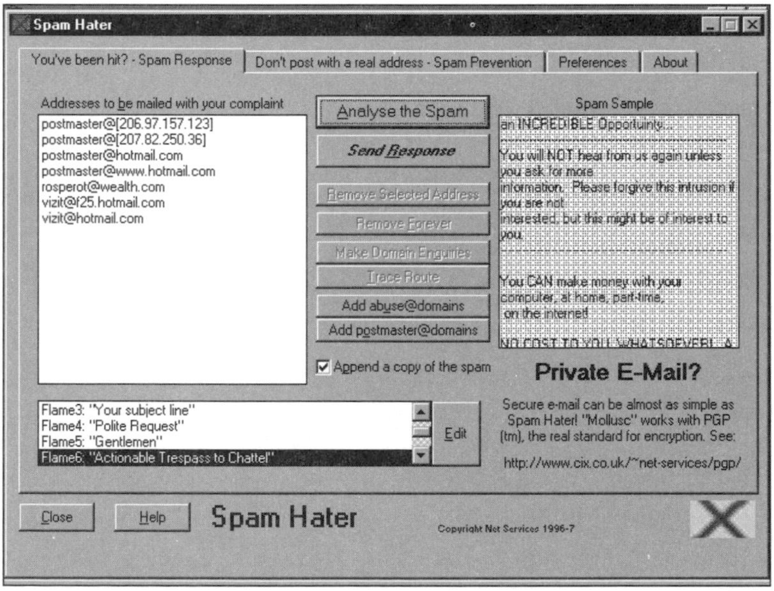

Figure 10.20 Spam Hater, an answer to spam.

Spam Hater works with a variety of email programs and online services, including AOL, CompuServe, Eudora, Free Agent, Microsoft Internet Explorer, Netscape, Pegasus Mail, and others.

Download a copy at **http://www.compulink.co.uk/~net-services/spam/**.

The software tools discussed here should add quite a bit to your ability to keep your privacy, control the Internet, and deal with some online problems. Now, let's delve a little deeper into how you can best put this arsenal of tools to work with techniques you've already learned, in Chapter 11.

Chapter 11

Internet Safety Tips And Tricks

Chapter 11

Browser, Email, And USENET Security

Controlling What Comes Into Your Email Box

Chat Room And IRC Safety

Getting Your Information Off The Net

Online Shopping And Financial Alternatives

Handling Online Crime

Internet
Safety
Tips
And
Tricks

Chapter 11

This chapter presents a categorized roundup of online safety tips and techniques. I'll also show you a few new tricks and techniques for protecting yourself in cyberspace, along with some useful resources I've collected and some interesting background information. You might consider it a "grab bag" of information about protecting yourself and your privacy.

There are a number of ways to approach these issues, many of which were discussed in earlier chapters. I'll recap some here and show you a few new tricks.

Browser, Email, And USENET Security

The first and most important means of preventing problems on the Internet is maintaining control of your personal information. This includes not only your full name, address, and telephone number, but also, in certain circumstances, your email address and other information.

Your Web browser and/or email program can distribute your email address and other information—without your knowing it—in several ways:

- When you send email to someone you don't know, it could be passed along to others or added to all sorts of mailing lists.

- When you post in Newsgroups or Internet BBSes, your email address (and sometimes your name) can be included in your message headers.

- Some Web pages can obtain your email address, name, and other information from your browser.

You can prevent your browser, email, and public messages from revealing personal information. I'll detail several ways to do so in this section.

CHANGE YOUR HEADERS

One of the simplest ways to keep your email address and other data to yourself is to keep it out of the From: and Reply-To: headers in your messages. Of course, without that information, no one can write back to you. Still, messaging without a return address or name in the headers does have its advantages:

- You can visit Web pages and FTP sites anonymously.

- You can post messages in USENET without revealing your identity. (I know public posting shouldn't be a contact sport, but a lot of people try to make it so. That being the case, keeping your identity to yourself is sometimes best.)

- You can send messages expressing your opinions (as with polls or forms) without having your return address attached.

Altering Netscape And Internet Explorer Mail Headers

You can delete information from message headers in Netscape and Internet Explorer as follows:

- *Netscape*—First select Mail and News Preferences... on the Options menu. Then click on the Server tab and remove or replace the first three fields. Click on the Identity tab and remove or replace the first three fields there. (Write down the information you're deleting; you'll want to replace it later so you can send and receive email and post Newsgroup messages.)

- *Internet Explorer*—Select Read Mail on the Go menu, then select Options on the mail client's Mail menu. Click on the Server tab and delete or replace any information in the seven fields in the tab. (Here again, copy the information you delete for later replacement.)

Don't Press That!

Have you ever seen a Web page that featured "voting" buttons? The page may ask for your opinion—for example, "Do you care whether the color of money is green?"—followed by two pushbuttons, labeled "Yes" and "No."

Such a page may be legitimate—or it may simply be a means of collecting your email address to add to a mailing list, using an email capture script. Clicking on such a button would send your email address to the person who set up the Web page. So, think twice before you press a button on a Web page.

Altering Headers Produced By Email Client Programs

Email client programs—such as BeyondMail, Eudora, and Pegasus for the PC, and the various Macintosh email clients—can be similarly modified to keep your real name and return address out of your messages. Each has a different approach to its setup, but altering the header information is not difficult. As is the case with altering browser settings, after you finish your "anonymous" tasks, you will want to replace any server and identity settings you changed or deleted.

Online-Service Email Areas

If you use an online service's email area for your outgoing email, you will find that removing your return address from the headers is difficult. You can, however, specify the name or nickname included with your email address. (But changing the actual email address is extremely difficult at best.) I recommend leaving it blank. (This, of course, does not apply if you are using your Web browser or an email client program to handle mail via the online service's SMTP—Simple Mail Transfer Protocol—server.)

Making Your Address Available In USENET Postings

If the only reason you need to keep your email address out of headers in USENET postings is to avoid address-collecting "spambots," you can still include your address so humans can read it. Spambot programs look for strings in a specific format: xxxxx@xxxxx.xxx. All you have to do is include your address in a different format: for example, xxxxx at yyyyy dot xxx. This fools the spambots, yet a person can easily figure it out.

Tempted To Use Anonymous Email As A Weapon? Don't!

As you may have guessed, altering your headers is also a way to send anonymous mail or postings with ill intent. Before you try to harass someone with anonymous mail, however, consider this: I have not told you *all* the ways to track down the sender of an "anonymous" message. These techniques are no secret to ISP and online-service technical staff, most of whom are more than willing to use them when someone tries to play email tricks involving their systems.

Use An Anonymous Remailer

For the ultimate protection of your email and Newsgroup postings, consider using an anonymous remailer. It hides your identity in both incoming and outgoing email. No one knows where you ultimately receive your email, nor where it really comes from.

For incoming email, an anonymous remailer accepts it for you and forwards it to an address you designate, without revealing that address to senders.

When you send email, it goes first to the anonymous remailer's server, which removes headers before sending it on to its destination. Thus, your email address and even your ISP remain unknown.

Anonymous remailers are also used for USENET postings. They are particularly useful for people who want to participate in personal discussions of sensitive topics in Newsgroups.

Where Do I Find One?

A few ISPs (**http://www.interlink-bbs.com**, for one) provide anonymous remailer services to their customers for USENET postings. Most people who use anonymous remailers subscribe to one of several public remailer services. These services are usually free, operated as a public service. For a list of anonymous remailers, visit **http://www.cs.berkeley.edu/~raph/remailer-list.html** or **http://www.compulink. co.uk/~net-services/care/**.

For those who want to ensure that even their system administrators can't read their anonymous messages, a special service that combines message encryption with a remailer service is available. This double security system is the John Doe Home Page (**http://www.compulink.co.uk/~net-services/care/**). It isn't free, but the cost is minimal if you are really concerned about your privacy.

(Note that anonymous remailers have strict rules against activities such as mailbombing, spamming, using email to harass someone, and distributing illegal materials by email. Try it, and you'll lose your account. Also, a court order can force the operator of an anonymous server to reveal your identity. So, these services are not shelters for illegal or unethical activities.)

Don't FTP Your Email Address

Most people are unaware that when they go to an anonymous FTP (which requires no specific user ID and password), their browsers use their real user IDs and host names (ISP names). Together, these make up your email address.

You can prevent your email address from being handed out this way by one of three methods:

- Use a proxy server, as described in the next section.

- Place a fictitious user ID in place of the one in your browser's mail setup.

- Use an FTP client program, such as WS_FTP, to access the site. This allows you to use any ID you wish. I recommend that you use an FTP client program, in any event, because it greatly enhances the reliability and available options for FTP transfers. (WS_FTP is available at: **http://www.ipswitch.com**.)

PROTECT YOUR INFORMATION WITH A PROXY SERVER

As described in Chapter 10, a proxy server is an agent or surrogate that shields you from being identified by the Web sites you visit. In conventional Web surfing, your system exchanges data with the Web-site host, and the Web pages you request are transmitted to you. On the surface, the only data you appear to be sending is the URL you type in. Wrong. The remote system is often collecting all sorts of information from your computer, including—but not limited to—your ISP name, email address, and the URL you visited previously.

How Does A Proxy Server Work?

A proxy server stands between you and Web-site hosts. Rather than your browser requesting pages from a server, the proxy server does it for you, then relays the pages to you. Every site you visit thinks it is being visited by the proxy server computer. *None* of your personal data is collected by the Web sites you visit.

The Anonymizer, A Simple Proxy Server

One of the more popular proxy servers (and by far the easiest to use) is The Anonymizer (**http://www.anonymizer.com/open.html**). Shown in Figure 11.1, The Anonymizer has a simple front end; go to the URL above, enter the URL you want to visit, and you're on your way—anonymously.

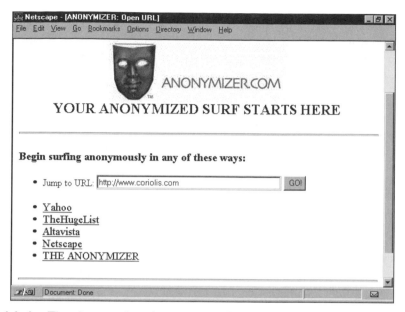

Figure 11.1   The Anonymizer lets you surf the Web anonymously.

The Anonymizer also provides an extensive listing of links you can jump to anonymously. In addition to allowing you to surf Web pages anonymously, it can also be used to access FTP sites anonymously.

You don't have to use The Anonymizer's front end. If you prefix the URL of a Web page you want to retrieve with the name of The Anonymizer's server (**http://www.anonymizer.com:8080/**), the result will be the same as if you had used the front end. For example, if you wanted to retrieve the page at **http://www.coriolis.com/webpsychos/**, you would enter this URL: **http://www.anonymizer.com:8080/http://www.coriolis.com/webpsychos/** (which is the index page for this book's site).

Either way you approach it, you would see the page you requested as "hosted" by The Anonymizer. Figure 11.2 shows how this looks, complete with a banner ad carried by The Anonymizer.

Other Proxy Server Applications

As noted in Chapter 10, proxy servers, such as Cyber Patrol (**http://www.microsys.com/proxy/proxserv.htm**), can also filter incoming Web content. (Rather than having a simple front end as The Anonymizer has, the Cyber Patrol proxy server requires you to configure your browser to work with it.)

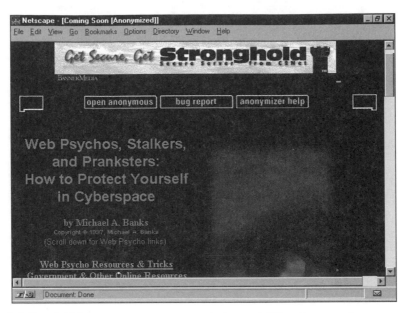

Figure 11.2   A Web page as accessed through The Anonymizer.

Many corporate Web servers use proxy servers to isolate themselves from other networks. The relationship of a proxy server to a corporate Web server in this application is similar to that of The Anonymizer to your Web browser. The proxy retrieves desired pages from the Web, then passes them on to the corporate server, without ever coming into contact with the servers from which pages are retrieved.

SNEAKING UP ON SUSPICIOUS WEB PAGES

As you know, some Web pages might not only swipe information from your browser and cookie file, but also perform more nefarious stunts. If you are suspicious of a Web page for any reason, consider sneaking up on it and viewing its content without exposing yourself to malicious applets or other vicious tricks.

You can do this by using Telnet to contact the server that hosts the page in question, through its port 80, the standard port for http access. Specify it by appending :80 to the end of the URL. Once connected, request the page using this format: GET <page> HTTP/1.0. The remote system will send the raw HTML code to your screen, then close the connection.

Say you wanted to request a page from **http://www.evilsite.com/buynow.html**, using Netscape. You would first use Telnet to access the host: **telnet:// www.evilsite.com:80**.

When the remote system connected, you would type "GET /buynow.html HTTP/1.0."

This will not work with all servers, but it's a great way to look at a page's source code without risking anything. I've used this technique several times, and it identified a potential problem with a Web page on more than one occasion.

Full Access To Browser Security

Not every technique discussed here is available if you use the built-in version of Microsoft Internet Explorer that America Online, CompuServe, and Prodigy offer. Those custom versions of the browser do not let you get at many browser settings.

If you find this limiting, just get a copy of Netscape or Explorer, and start it up after you use your online service's software to log on. Either browser will hook into the PPP (Point to Point Protocol) connection provided by the online service. (You can't use an email client program under these circumstances, except with CompuServe; you can use its SMTP to send email only using an email client. Thus, you can change headers on mail sent from a CompuServe account.)

If you do make the switch, remember that you lose any benefits the online service provided through its Internet gateway.

There is currently one exception to being unable to use an email client program with an online service. That exception is CompuServe; you can use its SMTP to send email only using an email client. Thus, it is possible to change headers on mail sent from a CompuServe account.

CREATE A "THROWAWAY" EMAIL ADDRESS

At times, for one reason or another, you may want to give an address to someone who might compromise it. Or, you may find yourself in a situation where you can't hide your online ID (chat rooms come to mind).

In either instance, you should have an alternate ID that you don't use for regular email. This extra ID, which I call a "throwaway ID," can serve all sorts of purposes. As you will see in the next few pages, you can use it to receive passwords and other information that automated systems may send to you via email. You can also use it to post to USENET Newsgroups and participate in chat rooms.

If you set up a throwaway ID as your surrogate for USENET and/or chat rooms, you can count on getting loads of spam and probably a little crackpot mail. Throwaway IDs are also handy for posting classified ads.

A throwaway ID is well worth the small extra expense. It protects your identity and your primary ID so that you can safely enjoy any Internet activity you wish. If the ID becomes a problem, or your ID is compromised through it, you simply throw it away and get another.

 A throwaway ID may not cost you anything. If you use an online service that lets you have more than one ID, such as AOL or Prodigy, you're already in business. Some ISPs allow more than one ID per account, too, or provide a discount for a second account.

Take the same precautions with this ID as you do with your regular account. Select an ID that is not offensive and doesn't give away any information about your sex, age, or interests that you don't want it to. Remove any information that an ISP or online service may have created for it in a finger listing or online directory. If you use your real name with your regular ID, don't post anything using the throwaway ID that may associate the two. In short, cover your tracks carefully. For a throwaway ID to be useful, it must never be linked to your regular ID, nor, usually, to your real name.

Controlling What Comes Into Your Email Box

Controlling what comes into your email box isn't a big safety issue, but it certainly can make life online easier. Exercising a little control can prevent you from ending up with several dozen spam messages in your inbox every week, and it may make you a little more difficult for a Web psycho to find.

Controlling your inbox contents starts with keeping your email address as private as possible. In addition to the tips in the preceding section, the following precautions will go a long way toward preventing your email address from getting too public—and being abused:

- If you do a lot of posting in USENET Newsgroups or other public message systems, consider using a throwaway ID for posting. That way you can ignore the spam and occasional crank or threatening email your postings may generate. If you can turn off or block all email to the throwaway address, do so. AOL and Prodigy allow you to block all email, and those who use conventional ISPs can do the same with the proper server-side scripts or programs (see Chapter 10).

- Don't sign every Web-site guest book you come across; this will only increase your load of unsolicited email, as guest-book entries are one of the many sources spammers use for compiling their address lists.

- To reduce or eliminate unsolicited commercial email—and the potential for other unpleasant email—delete any online profiles you may have posted about yourself. Double-check your ISP or online service to make sure that your name and other information weren't automatically entered in an online directory or finger listing when you signed up.

- When you sign up for a members-only Web site, provide as little information as possible. Omit important information, such as your real name, address, telephone number, and email address. If the sign-up process won't go through without some or all of those items, consider faking the information. At the very least, fake your email address—many companies that collect such information about you also sell it to other companies. If the Web site wants to email your password to you, consider just moving on—or having the password sent to a throwaway email address.

- If you use an online service, make full use of any email blocking features offered.

- If you use a conventional ISP, look into methods of filtering your email. I covered several in Chapter 10.

If you would rather not bother with any of the preceding, you can always practice "selective deletion"—that is, delete anything you don't like. (Many spammers recommend that you do this, rather than ask them to stop sending their trash to you.) Of course, you may eventually find yourself devoting several hours to this task every month.

Chat Room And IRC Safety

Aside from the aggravation and annoyance that some people bring into chat rooms, the biggest concern is having your email address, and thus your identity, compromised. Chat rooms on online services or the Web can attract some real weirdos. Get the wrong person's attention—good or bad—and you could have an annoying pest on your hands at best, or a stalker at worst.

The strongest protection against such harassment is to use a throwaway ID. If you find that you have attracted undue attention from a chat-room habitué, you can ignore any email pandering. If the situation gets really difficult—perhaps this person looks for you in chat rooms every night—you can always just throw the ID away and create another.

Who's Online?

If you're on an online service, you probably know of various commands to show you who's in various chat rooms, and maybe in a chat area, whether or not you are in a chat room. The same is true of IRC chat rooms on the Web. Among other places, you'll find "who's online" directories for IRC chats at **http://www.four11.com**. Its Net Phone Directory lets you see who's online, using Connectix Videophone, CU-SeeMe, Intel Internet Phone, AudioVision/VideoLink, Microsoft NetMeeting, or H.323-compliant net phones.

Also available are commands to identify people using nicknames. You can see the ID of the person using a given nickname or, on some systems, of everyone in a chat room.

The point? You can use a nickname, but you can't hide your online ID in a chat room.

In addition to using a throwaway ID, you can protect yourself in two other ways:

- Learn all the important commands available in the chat room. These include the commands to show who is in the room and the IDs behind nicknames; to "ignore" or "gag" specified participants so you won't have to see what they are typing to you or sending as whispers; and to send a whisper, should you need to communicate with someone privately.

- In an IRC chat, make sure you know how to contact the "op," the person in charge of the chat room. On an online service, learn whom you should contact—and how—if any problems come up. This way, you have some recourse if someone is harassing you or disturbing the group at large.

A final note: Until you get to know the people in a chat room, listen more than you talk. You needn't "lurk," but you should take time to get to know the protocols and people of the chat room. If rules are posted, read and follow them. That way, you won't offend anyone.

Getting Your Information Off The Net

You know from reading earlier chapters that the Internet has certain key places to look for information about people online. These include online member directories and finger listings, BBS and Newsgroup postings, and Internet email directories. You have some control over information in these areas—you can remove it or take steps to ensure that it eventually goes away.

And well you should, for the longer you leave information on the Internet, the farther it can spread. If it's online, you have absolutely no control over how your information is used.

DIRECTORIES, PROFILES, AND LISTINGS

The starting point for removing information is your ISP or online service. Remove any finger, profile, and directory information that exists.

If you think that no information about you is available online, look again. On ISPs that enable finger listings, new users' names and IDs are automatically entered in the ISP's finger directory. Similarly, an online service may automatically include you in its member directory. As for online profiles, don't put one up; if you have, delete it.

When you join a forum on an online service, you may be asked to provide your name. (This is the case with CompuServe and DELPHI.) I suggest providing your first name only.

Public Postings

If you feel your postings on an online-service BBS have compromised your privacy, you can usually go back and delete them. (Chances are, they will have disappeared after a few weeks, anyway.) If the questionable postings are on a Web-site BBS, ask the person who runs it to delete them.

If past USENET postings are bothering you, you're probably out of luck. Several services archive USENET postings, and one—Deja News—is intent on archiving and making available in searchable format every posting ever made to any USENET Newsgroup.

Supposedly, you can have Deja News remove your postings by sending a detailed request to **comment@dejanews.com**. But the company has not responded to those requests in at least three instances I know of. Anything already archived may well be in the searchable Deja News database forever.

Even if you can't get postings removed from the archives, you can ensure that a posting will not be archived. All you have to do is include this header in each of your postings: x-no-archive: yes.

If you can't set up your software to include that header, simply make it the first line in your message.

You also want to avoid placing classified ads on online services or Web pages. These sometimes stay around forever, and, as with other types of public postings, they are sources of email addresses for spammers.

If you have to post in any of these venues, consider using a throwaway account. Never post anything that might be embarrassing, or worse, in five years.

INTERNET EMAIL AND TELEPHONE DIRECTORIES

Chapter 8 detailed a number of email directories and databases available as Web sites. These directories let you search for email addresses based on a person's name. Some also let you search for the name of the person who has a given email address. A few contain additional information on people listed and cross-reference to Internet telephone directories.

Most of the directories will remove your name and email address(es) from their listings if you ask. You will have to look around each directory's site to find the address to email your remove request. (It's usually in an About or Help section.)

Note that you may have to be persistent with some of these services. I suspect that removing names from their databases is low on their lists of priorities.

Online name/address and telephone directories are a different story. Options to remove entries may be nonexistent, or you may be required to submit a request in writing. Check individual sites for details.

Online Shopping And Financial Alternatives

Online shopping has yet to achieve its full potential, largely because of the public's perception of potential risks in transmitting credit-card information over the Internet. At present, a few niche marketers—offering books, computer equipment, items that can't be found elsewhere, and a few other types of merchandise—do well. Those who do best offer value-added factors, such as free shipping or discounts, to help consumers overcome their resistance to buying online.

Online shopping will not fully evolve until convenient and secure payment systems are available. I suspect these will be in the form of debit-type arrangements, under which "e-cash" units are purchased offline and tendered online via secure servers. (For more information on such systems, visit **http://www.ecash.com** and **http://www.firstvirtual.com**.)

Until this sort of system is generally available, the best alternative is to shop around online, but purchase through conventional offline channels.

Handling Online Crime

The Internet has no police—at least not in the traditional sense. You won't, for example, find your city, county, or state police forces patrolling the Internet. Nor do the FBI (**http://www.fbi.gov**) and the Secret Service (**http://www.ustreas.gov/treasury/bureaus/usss/usss.html**) maintain Internet offices where you can file complaints, even though both agencies have been known to investigate crimes that used online services and/or the Internet. (Of course, if they did have Web sites where you could complain about someone, say, harassing you online, the agencies would quickly be overwhelmed by complaints.)

So, what if you are the victim of problem email? What if you get threats via email or in a chat room? What about someone who tracks you down online and starts making harassing telephone calls—or worse?

At some point, you might decide to call your local police, but you might be disappointed. Overworked, understaffed, and often underpaid, many local or regional police departments do not have the staff, knowledge, or resources to handle Internet crimes. They have their hands full with crimes in the real world, crimes that are easier to prosecute than harassing email messages.

Furthermore, explaining the nature of Internet crimes to police, prosecutors, judges, and juries can be a little difficult.

Not that these agencies don't want to help; often, there is nothing they can do. A dearth of laws that clearly address online crimes is in large part responsible for the fact that Internet crimes are not always treated the same—or as seriously—as real-world crimes. Only when the criminal activity moves into the real world—into the sphere of conventionally defined criminal activity—do some agencies take action. When the stalker starts making telephone or physical contact, when the con artist starts taking in money through the mail, or when threats are backed up by action, then the system kicks in.

Unfortunately, this can be too late.

This situation will be remedied over the next few years as more and more states enact laws that clearly address Internet issues. That, combined with increasing

Internet literacy, will eventually help conventional law enforcement move into cyberspace.

Until then, you have limited choices: You may have to approach online criminal acts in a vigilante mode (usually fruitless); ignore a problem until it touches the real world; or seek other help.

Where can you find help? Read on.

RESOURCES FOR VICTIMS OF PERSONAL CRIMES ONLINE

Crime watching and crime fighting have evolved right along with crime itself on the Internet. Several organizations and public (if not legally empowered) agencies online devote all or most of their resources to helping victims of online crime and preventing online crime through education and sharing information on criminal activities.

The next few pages offer a look at organizations and agencies that can help if you are a victim of a *personal* crime online. Personal crimes include stalking, threats, harassment, and mailbombing. They also include various forms of impersonation—someone sending email with your name on it, posting with your name, impersonating you in chat rooms, or signing you up for mailing lists or other online offers. (Victims of fraud and spam are referred to Chapters 7 and 8.)

CONVENTIONAL LAW-ENFORCEMENT AGENCIES

While getting help from conventional law-enforcement agencies may at times be difficult, it is not impossible. The reaction you get to reporting an online crime will depend in large part on the level of computer literacy of the person you talk with. More and more police agencies have an officer who is designated to look into online crimes, either officially or unofficially. This is usually someone who knows the Internet and can help translate what is happening to you online into real-world terms—and who can point out which conventional laws may apply, thus assisting you in filing a complaint. The same person can often give you advice to help reduce or eliminate the problem.

Attitude is another determining factor. If no one with an agency really takes the Internet seriously, you're not going to get far. If you can clearly explain what is happening to you, perhaps putting it in real-world terms, you may be able to convince the agency to seek out additional resources and help—such as the FBI, whose interest is aroused when a crime crosses state lines, or the Secret Service, which is mandated to investigate fraud and other crimes that use your computer systems and the Internet.

You may, however, have to seek out another agency yourself, or even take your problem to the local prosecutor's office. Here again, the help you receive will depend on the level of computer and Internet literacy you encounter, and you may have to do quite a bit of "educating" about the facts of your case and how it affects you in a real-world sense. You might have to research applicable laws—old or new—to present a convincing case.

Ideally, though, your local police will be able to advise and help you—and put a stop to the problem quickly.

Law Enforcement And Online Crimes

Conventional law enforcement does, by and large, recognize online crime. In many instances, however, such crime cannot be prosecuted nor even addressed by police action unless existing laws can be applied. This is either because a given jurisdiction has no laws that apply, or because making the charges stick is simpler using familiar laws. (Florida, for example, has a number of computer crime laws, but they have been used only three times since 1979. High-tech crimes of any type are usually prosecuted under existing laws.)

Online–Service And ISP Sysops

Don't discount the potential for your online service's or ISP's management to help you if you are being victimized online. The same is true of the management at the perpetrator's ISP. Sysops have a number of options, beginning with warning the perpetrator to stop, or else. Beyond that, they can kill the perpetrator's account or block certain privileges (such as email). They can also be a good source of evidence, should you be forced to take your problem to the police or courts.

Check your ISP's Web site or your online service's member information for email addresses of contacts if you have problems online. For other ISPs or online services, you can complain to the postmaster at the site or use the Web interface to Whois (**http://rs.internic.net/cgi-bin/whois**) to see who is responsible.

Places To Get Help Now

When you are a victim of online crime, you need to get help immediately. As with any crime, you want to get people looking into it before the trail cools. A perpetrator may be using a throwaway account, so you want to get moving before he or she decides to dump it and disappear. (This is not to say that you can't track someone down via an account they're no longer using, but getting information on an active account is easier.)

You also want to share information with as many people as possible. Online organizations and agencies are the best starting point. Sometimes, sharing information can contribute substantially to handling an online criminal or Web psycho. (Indeed, the now-famous case of Jane Hitchcock, who suffered criminal harassment via the Internet, in addition to offline harassment, was helped by a number of online acquaintances.) By sharing your information, you alert other potential victims, while serving as a reminder that online crime is real and must be dealt with.

The following resources are among the best available on the Web. They can provide immediate help, advice, referrals, and more. If your case warrants, they will publicize it.

Each of these organizations is worth visiting, even if you aren't the victim of an online crime. Their frequently updated educational and advisory resources offer information that can help you prevent online crime. In addition, most welcome volunteers. Chapter 9 also included information on most of these groups.

CyberAngels

Founded in 1995 by members of the International Alliance of Guardian Angels, CyberAngels (**http://www.cyberangels.org**) focuses on Internet safety. This includes educating new Internet users, crime prevention, and helping victims. As you can see in Figure 11.3, CyberAngels offers a wide variety of services and resources.

CyberAngels is particularly active in patrolling the Web; members observe and report criminal activity ranging from child pornography to online stalking and sexual harassment. They also actively support and advise online victims; among other services, they operate a Tracing Unit, which assists victims in tracing online attackers. (The volunteers in the Tracing Unit use many of the same techniques you've learned about in this book.)

The Web site also provides a wealth of links to cyberstalking and anti-harassment resources, news reports of Internet-related crimes, and education, information, and safe-surfing resources. There is also a section on current active cases handled by CyberAngels.

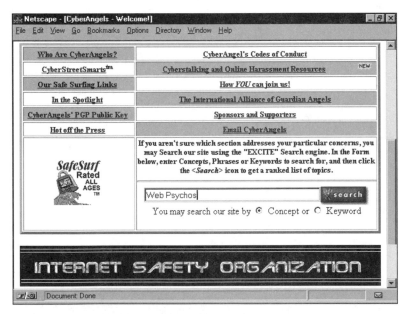

Figure 11.3   A page from the Web site of CyberAngels, an online crime-fighting organization.

Per their mission statement, CyberAngels also works to protect children from online criminal abuse (particularly involving child pornography), preserve and promote netiquette, preserve freedom of speech, and teach new Internet users "Cyberstreetsmarts."

For more information about CyberAngels, or to join, send email to **gabriel@cyberangels.org**.

Cybergrrl Webstation

The Cybergrrl Webstation is a wide-ranging resource for women on the Web, concentrating on making the Internet safe and fun. It also offers free membership in the Cybergrrl Network, providing a chat room and forum, in addition to other resources.

Billed as "The Premier Place for Women and Girls Online," the Cybergrrl Webstation resources extend to women's topics beyond the Web, as shown in Figure 11.4.

Other Cybergrrl resources include health information, categorized news, features, and information specifically for women. The site also includes a categorized search

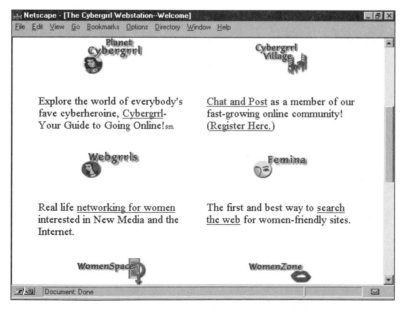

Figure 11.4   The Cybergrrl Webstation.

engine, an entertaining online serial ("The Adventures of Cybergrrl"), a newsletter, and numerous other resources of interest to women on the Web.

For more information about Cybergrrl, stop by the Web site, or email **cybergrrl@cgim.com.**

ScamWatch

ScamWatch (**http://www.scamwatch.com**) is a place to collect and share information and experiences involving online consumer fraud. The organization provides a Web site (Figure 11.5) offering assistance with issues related to fraud and scam. This includes business-to-business fraud as well as consumer-related fraud.

Visitors can post information about suspected scams for others to read, and peruse extensive information about fraud—including rebuttals from anyone accused of perpetrating a fraud who wants to explain their side of the story. The site has a large number of links to related sites and resources.

ScamWatch investigates and verifies scams and frauds and turns them over to the appropriate commercial or government agency. The organization also posts site reviews and ratings, alerts, and other information on Internet scams.

For more information, contact **comments@scamwatch.com.**

Figure 11.5   ScamWatch menu.

Vice Squad

The Vice Squad site (**http://207.15.223.224/vicesquad.htm**) is a clearinghouse for information on online crime and fraud. You can report incidents here, and get information on current Webwide problems.

The Vice Squad also provides general information about online crime and fraud.

Web Police

Web Police (**http://www.web-police.org**) is allied with other organizations that deal with fraud, scams, and related issues online. Web Police takes reports on Web crimes and incidents, investigates them, and turns them over to the appropriate agencies. Members also stand ready to advise victims and take action where possible.

The organization's Web site, shown in small part in Figure 11.6, offers extensive resources having to do with all categories of online crime, frauds, and scams.

It also provides news bulletins, a public forum, a chat room, and more, including links to like-minded online organizations. A frequent email newsletter keeps

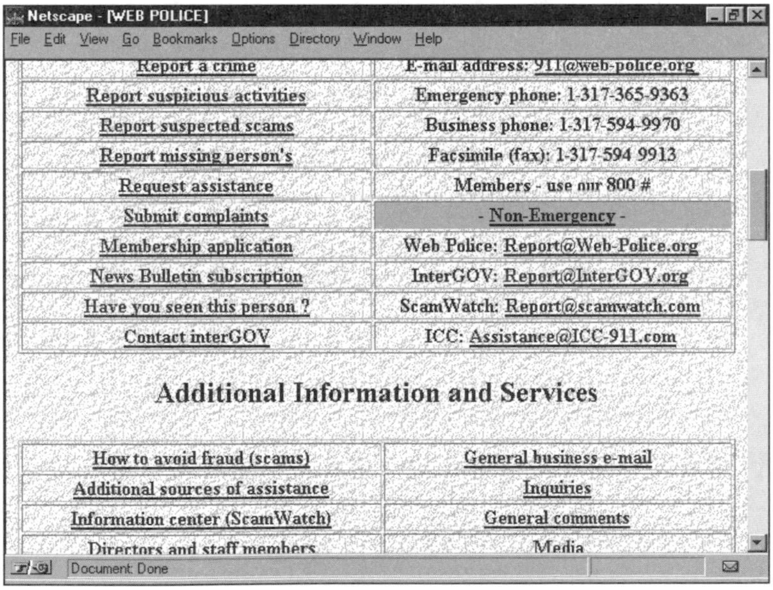

Figure 11.6   Web Police menu.

members and other interested parties abreast of online crime developments, along with news of additions and improvements to the Web Police service.

For more information, email **comments@web-police.org**.

Keeping Parolees Off The Internet

If you have any doubt as to the seriousness of online crime, consider the United States Parole Commission's stand on the Internet. The commission—which does not allow federal parolees to associate with known criminals, drink excessively, or own guns—has decided that accessing the Internet is a potentially dangerous activity. Thus, federal parolees are now prohibited from accessing the Internet via computer.

Women Halting Online Abuse (W.H.O.A.)

W.H.O.A. (**http://whoa.femail.com/index.html**) addresses Internet issues exclusively from the woman's viewpoint. A lot of emphasis is placed on education—particularly regarding online harassment of women—and on encouraging ISPs and online services to create problem-free environments. Figure 11.7 shows a portion of W.H.O.A.'s Web site.

W.H.O.A.'s resources are quite extensive. In addition to organizational announcements and papers, the site offers a Safe Site List, shown in Figure 11.8, featuring sites that have adopted and enforced anti-harassment policies.

Balancing out the Safe Site List is the Unsafe Site List, listing sites that have a history of harassment and abuse. It includes some actions you can take to fight back, as well.

The Web site also features W.H.O.A.'s Voluntary Anti-Harassment Policies for Web sites and ISPs, as well as articles and personal stories about online harassment, abuse, and stalking. This is complemented by information on how to get help and support if you have been harassed.

W.H.O.A. has direct links to the Women's White Pages Directory (**http://www.femail.com/fesearch.htm**) and the Women's Web Site Directory (**http://www.femail.com/sites/**). A collection of links to educational and other resources rounds out the W.H.O.A. site's offerings.

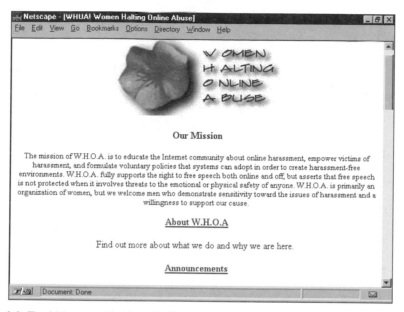

Figure 11.7   Women Halting Online Abuse is an educational and proactive online organization for women.

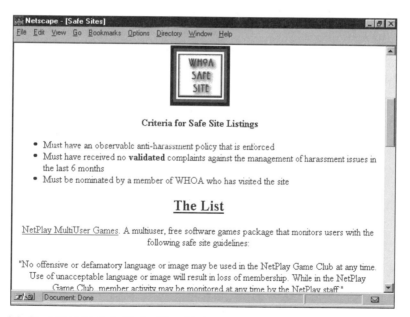

Figure 11.8   W.H.O.A.'s Safe Site List.

To get more information or to become a member of W.H.O.A. (membership is free), email **whoa@femail.com**.

Help Yourself

Don't forget that preventing online crime, as well as dealing with it if you are a victim, starts with you. Apply what you have learned in this book and avail yourself of the educational resources provided at such sites as CyberAngels, W.H.O.A., and others discussed here. Simple education—and using what you learn—can prevent most online problems.

Take Action

When you do have a problem, do not hesitate to take action. Report problems to the appropriate agencies or organizations immediately; they can provide valuable advice and take action to help you.

Investigate

Start your own investigation right away. The minute you receive a threatening or harassing communication, start a file of evidence, adding communications as they come in. Research the perpetrator, as well as his or her actions. Use the resources discussed throughout this book to track him or her down. Collect as much information about him or her as possible; anything you learn may be useful later. Sometimes, just knowing that you know who they are and where they live is enough to deter criminals.

Zero Tolerance?

Whatever you do, don't fold up and fade away when you are attacked, harassed, or threatened online. Every time an online psycho gets away with a crime, he or she is encouraged to do it again, convinced of his or her ability to continue harming others with impunity. Maybe what happened to you wasn't so bad—but you have no way of knowing what was done to others or how far the criminal may go with the next victim.

How much or how little of the information here (and, indeed, throughout this book) you use is up to you. The precautions you take depend on two things: the amount of risk you can live with comfortably, and how much you value your privacy. It's your call.

Appendix

Web Sites And
Other Online Resources

Appendix

Web Sites And Other Online Resources

Appendix

The following is a compendium of Web sites and other online resources mentioned in this book, organized by category. Several resources appear in more than one category.

The categorics are:

- Anonymous Remailers

- Cash and Banking

- Email Address Directories

- Email Filtering Tools

- Education and Information

- FAQs

- Fraud and Scam Information

- Government Sites

- Investigative Services' Web Sites (Fee-Based)

- IRC Information

- ISPs and Online Services

- Miscellaneous Sites

- Name/Address/Telephone Directories

- Privacy Organizations' Sites

- Search Engines

- Security Organizations' Sites

- Services

- Software

- Spam

- Specialized Search Tools

- USENET Newsgroups and Newsgroup Information

- Virus Information

- Web Tools

- Yellow Pages and Business Directories

These links, along with addenda and updates, are available online at **http://www.coriolis.com/webpsychos/links.htm**.

ANONYMOUS REMAILERS

Anonymity and Privacy on the Internet—**http://www.stack.nl/~galactus/remailers/**
Anonymous Remailer List—**http://www.cs.berkeley.edu/~raph/remailer-list.html**
Anonymous Remailer List—**http://www.compulink.co.uk/~net-services/care/**
InterLink Member USENET Remailer Service—**http://interlink-bbs.com/anonremailer.html**

The John Doe Home Page (Remailer/Encryption Service)—**http://www.comp ulink.co.uk/~net-services/care/**

CASH AND BANKING

The Ecash Home Page—**http://www.digicash.com/ecash/ecash-home.html**

First Virtual Bank—**http://www.fv.com/demo/**

First Virtual Holdings, Inc.—**http://www.firstvirtual.com**

Online Credit Card Authorization Service—**http://www.ecash.com**

EMAIL ADDRESS DIRECTORIES

All-in-One Email Address Search Page—**http://www.albany.net/allinone/ all1user.html**

Bigfoot Email Directory—**http://bigfoot.com**

The E-Mail Address Book—**http://www.emailbook.com/**

ESP Mail Search Program (UK)—**http://www.esp.co.uk**

Four11 Email Directory—**http://www.four11.comfs**

Internet Address Finder—**http://www.iaf.net**

Infospace Email Directory—**http://email.infospace.com/info/index.htm**

Infospace Web Page Submission Form—**http://www.infospace.com/submit.html**

The Internet Sleuth Email Search—**http://www.isleuth.com/**

Lycos EmailFind Email Directory—**http://www.lycos.com/emailfind.html**

The National Address Browser—**http://www.semaphorecorp.com/default.html**

Netfind Email Directory—**http://www.nova.edu/Inter-Links/netfind.html**

People Finder Email Directory—**http://www.peoplesite.com/indexnf.html**

WhoWhere? Email Address Directory—**http://www.whowhere.com**

Who's Who Online—**http://www.whoswho-online.com/**

WED World Email Directory—**http://www.worldemail.com**

The Women's White Pages—**http://www.femail.com/fesearch.htm**

Yahoo People Search Email Directory—**http://www.yahoo.com/search/people/ email.html**

EMAIL FILTERING TOOLS

Adcomplain Unix Email Script—**http://agora.rdrop.com/users/billmc/adcomplain**

The ELM Page—**http://www.math.fu-berlin.de/~guckes/elm/**

Infinite Ink's Mail Filtering and Robots—**http://www.jazzie.com/ii/internet/ mailbots.html**

Laus's Mail Filters—**http://www.cs.helsinki.fi/~wirzeniu/mailfilter.html**

Paul Milligan's Anti-Spam Trick for Web Pages—**http://www.mindspring.com/ ~pjm/webtrick.html**

Paul Milligan's procmailrc Spam Filter with Fgrep—**http://www.mindspring.com/ ~pjm/myproc.html**

Paul Milligan's procmailrc Spam Filter without Fgrep—**http://www.mindspring. com/~pjm/myproc2.html**

EDUCATION AND INFORMATION

The Anonymizer Browser Snoop Page—**http://www.anonymizer.com/cgi-bin/ snoop.pl**

Center for Democracy and Technology (CDT) Demo of Web Page Snooping— **http://www.13x.com/cgi-bin/cdt/snoop.pl**

Codex Surveillance & Privacy Page—**http://www.thecodex.com**

Computer Virus Myths Home Page—**http://www.kumite.com:80/myths/**

Definitions of Abbreviations Used in Online Communications—**http:// wombat.doc.ic.ac.uk/?Free+On-line+Dictionary**

Definitions of "Smileys"—**http://cuisun9.unige.ch/eao/www/Internet/ smileys.html**

DigiCrime, Inc.—**http://www.digicrime.com/**

FAQ: How to Find People's Email Addresses—**http://www.qucis.queensu.ca/FAQs/ email/finding.html**

Infinite Link's Mail Filter FAQ—**http://www.jazzie.com/ii/faqs/archive/mail/ filtering-faq/**

Internet Engineering Task Force Standard for Tracking Cookies—**http:// ds.internic.net/rfc/rfc2109.txt**

Masha Boitchouk's Guide to Finding Email Addresses—**http://sunsite.unc.edu/ ~masha/**

Microsoft Security Advisor—**http://www.microsoft.com/security/**

NetscapeWorld—**http://www.netscapeworld.com/**

Platform for Internet Content Selection (PICS) Information Page—**http:// www.w3.org/pub/WWW/PICS/**

Probe Internet—**http://pihome.com/pirc/incoming/piin.html**

The Recreational Software Advisory Council (RSAC)—**http://www.rsac.org/ratingsv01.html**

RSA Data Security's Web Site—**http://www.rsa.com/**

The Stalker's Home Page—**http://www.glr.com/stalk.html**

Vince Zema's Netiquette Primer—**http://www.primenet.com/~vez/neti.html**

FAQs

The BotSpot FAQ on Internet Robots—**http://www.botspot.com/faqs/**

The BIZ Newsgroup FAQ—**ftp://ftp.xenitec.on.ca/pub/news/faqs/biz.faq**

The Data Security FAQ—**http://www.qualix.com/sysman/info/securityfaq.html**

FAQ: How to Find People's Email Addresses—**http://www.qucis.queensu.ca/FAQs/email/finding.html**

Infinite Link's Mail Filter FAQ—**http://www.jazzie.com/ii/faqs/archive/mail/filtering-faq/**

IRC FAQ—**http://www.compusmart.ab.ca/aboutsmartnet/faqirc.htm**

Mail Filtering FAQ—**http://www.cis.ohio-state.edu/hypertext/faq/usenet/mail/filtering-faq/faq.html**

Net Abuse FAQ—**http://www.cybernothing.org/faqs/net-abuse-faq.html**

Newsgroup FAQ—**ftp://ftp.cs.columbia.edu/archives/faq/news/announce/newusers**

Newsgroup FAQ—**http://ancho.ucs.indiana.edu/FAQ/USAGN/**

Newsgroup FAQ—**http://www.spirit-lake.k12.ia.us/html/jbolluyt/newsgrp.htm**

Newsgroups FAQ—**http://www.ucsalf.ac.uk/usenet/computer-security/**

Spam FAQ—**http://www.vix.com/spam/faq.html**

Unix Mail Filtering FAQ—**http://www.cs.ruu.nl/wais/html/na-dir/mail/filtering-faq.html**

World Wide Web Security FAQ—**http://www-genome.wi.mit.edu/WWW/faqs/www-security-faq.html**

FRAUD AND SCAM INFORMATION

The AIMC Consumer Corner—**http://aimc.com/aimc/consumer.html**

Consumer Fraud Alert Network (1)—**http://www.pic.net/microsmarts/fraud.htm**

Consumer Fraud Alert Network (2)—**http://www.world-wide.com/Homebiz/fraud.htm**

Consumer World—**http://www.consumerworld.org**

Fraud Watch Newsletter—**http://www.silverquick.com**

The Internet Commerce Commission—**http://www.icc-911.com**

Internet ScamBusters—**http://www.scambusters.org**

The Netcheck Commerce Bureau—**http://www.netcheck.com**

Netchex—**http://www.netchex.com/index.html**

National Fraud Information Center (NFIC)—**http://www.fraud.org/**

National Fraud Information Center, Email Fraud Report—**nfic@internetMCI.com**

ScamWatch—**http://www.scamwatch.com**

SEC Internet Investor Scam Page—**http://www.sec.gov/consumer/cyberfr.htm**

The Vice Squad—**http://207.15.223.224/vicesquad.htm**

GOVERNMENT SITES

Computer Incident Advisory Capability (CIAC)—**http://ciac.llnl.gov/ciac/**

Federal Bureau of Investigation (FBI)—**http://www.fbi.gov**

Federal Trade Commission (FTC)—**http://www.ftc.gov**

National Computer Security Association (NCSA)—**http://www.ncsa.com**

National Security Agency (NSA)—**http://www.nsa.gov:8080/**

Secret Service—**http://www.ustreas.gov/treasury/bureaus/usss/usss.html**

Securities & Exchange Commission (SEC) Web Site—**http://www.sec.gov/**

SEC Internet Investor Scam Page—**http://www.sec.gov/consumer/cyberfr.htm**

INVESTIGATIVE SERVICES' WEB SITES (FEE-BASED)

American Information Network—**http://www.ameri.com**

Codex Surveillance & Privacy Page—**http://www.thecodex.com**

Informus Free Sample—**http://www.informus.com/ssnlkup.html**

Informus Lookup Services—**http://www.informus.com/avlsrch.html**

Informus Links to Private Investigators—**http://www.inil.com/users/dguss/gator14.htm**

Infoseek—**http://www.infoseek.com/**

The National Association of Investigative Specialists (NAIS) Member Directory—
http://www.pimall.com/nais/dir.menu.html

The Private Investigator's Home Page—**http://www.pihome.com/pihome/index.cgi**

IRC Information

IRC Information—**http://www.thenet.co.uk/~bvr/index2.html**

IRC FAQ—**http://www.compusmart.ab.ca/aboutsmartnet/faqirc.htm**

IRC User Guide—**http://lucy.swin.edu.au/csit/opax/userguide/irc.html**

ISP's And Online Services

AOL Members Home Page Directory—**http://home.aol.com/index.html**

CompuServe Members Home Page Directory—**http://ourworld.compuserve.com**

DELPHI Members Home Page Directory—**http://people.delphi.com/**

One Net—**http://www.one.net**

Panix.com's Site-Wide Email Filters—**http://www.panix.com/e-spam.html**

Prodigy Members Home Page Directory—**http://pages.prodigy.com**

Miscellaneous Sites

The AOL Lamer Page—**http://hnet.hutton.com/~mredrain/aolmr.html**

Baen Books—**http://www.baen.com**

Better Business Bureau—**http://www.bbbonline.org/**

The Computer Law Observer—**http://www.lawcircle.com/observer**

Interactive History Exhibit: Turks & Tatars—**http://www.uoknor.edu/
cybermuslim/russia/rus_home.html**

The Lamer Page—**http://hnet.hutton.com/~mredrain/metoo.html**

List of Listserve Mailing Lists—**http://www.ttu.edu/~library/subject/listserv.htm**

Web Psychos, Stalkers, and Pranksters Pages—**http://www.coriolis.com/
webpsychos/**

Name/Address/Telephone Directories

American Directory Assistance: People Search—**http://www.lookupusa.com/
lookupusa/adp/peopsrch.htm**

Database America's PeopleFinder Name/Address/Telephone Directory—**http://www.databaseamerica.com/html/gpfind.htm**

InterNIC White Pages Directory Services—**http://ds.internic.net/tools/wp_text.html**

Lycos PeopleFind Name/Address/Telephone Directory—**http://www.lycos.com/pplfndr.html**

Phone*File Name/Address/Telephone Directory—On CompuServe, **GO PHONEFILE**

Pro CD's Select Phone Web Site—**http://www.procd.com/pi/td/td.htm**

SearchAmerica Name/Address/Telephone Directory—**http://www.searchamerica.com/**

Switchboard Name/Address/Telephone Directory—**http://www.switchboard.com**

Switchboard Name/Address/Telephone Directory Search Page—**http://www.switchboard.com/bin/cgiqa.dll?CHKKNOCK=1&MEM=1&**

Telephone Directories on the Web—**http://www.contractjobs.com/tel/**

Yahoo People Serarch U.S. White Pages/Individuals—**http://www.yahoo.com/Reference/White_Pages/Individuals**

Yahoo People Search U.S. White Pages—**http://www.yahoo.com/search/people/**

PRIVACY ORGANIZATIONS' SITES

Anonymity and Privacy on the Internet—**http://www.stack.nl/~galactus/remailers/**

Andre Bacard's Privacy Site—**http://www.well.com/user/abacard/**

Computer Professionals for Social Responsibility (CSPR) Privacy and Civil Liberties Page—**http://snyside.sunnyside.com/dox/program/privacy/privacy.html**

The Electronic Frontier Foundation—**http://www.eff.org**

Electronic Privacy Information Center (EPIC)—**http://www.epic.org/**

FACTnet International (Fight Against Coercive Tactics Network Inc.)—**http://www.factnet.org/**

The International Electronic Rights Server—**http://www.privacy.org/**

The Internet Commerce Commission—**http://www.icc-911.com**

Internet Privacy Coalition—**http://www.privacy.org/ipc/**

Internet Privacy Law—**http://www.mother.com/~ono/tjw.htm**

Internet ScamBusters—**http://www.scambusters.org**

The Junkbusters Alert on Web Privacy—**http://www.junkbusters.com/cgi-bin/ privacy**

Junkbuster Privacy Resource Links—**http://www.junkbusters.com/ht/en/ links.html**

The Privacy Forum—**http://www.vortex.com/privacy.htm**

The Privacy Page—**http://www.unimaas.nl/~privacy/index.htm**

Privacy Rights Clearinghouse—**http://www.privacyrights.org/**

Yahoo's List of Privacy Sites—**http://www.yahoo.com/Government/Law/Privacy/**

SEARCH ENGINES

AltaVista—**http://altavista.digital.com**

C:Net's—**http://www.search.com**

Excite!—**http://www.excite.com**

HotBot—**http://www.hotbot.com/**

InfoSeek—**http://www.infoseek.com**

Lycos—**http://www.lycos.com**

Magellan—**http://www.mckinley.com/**

Webcrawler—**http://wc1.webcrawler.com/**

Yahoo—**http://www.yahoo.com**

SECURITY ORGANIZATIONS' SITES

Codex Surveillance & Privacy Page—**http://www.thecodex.com**

Computer Incident Advisory Capability (CIAC)—**http://ciac.llnl.gov/ciac/**

CyberAngels—**http://www.cyberangels.org**

The Cybergrrl Webstation—**http://www.cybergrrl.com**

The Vice Squad—**http://207.15.223.224/vicesquad.htm**

Web Police—**http://www.web-police.org**

Women Halting Online Abuse (W.H.O.A.)—**http://whoa.femail.com/index.html**

SERVICES

Bess Safe Surfing ISP—**http://www.bess.com**

Hallmark Free Reminder Service—**http://www.hallmarkreminder.com**

iName Lifetime Email Address—**http://iaf.iname.com**

Anonymizer Proxy Server Interface Page—http://www.anonymizer.com/open.html

The Internet Junkbusters Proxy Server—http://www.junkbuster.com

Juno Free Internet Email Service—http://www.juno.com

Microsoft Security Advisor—http://www.microsoft.com/security/

The Microsystems Cyber Patrol Proxy Server—http://www.microsys.com/proxy/proxserv.htm

NetscapeWorld—http://www.netscapeworld.com/

The SafeSurf Web Page Rating System—http://www.safesurf.com

Software

BeyondMail Email Program—http://www.coordinate.com/bmail/

Boutell Software's Wusage Web Server Statistic Software—http://www.boutell.com/wusage/

Cyber Patrol Safe Surfing Software—http://www.cyberpatrol.com

CYBERsitter Safe Surfing Software—http://www.solidoak.com/

daxHOUND Internet Content Selection Tool—http://www.netshepherd.com/products/daxHOUND2.0/daxhound.HTM

Email for Kids Email Program—http://www.connectsoft.com

Eudora and Eudora Light Email Programs—http://www.qualcomm.com

Internet WatchDog Safe Surfing Software—http://www.charlesriver.com/titles/watchdog.html

KidWeb Web Browser—http://www.connectsoft.com

KinderGuard Safe Surfing Software—http://www.intergo.com/wow/kguard.htm

McAfee Anti-Virus Products—http://www.mcafee.com

Net Nanny Safe Surfing Software—http://www.netnanny.com

NetShepherd Web Rating Service—http://www.netshepherd.com/

Pegasus Email Program—http://www.pegasus.usa.com/

PGP Cookie Cutter—http://www.pgp.com

PGP Download Site—http://bozo.mit.edu:9999/pgp

PGP Front Ends (DOS and Windows)—http://www.seattle-webworks.com/pgp/pgplinks.html

PGP Home Page—http://www.pgp.com/

PGP Public Keys Server—http://rs.internic.net/support/wwwpks/

Rated-PG Safe Surfing Software—http://www.ratedpg.com/

Spam Hater Download—**http://www.compulink.co.uk/~net-services/spam/**

Spam Hater Software Info—**http://www.hitchhikers.net/hotsoftware. shtml#Spammers**

SurfWatch—**http://www.surfwatch.com**

Symantec Anti-Virus Research Center (SARC)—**http://www.symantec.com/ avcenter**

Symantec/Norton Anti-Virus Products—**http://www.symantec.com/**

Time's Up! Web Surfing Timer—**http://www.timesup.com/**

TSW's eFilter—**http://catalog.com/tsw/efilter/**

Web Tracker Individual Web Site Statistics—**http://www.fxweb.holowww.com/ tracker/index.html**

Webtrends Web Server Statistic Software—**http://www.egsoftware.com/**

WS_FTP Telnet Client Download—**http://www.ipswitch.com**

Spam

Anti-Spam Site—**http://www.ca-probate.com/aol_junk.htm**

Anti-Spam Site—**http://knet.flemingc.on.ca/~surly/junkmail.html**

Anti-Spam Site—**http://com.primenet.com/spamking/slatinfo.html**

The Blacklist of Internet Advertisers—**http://math-www.uni-paderborn.de/ ~axel/BL/**

Domains Blocked by AOL Due to Spam—**http://www.idot.aol.com/preferredmail/**

Mark Eckenwiler on Applying the U.S. Junk Fax Law to Spam—**http:// www.panix.com/~eck/junkmail.html**

Dan Gilmour on Spam as Extortion—**http://www.sjmercury.com/business/ gillmor/dg072196.htm**

Internet Spam Boycott—**http://www.vix.com/spam/**

Paul Milligan's Anti-Spam Trick for Web Pages—**http://www.mindspring.com/ ~pjm/webtrick.html**

Paul Milligan's procmailrc Spam Filter with Fgrep—**http://www.mindspring.com/ ~pjm/myproc.html**

Paul Milligan's procmailrc Spam Filter without Fgrep—**http://www.mindspring. com/~pjm/myproc2.html**

Panix.com's Site-Wide Email Filters—**http://www.panix.com/e-spam.html**

Howard Rheingold on the Tragedy of the Electronic Commons—**http:// www.well.com/user/hlr/tomorrow/tomorrowcommons.html**

Spam Hater Download—**http://www.compulink.co.uk/~net-services/spam/**

Spam Hater Software Info—**http://www.hitchhikers.net/hotsoftware. shtml#Spammers**

Spam FAQ—**http://www.vix.com/spam/faq.html**

USENET Advertising How-To—**http://www.cs.ruu.nl/wais/html/na-dir/usenet/ advertising/how-to/part1.html**

USENET Newsgroup on Net Abuse and Spam—**news.admin.net-abuse.announce**

Specialized Search Tools

Ahoy Internet Home Page Directory—**http://ahoy.cs.washington.edu:6060/**

Deja News Search Form—**http://www.dejanews.com/forms/dnq.html**

Reference.com (The USENET/Email List/Web Forum Email Directory, aka the SIFT Directory)—**http://www.reference.com/**

The Seeker, Specialized Email Address Directory—**http://www.the-seeker.com/**

The USENET Address Database—**http://usenet-addresses.mit.edu/**

Women's Web Site Directory—**http://www.femail.com/sites/**

USENET Newsgroups And Newsgroup Information

The BIZ Newsgroup FAQ—**ftp://ftp.xenitec.on.ca/pub/news/faqs/biz.faq**

Net Abuse and Spam Newsgroup—**news.admin.net-abuse.announce**

Newsgroup FAQ—**ftp://ftp.cs.columbia.edu/archives/faq/news/announce/ newusers**

Newsgroup FAQ—**http://ancho.ucs.indiana.edu/FAQ/USAGN/**

Newsgroup FAQ—**http://www.spirit-lake.k12.ia.us/html/jbolluyt/newsgrp.htm**

Newsgroups FAQ—**http://www.ucsalf.ac.uk/usenet/computer-security/**

Yahoo Newsgroup Listing—**http://www.yahoo.com/news/usenet**

Virus Information

Computer Incident Advisory Capability (CIAC)—**http://ciac.llnl.gov/ciac/**

Computer Virus Myths Home Page—**http://www.kumite.com:80/myths/**

McAfee Anti-Virus Products—http://www.mcafee.com

National Computer Security Association (NCSA)—http://www.ncsa.com

Symantec/Norton Anti-Virus Products—http://www.symantec.com/

Symantec Anti-Virus Research Center (SARC)—http://www.symantec.com/avcenter

WEB TOOLS

Finger Gateways

Advanced HTTP/HTML Research Server WWW Finger Gateway with Faces—http://httptest.bsdi.com/finger/gateway

WWW Finger Gateway with Faces, Indiana University—http://cs.indiana.edu/finger/gateway

CAN Services Finger Gateway—http://www.cans.com/cgi-bin/cfa-finger

WWW Finger Gateway with Faces—http://www.cs.indiana.edu:800/finger/gateway

Internet Tools Gateway/Finger—http://www.magibox.net/~unabest/finger/query.cgi

The Unofficial WWW Project Vincent Ginger Gateway—http://www.public.iastate.edu/cgi-bin/finger?

MIT Student Processing Board Finger Gateway—http://www.mit.edu:8001/finger?

NSLookup Gateways

University of Antwerp NSLookup Gateway—http://www.uia.ac.be/ds/nslookup.html

Internet Tools Gateway/NSLookup—http://www.magibox.net/~unabest/finger/query.cgi

NSLookup Gateway, Warsaw—http://ldhp715.immt.pwr.wroc.pl/util/nslookup.html

Sample Ph Directories

Miami University—http://www.muohio.edu/directory/

Cornell University—http://www.cornell.edu/Direct/search_ph.html

UCS—http://msgwww.ucs.indiana.edu/messaging/projects/addrbook/ph.html

Traceroute Gateways

University of Wisconsin, Department of Medicine Traceroute Gateway—http://www.medicine.wisc.edu/cgi-bin/traceroute

Internet Tools Gateway/Traceroute—http://www.magibox.net/~unabest/finger/query.cgi

Speedyweb Corporation Traceroute Gateway—http://www.llv.com/~lasvegas/traceroute.cgi

Whois Gateways

Gopher Search of the InterNIC Whois Database—gopher://rs.internic.net/7waissrc%3A/rs/whois.src

Internet Tools Gateway/Whois—http://www.magibox.net/~unabest/finger/query.cgi

University of Michigan Whois Gateway—http://www.hgp.med.umich.edu/cgi-bin/whois

InterNIC Web Interface to Whois—http://rs.internic.net/cgi-bin/whois

Miscellaneous

Host Name to Latitude/Longitude Lookup—http://cello.cs.uiuc.edu/cgi-bin/slamm/ip2ll

IP Address to Host Name and Vice Versa—http://cello.cs.uiuc.edu/cgi-bin/slamm/ip2name

Yellow Pages And Business Directories

American Yellow Pages—http://www.lookupusa.com/lookupusa/ayp/aypsrch.htm
The AT&T 800 Directory—http://www.tollfree.att.net/dir800/
Bellsouth Net Yellow Pages—http://yellowpages.bellsouth.com/
BigBook Yellow Pages—http://www.bigbook.com
Biz*File Yellow Pages—On CompuServe, **GO BIZFILE**
Europages Business Listings—http://www.europages.com/home-en.html

First Worldwide International Yellow Pages—**http://www.worldyellowpages.com/
yellowpg.html**
GTE Super Pages Yellow Pages—**http://yp.gte.net/**
Infospace Yellow P9ages—**http://www.infospace.com/info/2index_yp.htm**
World Wide Yellow Pages—**http://www.yellow.com/**

Index